HELLENIC STUDIES 93

LOVE IN THE AGE OF WAR

Recent Titles in the Hellenic Studies Series

http://chs.harvard.edu/chs/publications

LOVE IN THE AGE OF WAR

SOLDIERS IN MENANDER

Wilfred E. Major

Center for Hellenic Studies

Trustees for Harvard University

Washington, D.C.

Distributed by Harvard University Press

Cambridge, Massachusetts, and London, England

2022

Contents

Contents

to M.
contra mundum

Preface

As this book went into its final production stages, the Russian military invaded Ukraine, sparking the most expansive military activity on European soil since World War II and projecting images of the horror of battle around the world. I was fortunate enough to come of age in the United States when, owing to the grim shadow of the Vietnam War, the prospect of engaging in war again was barely conceivable. I could scarcely imagine except in nightmares that as an adult I would become a teacher before generations of students who live the reality of war in their world daily, most of whom have loved ones directly affected by one or more wars, and some of whom have participated themselves. History guarantees that the consequences of this and other wars will extend beyond my lifetime and the lifetimes of everyone on the planet today, a heartbreaking reality. I have never wished more that my academic work would be completely dissociated from the future, but if it is to resonate, my highest wish is that whatever its impact, it will be positive for anyone suffering the consequences my generation's failure to make the world more peaceful.

Acknowledgements

All scholarly studies in Classics have long and deep roots, but this one may have a longer gestation and a taller mountain of debts than most. The core thesis of this book appeared in an article some twenty-five years ago, itself the development of a paper that I had delivered two years earlier in 1995. The expansion and improvements since then surely leave me in debt to many more than I will be able to acknowledge adequately, so first I offer my humblest apologies for shortcomings and omissions in what follows.

The writing of this volume began in earnest in 2017 and its completion was possible only with some substantial support to allow time to focus on the project. An ATLAS grant (Awards to Louisiana Artists and Scholars) from the Louisiana Board of Regents allowed me to spend the spring and summer of 2019 as a Visiting Scholar at Stanford University. The thorough kindness and generosity of the Stanford community exceeds my ability to express adequately. Absolutely everyone, even in the briefest encounters, was open and supportive, but extra thanks go to some who patiently listened and assisted with the work specifically on this project, including Valerie Kizka, Grant Parker, Josh Ober, Susan Stephens and especially Hans Bork. During that same stay, I enjoyed a marvelous visit and opportunity to lecture and participate in a class at University of California, Davis. Rex Stem, who had been a dear colleague previously at Louisiana State University, affably coordinated my visit. His subsequent premature death is surely one of the greatest recent losses to the profession and to humanity in general, and I can never be thankful enough for having his company while he was his full self. Conversations with others during that brief stay, especially Valentina Popescu and her students, became uniquely valuable in developing the work in this volume.

Among the greatest and most humane benefits of studying an ancient playwright is the community of scholars who are also practitioners of theater. Absolutely every moment of labor that went into this work has been pleasurably enhanced by my time and experience with those who participate in the Society for Classical Studies' Committee on Ancient & Modern Performance (CAMP). This community overlaps with those who participated in several conferences where I tested and tried out ideas about Menander's plays, including at Amy

Acknowledgements

Cohen's Ancient Drama in Performance in coordination with the Randolph Greek Play (2012, 2016, 2018, and 2021) and Greek Drama V in 2017 with the sublime hosting of Hallie Marshall and Toph Marshall at the University of British Columbia in Vancouver. Under their editorial hand, moreover, some preliminary steps toward this volume, especially data in Chapter 2, first saw publication in the proceedings from that conference ("The Pre-History of the *Miles Gloriosus* in Greek Drama," *Greek Drama V: Studies in the Theatre of the Fifth and Fourth Centuries BCE.* [London: Bloomsbury Academic 2019:215-24]). Finally, my debt to this community would not be expressed adequately without specific gratitude to John Given and the righteous inspiration of Mike Lippman. Break a leg, all y'all.

Two decades at Louisiana State University in Baton Rouge, Louisiana, have inevitably involved hurricanes, some delivered by earth's elemental forces and some by human choice. My resilience through these onslaughts has been possible only because of the astonishing strength and humanity of a number of individuals in that community. Among students I must mention Joseph Bemis, Tommy Dihn, Rachel Milpro, and (Marie) Clare Plunkett, who, every single day during the most tumultuous semester of the Covid-19 pandemic, brought themselves in person along with dedication and good spirit, for an experimental class on the history and legacy of ancient Greek soldiers. Ms. Plunkett furthermore created an Honors thesis, live performance (among whose performers was Mr. Bemis) and intermediate Greek reader of Menander's *Epitrepontes* that same year (watch the Dickinson College Commentaries series for the finished project). While this study does not feature that particular play extensively, it does benefit greatly from Ms. Plunkett's work and inspiration. Likewise, countless conversations and convivial occasions with my colleague Kristopher F. B. Fletcher permeate my work in the best way. Seemingly less direct but no less valuable have been the friendship, musical joy and collegiality of fellow musketeer Paolo Chirumbolo. A special shout out to Jeremy King for his unique contribution. *Debido a sus papeles como académica, profesora, y vampiro-agente (a escondidas) con talentos inigualables, el presente trabajo se ve ampliado, profundizado, e iluminado por las contribuciones de la Dra. Laura Martins (¡che, boluda!). Ella ha contribuido profundamente al aprecio que tengo por el arte y la belleza en el mundo. Este libro, y aun mi propia vida tal como está, no existirían si no fuera por su apoyo.*

As the manuscript crashed through various revisions, more contributions ensued, including those of anonymous readers and editors who made improvements on every page that follows. Among those whose name I happily know in these final stages are Casey Due, who patiently and faultlessly shepherded the manuscript through the most challenging months of the pandemic, and Jill Robbins, who has been uniformly cheerful and energetic down to this final stage. Jeff Carnes brilliantly and selflessly generated yet another excellent index for me on short notice. The chart and illustrations that grace these pages come from the (digital) pen and artistic talent of Marianne B. Sowa, who otherwise improves the world in her work in and beyond NASA, to the envy of us in Classics. Her contributions to my life and work are elsewhere encapsulated in this volume's dedication.

All this prodigious energy and talent should surely have resulted in a volume without the faults that remain, but I am so frightfully deficient across such a broad spectrum that I can take credit only for the unnecessary shortcomings that abide. Among those shortcomings, some partly result from timing. The manuscript for this work was mostly complete in the summer of 2019, so only a limited amount of scholarship that came to my attention since then (some of which was in fact published earlier than that date) finds mention here. Such omissions are thus in no way an opinion of the quality of that work or the contributions by their authors.

Last but not least, a confession: In this work about soldiers and military life, I claim absolutely no time in military service nor deep immediate connections with family and friends in such service, nor systematic and prolonged experience with the soldiers and their families whose dedication ensure the safe environment in which I have always lived and worked. I claim only that I have tried to listen and learn attentively and respectfully at every opportunity so that my work might make some measure of recompense to that unique community. At one point among the conversations that I did have, one veteran, after I had told him about this project, began haltingly to offer feedback, but suddenly stopped and said directly, "Listen, just tell the truth. That's all anybody really wants." Not a moment has gone by since without those words and that voice in my mind, so my sole promise and guarantee is that in everything that I have written here, with all the errors, problems and points of disagreement inevitably contained within, I have never ceased my efforts to speak the truth.

List of Figures

Introduction

IN 280 CE, LUCIA AMATIA PROSDOKIA died at the age of twenty-six in northern Lydia. On her tombstone, her husband, Poplius Claudius Thrasyboulos, identifies himself as a soldier (στρατιώτης) at the rank of ὀπτίων in the Roman army (Latin *optio*, roughly second-in-command in a century) and also mentions that Lucia's father was a comic actor from Alexandria (κωμῳδοῦ παραδόξου Ἀλεξανδρέως). Forty years later, Thrasyboulos himself died, and when their daughter set up his tombstone, his military career and connection to stage comedy appear prominently. He received exceptional honors for his military campaigning from noble, powerful kings (στρατιῆσιν ἀρίσταις ἔξοχα τιμηθέντα κλυτοῖς βασιλεῦσι μεγίστοις). The epitaph then highlights Thrasyboulos as a performer of the "wise" Menander (ὑποκρινάμενον σοφὸν ἄνδρα Μένανδρον).[1] The combination of a prominent military career and a record of acting Menander is intriguing. In a purely literary or theatrical context, if presented with a man honored by great kings and bestriding a stage in Greek New Comedy, scholars would routinely characterize such a man as a braggart soldier, a *miles gloriosus*. In the real world of these funerary contexts, the combination is in fact duly reverent. Moreover, while it seems unlikely that Thrasyboulos could have been both a successful military officer and a professional actor of Menander, his tombstone juxtaposes exactly these two roles.

It would be illuminating to glean how military life and performing Menander interwove in the life of Thrasyboulos and his family, but these two grave markers give more clues than answers. The current study will argue for an understanding of Menander's plays that could have made Thrasyboulos' engagement with the wise playwright something that resonated with his military experience, but not because he acted like a bragging fool on or off stage. Rather, Menander's comedies could have provided him thoughtful dramatizations of men who had been militarized, on the one hand, but struggled, on the other hand, to be successful civilians, accepted as devoted husbands, a conflict between past success and aspirations for the future.

---

[1] For text, commentary, and photos, see Petzl 2002:93–99 nos. 1–2, cf. Dunbabin 2016:70 and n. 92. The epitaph forms a six-line hexameter poem.

That Thrasyboulos could have felt Menander's soldier characters were relatable runs counter to the majority critical opinion of New Comedy in modern times, an assumption that it was formulaic and escapist, especially when compared to the robustly topical and scandalous comedy that preceded Menander by a century. Even one of the more acute analyses of the legacy of military life in Menander, Sharon James's study of the *Aspis*, finds the resolution of the play "a fantasy." (James 2014:237). The perception of Menander's comedy in antiquity, however, was the opposite. Menander, often paired with his tragic predecessor, Euripides, ranked among the more accessible and immediate literary figures. Whether in Aristophanes of Byzantium's famous quote that finds little distance between life and Menander ("Which of you imitated the other?") or the performances and artistic renditions of Menander's plays that still abounded in Thrasyboulos' day, six centuries after the playwright's death, Menander was firmly and deeply embedded in the ancient Greek world, at least until the Christianization of that world correlated with the end of theatrical performances and the end of preserving Menander's scripts.[2]

However close his plays seemed to life, there remained aspirational elements to them. Resolutions to conflicts about citizenship, marriage, inheritance, finances, and more did not routinely occur as happily as they do in Menander's plays. There are brief occasions when characters in Menander's plays measure the distance between themselves and those aspirations. One such character is Knemon, the title grouch of *Dyskolos*, whose body becomes broken to the point that he says that he is near death (729–730), and at the end of his lengthy speech concludes:

εἰ τοιοῦτοι πάντες ἦσαν, οὔτε τὰ δικαστήρια
ἦν ἄν, οὔθ' αὑτοὺς ἀπῆγον εἰς τὰ δεσμωτήρια,
οὔτε πόλεμος ἦν, ἔχων δ' ἂν μέτρι' ἕκαστος ἠγάπα.
ἀλλ' ἴσως ταῦτ' ἐστ' ἀρεστὰ μᾶλλον· οὕτω πράττετε.

743–746

If everyone were like this, there would be no courts, no one would haul themselves off to prisons, there would be no war. Instead they would each cherish and keep to themselves. Maybe things are better this way. Go on this way then.[3]

---

[2] See Nervegna 2013 for a thorough study of Menander's legacy in the pre-Christian Greek world and Petrides 2014a:15–16 for helpful analysis of the resonance and context for Aristophanes of Byzantium's characterization.

[3] All translations are my own except where indicated.

Commentators have recognized that these lines strike a tone rare in Menander. Handley says, "it is possible that events of the immediate past made the lines strike the audience with immediate vividness," (1965:261), having in mind the violent trial of the democratic leader Phokion, which had taken place in the same theater where *Dyskolos* was performed (Handley 1965:7–8; cf. Chapter 1). In the absence of courts, some have seen a reference to the new political system under Macedonian governance (Scafuro 1997:15). Gomme and Sandbach conclude about the last line, "This line must be addressed to the audience, oddly though this may strike the modern reader" (1973:248).

Knemon speaks of court trials and war, but Menander always sets his plays near the homes of one or more of his characters, never in a war zone or in a courtroom. The consequences of battle or a trial nevertheless afflict numerous characters in his plays.[4] Like Knemon, soldier characters—who feel isolated, betrayed, and suicidal when their prerogatives as soldiers have left them isolated from their families and communities—are central characters, indeed protagonists in Menander's plays. Also, as Knemon says, when these and other characters take care of their own business, they find peace and acceptance away from war and litigation. The homes on stage become places of this refuge and happiness.

This study seeks to articulate why and how soldiers and the consequences of war play out repeatedly, forcefully, and prominently in Menander's comedies. It will even suggest that this dynamic was a critical part of Menander's appeal and endurance in culturally Greek communities for centuries, a quality that was obscured when Menander became known overwhelmingly through Roman adaptations, a process of reception which transformed the characters and narrative trajectories of these soldiers on stage.

Analyzing Menander's plays toward this end involves focusing on where two components of his identity interact, two spheres of activity that are worth studying distinctly as well as in their interactions: his identity as an Athenian citizen, with an ideologically oriented view on the political life in his polis, and as an active playwright.

The first area of activity derives its structure from Menander's ideological orientation as a citizen of Athens. The political and military turmoil in Athens during Menander's lifetime testifies to the diverse positions staked out by various factions in the city. With each phase of political upheaval, individual citizens' ideological priorities could put them further in or out of favor with the group in power at the moment. In such an environment, not being aligned with the ideology dominant at a given time could and did lead to practical

---

[4]   Scafuro 1997, James 2014.

consequences for individuals, though the specific consequences could vary widely. Menander was not immune from this dynamic, even being arrested for his perceived loyalties after one such change of regime. As I concluded previously in an argument that I refresh and update in Chapter 1, Menander operated and composed plays based on a political vision that prefers Athenian citizens to pursue domestic prosperity in an environment stabilized by Macedonian imperial control. Accordingly, Menander dramatizes prosperity as resulting from citizens attending to their private or domestic affairs, a conclusion congruent with an ideological vision that prefers citizens to behave in just this way.

Unlike most of his fellow citizens, though, Menander was an active playwright. As such he knew the craft and culture of the theatrical community in Athens. Menander's plays were, as all plays are in various proportions, innovative and contemporary, yet continuations of techniques established prior to Menander's career and prior to the theatrical experience of his spectators. While it is perhaps unnecessary to emphasize that Menander composed for a theatrical community that had been vital and evolving for generations further back than anyone in his day could have living memory of, it is crucial to understanding Menander's plays that he had a body of prestigious and popular theatrical traditions to reach for and redeploy. Thus his identity as a playwright is shaped substantially by his choices, aversions, and innovations with respect to theatrical tradition, as far as these can be delineated.

Soldier characters provide a rich opportunity to analyze how these two spheres, Menander's political priorities and his redeployment of theatrical practices, interact. For Menander as a citizen with political priorities, soldiers represent a threat to the stable, peaceful domestic life that is the resolution of conflict at the end of all of his plays. To dramatize these soldiers on stage, Menander the playwright deployed techniques and invoked patterns established in his theatrical community. For example, ancient sources preserve testimony that Menander included "Ajax laughter" in his *Perinthia*, but Menander never put a mytho-historical character like Ajax on his stage. He never put a soldier on the battlefield on his stage. He never had a character commit suicide on stage (as Sophocles' Ajax does). But Menander did have a character refer to the ironic laughter born of pain and suffering that an actor used when performing Ajax on stage.[5] In another play, *Sikyonios*, another scene with motifs reworked specifically from Euripidean tragedy turns on the citizenship and military identity of a man, with a conflict that hinges on the political debate about clemency and oligarchy (see analysis in Chapter 3).

---

[5] See Chapter 2 for more on this event and on tragedy in Menander vis-à-vis soldier characters.

Menander made these and thousands of other choices as he composed his scripts. One key goal of this study is to articulate these choices as thoroughly and accurately as possible, so as to delineate something of the action and movement of the plays that were performed from those scripts. This process adds knowledge to the conversation that Menander, as a playwright and citizen, had with the Athenian community. In turn, Menander's choices illuminate the subsequent options that later playwrights had when Menander's plays became part of the their theatrical tradition. This perspective will recast scholars' understanding of what Plautus and Terence, each of whom absorb and redeploy Menander's soldier characters in distinct ways in their own plays, could and did do on Italian stages several generations after Menander.

Menander's choices in dramatizing soldiers and the choices that Plautus and Terence made subsequently are not those expected by the current categorizing of soldier characters in Greek and Roman comedy, specifically, that they are fundamentally braggart soldiers, always a species of *miles gloriosus*. Menander's soldier characters were not exclusively or even predominantly of this type. Consequently when Plautus and Terence composed plays where such braggarts are the dominant type, the soldiers they adapt from Menander stand apart and require fresh analysis to understand their distinctive traits and behaviors.

There is a corollary to these claims (that Menander shaped his soldiers in a distinctive way, that soldiers on the Roman stage took on a form distinct from that in Menander): the soldiers that we can now stage from Menander's plays have fresh and powerful resonance in the ongoing cultural discourse about soldiers in the twenty-first century. Menander's soldier characters are in fact all former mercenaries who are struggling to live a stable domestic life with the approval of their local communities. Actions and prerogatives that these characters invoke based on their military identity range from ineffective to counterproductive during these plays. In turn, Menander guides these protagonists along a path toward stability in their own homes and toward peaceful, respectful relationships with their neighbors in civilian life. As such, Menander's plays should join the fruitful ongoing conversations that use Greek epic and tragedy to contextualize, probe, and improve the lives of veterans today as they navigate the tensions embedded in transitioning from military to civilian life.

As Menander's soldiers and comedies have played little role in the conversations by and about veterans transitioning to civilian life, it is not intuitively obvious that soldiers from Greek comedy have a role in the modern conversation, nor is it obvious what that role should be. It is a topic of ongoing debate whether stories of soldiers from ancient Greece even provide legitimate and relevant contributions to this conversation. Clinical psychiatrist Jonathan Shay pioneered dialogue on this issue when he observed parallels between combat veterans under his care, who were suffering persistent struggles in civilian life because of carryovers from traumatic events in combat situations, and narrative patterns of warriors from ancient Greece, primarily drawing on the epic poetry of Homer and focusing on Achilles in the *Iliad* (1994) and Odysseus in the *Odyssey* (2002). Shay argued that Achilles experiences a betrayal that in modern combat soldiers is a non-trivial trigger of post-traumatic stress disorder (PTSD), a phenomenon that Shay preferred to characterize as "psychological injury" and subsequently "moral injury" (2014). Achilles' behavior in the *Iliad* after leadership (in the form of Agamemnon) inflicted this injury parallels that of military men in combat after analogous betrayals. More than just cataloging these parallels, Shay argued that the *Iliad* and other works reflected ancient Greek communal activities that identified and dealt with the causes and effects of combat-induced injuries to soldiers' psychological health. Furthermore, Shay used his observations of these parallels between experiences described in antiquity and by his twentieth-century patients to lobby health and military professionals so that they would modify policies in order to treat and prevent these injuries. During this process he used passages in the *Odyssey* that address more events typical of soldiers afflicted with psychological injury, most prominently afflictions that render Odysseus himself an undependable and failed commander. Among Odysseus' failures is his inability to rejoin his home community and family in a peaceful or settled way. Among Greek mytho-historical warriors, peaceful and stable retirement after combat is a rarity, suggestive of the enormity of the tradition that Menander recasts in his plays when he has soldiers succeed in reaching just this conclusion.

Like Shay but more forcefully, historian Lawrence Tritle has invoked personal combat experience and drawn in voices from ancient Greek historiographic sources to broaden the claim that these ancient narratives document the recognizable phenomenon of soldiers afflicted with combat-induced PTSD. In response have come notes of caution and skepticism about the methodology and sureness of the parallels between the experiences of modern combat veterans and those of ancient Greek predecessors on the battlefield. Jason Crowley, for example, has drawn up a psychological portrait of ancient Athenian hoplites that is not entirely consistent with the suppositions of Shay and Tritle and arguably exposes the parallels they draw as more asserted than plausibly argued.[6]

This schism has a parallel in scholarship on ancient Greek theater, where scholars differ on the extent to which metrics are valid for assessing the overlap

---

[6] Crowley 2014; for a review from the perspective of clinical psychologists, see Ustinova and Cardeña 2014.

between the experiences of moderns and those of ancient theatergoers.[7] Peter Meineck has explored these issues both for the experiences of theatergoers and for combat veterans. On both fronts he is keenly aware that one community's cultural norms have isolated or superficial resemblances which need not testify to broader and deeper analogies with those of other cultural communities. With regard to humans in combat and in a theater, Meineck accordingly concentrates on the structures and flexibility of human psychological mechanisms, although he is prudently attuned to the limitations and even hazards in these endeavors. As a note of caution, he cites Evan Watters's exposé of well-intentioned health professionals who traveled to Sri Lanka following the devastation of a tsunami in 2004, but who too often were counterproductive with individuals in local populations whose communities had mechanisms and therapeutic procedures unrecognized by those trained exclusively in Western methods. With both theater and combat experience, however, there are traditions and engagement beyond the commonality of human biology, and extrapolations can be made from that commonality. Shay's patients, as members of American military forces, were acculturated in institutions directly descended from ones which over the centuries engaged to varying degrees with the military traditions of the ancient Mediterranean, including Greek traditions. This does not make correspondences between ancient Greek soldiers and twentieth-century American soldiers obvious, inevitable, or even straightforward to identify, but there are threads of continuity. The well-intentioned health professionals interacting with the Sri Lankans also had analogous threads of continuity, but the native populations had their own deep roots and connections, with less overlap with ancient Mediterranean traditions than that of their caregivers. Meineck himself makes this point for theater: "while establishing a cultural distance is vital ... in many ways Greek drama is the progenitor of the theatre we experience today" (2018:17).

Likewise when Shay and Tritle map the experiences of twentieth-century patients onto military narratives from Greek antiquity, they are in some sense mapping experiences onto one area of the ancestry of those patients. Moreover, combat and theater are not mutually exclusive spheres of activity, though the overlap was demonstrably greater in classical Athens than most any other time or place.[8] Shay rationally points to the theater as an arena where ancient Greek communities transmitted their knowledge and explored what they knew about the effects of trauma in human life following combat (1994:194, 329–330).

---

[7] See Carter 2011:1–17 for a helpful list of points of contention that need not be binary oppositions.
[8] Raaflaub 2001, esp. 329–339 and Konstan 2010.

In the scholarly exploration of Greek theater as a venue for communal activity directed toward "moral injury" and its consequences among soldiers, Athenian tragedy has garnered the most attention. Meineck, for example, summarizes: "Athenian tragedy offered a form of performance-based collective 'catharsis' or 'cultural therapy' by providing a place where the traumatic experiences faced by the spectators was reflected upon the gaze of the masked characters performing before them."[9] In this model, Sophocles' tragedy about Ajax showcases, for example, how moral injury affects even a warrior as traditionally successful as Ajax for the Athenian theatrical community, which overlaps substantially with the politically franchised community.[10] Bundled with Ajax's betrayal, humiliation, and suicide in the play are discussions of the culpability and responsibility of his fellow warriors and others in the community. As Sophocles stages the tale, Odysseus, Ajax's bitter rival, is reluctant to gloat over Ajax and ultimately stands up to the army's leaders, Agamemnon and Menelaus, for the principle of respecting Ajax's legacy after his death. Ajax's half-brother Teucer also stands up for Ajax, and his status as illegitimate offspring in terms of royalty becomes an additional point of conflict in the play. Social legitimacy and authority also haunt Tekmessa, Ajax's wife, a woman whose status as a legitimate and protected spouse depends on Ajax being alive and present. Her tenuous hold on social legitimacy devolves to their young son, Eurysakes. The status, acceptance by the community, and even survival of Tekmessa and the boy become uncertain once Ajax has committed suicide. The status and acceptance of a soldier's wife, whose status as a spouse depends entirely on the soldier's presence and military authority, will be key issues that Menander dramatizes in his comedies that feature troubled soldiers. As I argue for Menander, his resolution of such tensions is bound up in his preference for a certain type of political stability. In Sophocles' play, any such political stability remains beyond the play's scope. Scholars have detected that this tragedy of Ajax encompasses conflicts that should spur dialogue about the ability or possibility of the Athenian democracy to promote just decisions in a collective fashion.[11]

Modern scholarly analysis of Athenian tragedy as a venue for communal discourse about the experience of combat veterans and the place for that experience in the community includes scholarly conversation via traditional professional channels (publications, scholarly meetings, etc.) but also extends to the

---

[9] Meineck 2012:7; a revised version of this paper appeared as Meineck 2016. See Meineck and Konstan 2014 and Caston and Weineck 2016 for the state of research along these lines for tragedy and other areas.

[10] Scafoglio 2017 provides an up-to-date analysis of Ajax in the epic tradition prior to Sophocles. On the play and combat trauma in particular, see Cole 2019.

[11] Anhalt 2018:115–148; cf. further discussion of Ajax in tragedy in Chapter 2.

performance of scripts coupled with outreach to current combat veterans, their families and loved ones, mental health professionals, and other interested members of communities around the world. Peter Meineck is again a prominent figure, as founder and artistic director of the Aquila Theatre. Through Aquila, the Ancient Greeks/Modern Lives project offers performances of sequences from the *Iliad* to deal with combat trauma suffered by ancient and modern veterans. Toward analogous goals, Bryan Doerries's Theater of War project has traveled the world using staged readings of Greek tragedy, of Sophocles' *Ajax* in particular, to facilitate healing conversations between combat veterans, family members, health professionals, and members of local communities.[12] As Doerries himself emphasizes, the conversations that are spurred by and follow the staged readings are the focused goal of his projects. These conversations testify that modern combat veterans and individuals bound up in their lives do readily identify their experiences with those dramatized in ancient Athenian tragedy, including Sophocles' *Ajax*. This ready identification does not automatically validate the position of Shay, Tritle, and others that ancient experiences were analogues to modern experience, but, insofar as the work of Meineck, Doerries, and others has led to positive therapeutic outcomes, it does provide a reason to evaluate other narratives from Greek antiquity for their potential to generate additional positive results.

Compared to the use of ancient Greek narratives in epic and tragedy for dialogue about the experiences of modern combat veterans, both in terms of scholarly analysis and community outreach, the use of Greek stage comedy is comparatively underdeveloped.[13] Alan Sommerstein has even characterized comedy as the "dog that didn't bark," charging that Greek comic playwrights sanitized the effects of war (2014b:225). This characterization is a judgment call and one, I argue, unfair to the Greek comic stage tradition. A community and culture need not and should not respond with a single, restricted narrative for its combat veterans. There is nothing inherently defective in comedy dramatizing the effects of war differently from epic and tragedy. Aristophanes, after all, repeatedly promoted peace and absence of war, which would cancel

---

[12] Doerries 2015; Aquila also staged *Ajax* in the early 1990s before Shay's work became widely known. Meineck's translation from these performances resulted in the published translation found in Meineck and Woodruff 2007. Meineck 2009 reflects on Doerries's project. Under Meineck, Aquila is also instrumental in the Warrior Chorus project, http://www.warriorchorus.org/.

[13] Raaflaub 2016 considers Aristophanes' *Lysistrata*, but primarily as a witness to the idea of a "homefront," a space and conception that tends to be defined in part by gender and is segregated from battlefield experience.

the traumatic effects of combat before they take place, a position no tragedian is known to have dramatized.

Greek "New" Comedy can seem like an even less likely venue for positive cultural negotiation about the lives of combat veterans. This is reputedly a theatrical world bounded by domestic neighborhoods, where military experience is always in the past and soldiers are reckoned stereotypically as idiots who thwart the goals of loving, if hapless, protagonists. In the case of Greek New Comedy's leading practitioner, Menander, Sommerstein portrays his soldiers as financially successful calculators, mercenaries in the most cynical sense.

The tentative suggestion that Menander's comedy can contribute to modern conversations about the effects of combat on individuals finds spark in the grisly description of a failed military attack recounted near the beginning of *Aspis*. James writes of the play, "Menander depicts the very specific social realities of combat-related ... PTSD, survivor guilt, and family trauma .... *Aspis* constantly recurs to loss, grief, and an ever-widening circle of survivors whose lives will be irremediably damaged by the soldier's death. The happy turn, in which the warrior returns unharmed, offered a comforting wish-fulfillment for many viewers, a fantasy of family rescue and reintegration" (2014:237; cf. discussion in Chapter 3). In part, James evokes a vision of communal therapy much like what Meineck proposes for tragedy (cf. a similar suggestion in Slagowski 2015), but the idea of "comforting wish-fulfillment" is a notion typically linked with comedy.[14] Implicit here is acknowledgment that Menander resolves the tensions resulting from battlefield trauma in a scenario that differs sharply from nearly all epic or tragic precedent. "Family rescue and reintegration" looms small among these precedents, and in this way Menander's choice to pursue it becomes striking and meaningful.

James's characterization of "family rescue and reintegration" as a "fantasy" for viewers should be revisited. This categorization implies that the resolution toward which Menander drives all his plays constitutes a vision that is pleasing but not realistic for the community to attain. To what degree the ideal world at the end of Menander's plays can be justly reckoned as an aspirational goal rather than an unattainable fantasy merits further discussion, not least for understanding what it means for Menander to have soldiers seek to prosper—and succeed in prospering—within just these environments. At one extreme a peaceful and prosperous neighborhood is not a fantasy of the order of a disgruntled citizen fleeing urban life to become a bird and ending up as ruler of the entire cosmos, as happens in Aristophanes' *Birds*. At the other pole,

---

[14] See Richlin 2018:43–47 for recent views of this sort of humor theory and New Comedy, though aimed more at the Roman iteration by Plautus.

testimony from antiquity often leans toward praising Menander for drama-tizing distinctively "realistic" characters (Nervegna 2013:217–218). Engaging this very issue, Petrides has argued for an intriguing way to have Menander inhabit the middle ground between these poles. On the one hand, Petrides summarizes, "Menander's comedy is, at the end of the day, almost as fantastical as Aristophanes'" (2014a:47). By this he does not mean that Menander's neigh-borhoods are as absurd as Cloudcuckooland. Rather, he means that Menander dramatizes a world that creative Greek minds of his day did envision. Above all, Menander facilitates stage action propelled by philosophical articulation of the systems of sensory understanding and social encoding, primarily drawn from Peripatetic philosophy. Petrides describes it this way: " ... Menander's 'realism' is as much creating a social reality as it is reflecting one; his verisimilitude is the disguise of, or the vehicle for, a discursive intent, and his ethical types, 'real-istic' as they may be in their external accoutrements, are eventually capsules of philosophical and political (in the widest sense) debate" (2014a:18). Put another way, Menander is modeling an aspirational community about which citizens can and should debate and toward which citizens should ultimately strive. In this context, Menander (1) seeks out areas about which his community has anxiety and needs to engage in discussion (2) models a resolution of this anxiety toward which the community can and should aspire.[15] Integrating soldiers into civilian life was one such area of communal anxiety. As documented in Chapter 2, before, during, and after Menander's career, militarized men were one such source of anxiety. In particular, military conflicts and the building of empires on unprecedented scales meant militarized men served as mercenaries at rising levels, rather than in the armies that were part of their polis-communities. This in turn led to an growing number of militarized men who still had mili-tary skills and were no longer in military service, but whose loyalty to a polis-military structure could be complex, indirect, and thus reckoned as suspect or unreliable, posing at least a perceived threat to civilian life in a polis. Menander dramatizes the tensions embodied in such men but steers dramatic action so that they become happy and stable husbands in peaceful domestic communi-ties. It is one thing, and fair enough, to criticize this vision of resolving this particular cultural anxiety as naïve or unrealistic, but that is insufficient to warrant categorizing these idealistic resolutions as escapist fantasy. It is even reasonable to say that Greek communities in Menander's time did not attain the stable, peaceful vision that he dramatized. Indeed, since Menander's motive in promoting this vision, as I will again argue, presupposed an imperial

---

[15] Cf. Hurst 2015:15–32, who proposes that Menander sought to educate the community in ways to expose the gap between appearance and reality.

domination that many today would consider a negative result for Greece, it is fair to judge Menander's aspirational goal as undesirable in modern terms. But it is still relevant that no surviving voice from antiquity judges Menander negatively on these grounds and, to the contrary, finds Menander an oasis from the cultural reality of the times. There was something reassuring, and not in an unattainably fantastic way, in seeing a troubled and dangerous former mercenary find contentment as a husband with a family and peace with his neighbors. How Menander struck this chord with his immediate Athenian community and with audiences across centuries involves his absorption of the theatrical tradition as a critical conveyor and focus of Greek cultural identity. The tradition of tragedy becomes folded into that of comedy. Petrides again: "Tragedy ... can be anywhere and everywhere in Menander, even behind the most mundane, that is, seemingly 'realistic' situations" (2014a:79). When it comes to soldier narratives, tragedy and epic were the preeminent sources for invoking and debating the paths following lives in combat on the battlefield. Menander taps into these narrative traditions, even, as Petrides says, in "mundane, that is, seemingly 'realistic' situations," but Menander's narratives culminate in a role and stability for these veterans rarely granted to them in earlier traditions. The power and creativity of this innovation should not be underestimated.

All these dynamics, then, will need assessment in analyzing soldier characters in Menander's plays and in recognizing how these characters and narrative trajectories differ from those in later traditions of stage comedy, even those traditions on the ancient Italian stage that adapted Menander's scripts. To understand and articulate these trajectories, the work of Shay, Meineck, Doerries, James, and others provide a number of axes by which to orient and chart Menander's dramatization of soldier characters and the trajectories of their narratives in his plays. Among the key axes for orienting Menander's narratives are (1) the traumatic persistence of military prerogatives in civilian life, (2) the theatrical precedent of tragedy dramatizing the damaging effects of this persistence, (3) the sociopolitical orientations embedded in any given stance on these effects, (4) Menander's break with the traditional narrative of destruction and failure resulting from these effects, and (5) the value of Menander's distinct narratives for ongoing modern activities where veterans and their communities use ancient Greek narratives to enhance and improve the lives of struggling combat veterans in the twenty-first century.

Among other aims, this study seeks to orient Menander's dramatization of soldier characters along at least these five axes. The specific orientations that I will argue are: (1) Menander's "soldier" characters are consistently and specifically militarized men who have been in mercenary service but whose military identity and prerogatives are now a barrier to their desired goal of a stable family life approved by a civilian community. (2) Menander deploys elements from previous theatrical dramatizations of this tension between military and civilian life, especially those found in tragedy. (3) Menander's ultimate dramatic goal is predicated on his ideological preference for peaceful civilian communities under stable Macedonian rule. (4) That Menander guides his plays to this resolution represents a sharp break from the dominant cultural narratives he reworked from tragedy and more broadly from epic. (5) Even with this break, Menander's soldier characters are further evidence for ancient Greek cultural and narrative patterns involving the aftermath of battlefield combat upon its participants and on the communities in which those participants reside. As such, they do not provide additional, distinct evidence that the psychology of ancient Greek soldiers can be mapped confidently onto that of combat veterans in the twenty-first century, thus not affecting the balance of debate about this issue one way or the other. Nonetheless, Menander's dramas do deserve evaluation regarding the merits of using them to foster community outreach and continued healthy dialogue among soldiers and community members to address the difficulties and anxieties about former soldiers leading lives positive for themselves and for those they engage with in the community.

As such, this study offers a counterbalance to the views of Sommerstein and James that Greek New Comedy was inadequate or escapist in dramatizing the consequences of combat on soldiers in civilian life. Menander's plays offer a valuable trajectory of ancient Greek cultural narratives about veterans after combat where the Greeks learned, preserved, and renegotiated their communities' perspectives on the morally injured soldiers among them. Furthermore, this radical reconfiguring of soldier narratives deserves consideration as a component of Menander's ongoing impact after his death. For centuries in the Greek-speaking world, Menander was second only to Homer and on par with Euripides as an embodiment of Greek culture, and soldier characters were among his most cited and recognized figures.

And yet, as implied by Sommerstein and James, to put Menander in a continuum with Homeric epic and classical tragedy today can seem less than intuitive, even outrageous or patently wrongheaded. Yes, it is acknowledged by modern scholars that Menander had prestige on par with Homer and Euripides, but the acknowledgment comes grudgingly as often as not, or as a concession or as a reminder about the strangeness of the ancient world, rather than a sensible and relatable phenomenon (see Chapter 1 on harsh judgments of Menander). This hesitation and distancing, at least regarding soldier narratives, is not irrational, but results from at least two interlocking historical forces on the modern understanding of Menander: (1) the loss of his scripts for more than a thousand years; and (2) the consequent reconstruction of his drama and legacy mostly via the Roman comedies of Plautus and Terence. The swaggering soldier in these Roman plays was a stock figure and came to cast a long shadow over soldier characters on European stages when Menander himself was no longer accessible. It was not illogical to reason that Menander's stage saw the progenitors of the Latin *miles gloriosus*. Not illogical, but, as this study will show, nonetheless wrong. The recovery of substantial portions of Menander's scripts over more than a century, along with visual representations of his plays, has made analysis of and conclusions about Menander possible that were previously beyond the evidence. Sommerstein is right that Menander's soldiers are mercenaries and distanced from their communities, but this is because Menander is addressing the community's need for dialogue and renegotiation about such men. Greek communities in his day and in subsequent eras were focusing on the perceived threat of mercenary soldiers, who were increasing in number during Menander's lifetime. These men were militarized and could indeed acquire financial resources, but tension remained about their loyalty to a community after their military experience. Menander and his audiences inherited cultural narratives about combat veterans, but these veteran men were all unquestionably bound to the communities of their birth. Most of these narratives, moreover, despite this intrinsic link between the veteran and his community, did not culminate in the veteran leading a stable, peaceful domestic life. Instead, for example, Odysseus wanders continually until his very last moments far from home, Agamemnon is slaughtered, Ajax dies before he can depart the battlefield psychologically or physically, and so on. Menander absorbed these narratives and redeployed them on his stage, but steered them to a completely different conclusion: the veteran becomes a husband in love, legitimized as a citizen in his community. This is a stunning revolution, too easily overlooked or deprecated, and yet all the more compelling because Menander's dramas became canonical as a vehicle of Greek cultural identity. This achievement deserves attention for what new perspective it can bring to continually improving communities' narratives and judgments about combat veterans today.

Accordingly this study has two broad goals: (1) to recontextualize and recharacterize Menander as a playwright who was, as great artists often are, both challenging and engaging to the audiences of his day, but also a harbinger of the Greek cultural world to come; (2) to unpack the novel dynamics about soldier narratives in ancient Greek culture that Menander deployed which resonated broadly in the Greek-speaking world until live theater was progressively shut down in the wake of rising Christian institutions. Menander's new narratives contrast with those in Homer and tragedy, but they are also extensions of them. This makes Menander valuable and useful today. It matters to soldiers today that epic and tragic warriors of the past not only achieved epic victories and tragic defeats but that the Greeks knew well that even the best warriors suffered moral wounds. Menander continued the narrative of warriors struggling when they tried to lead settled, domestic lives, but he significantly changed the trajectory and outcome. His soldiers become reconciled to their communities and find homes and families where they love, are loved, and accepted in the community for what comes to be revealed as their true identities.

The narratives of Greek epic and tragedy give precedent and authority to certain types of soldier narratives that have proven beneficial and healing to veterans of combat in this century. But every individual is different. The narrative that benefits one might not benefit another. Menander's plays offer a different narrative, but one that we should recognize carries its own prestige of precedent and authority. Some may benefit from this narrative who would not from epic and tragedy. It is not a matter of privileging the narrative trajectories of epic, tragedy, or comedy at the expense of the others. Adding Menander to the canon creates an additional tool and method for facilitating the communal work that most benefits those who need and deserve it. This study aims to lay the foundation and graph the dynamics for such work. In the Epilogue and Appendix I will return with some more concrete hopes and ideas for turning these findings into activities.

Until then, it is worth summarizing the trajectory of this study.

Chapter 1, "Menander in a Macedonian World (Revisited)" updates and expands my argument that the ideological vision of Menander's plays supports control of Athens and Greece by the Macedonian imperial forces of his day. Consequently, Menander characterizes his soldiers as a particular kind of threat to the stable domestic life Macedonian rulers wanted for the Greeks, many of whom were instead fomenting rebellion. In response to this perceived threat, Menander reconfigures inherited cultural trajectories to yield to a vision of the soldier as a stable, legitimate domestic citizen.

Chapter 2, "Setting the Stage for the Menander's Soldiers" reviews the history and cultural anxiety about mercenary soldiers in Menander's time to provide context for the soldier characters in Menander's plays, all of whom are former mercenaries. This chapter also clears away the expectation that a soldier in Menander should be an arrogant buffoon (*miles gloriosus*). There is in fact no evidence that this type was the norm prior to or during Menander's career. This chapter then focuses on some mechanisms that will be critical for seeing what Menander as a playwright does and does not do with his soldiers. Scholars have increasingly identified a large toolbox of techniques from tragedy which Menander reconfigured in composing a distinctly new brand of stage comedy. Tools both visual and verbal play a role in dramatizing soldiers' stories. In contrast, the second part of the chapter analyzes how Menander deploys true arrogant buffoons (*alazones*) in his plays, using the most prevalent example of the type, cooks. This examination illustrates how Menander deploys cooks as braggarts to signal the level of tension in a household to his spectators. If a household is stable, members can control the employment of a cook, but otherwise the arrogance of a cook fuels the tensions that are present. This use of braggart characters throws into relief the depiction of soldiers, who are not *alazones* but desperate protagonists in love seeking the fulfillment of their erotic desires in a domestic environment.

Chapter 3, "Love in the Age of War: Soldiers in Menander," turns to detailed analysis of every scene in Menander's preserved writings that involves a soldier character or refers to a soldier. The protagonist Polemon in *Perikeiromene* serves as a paradigm for all other soldier characters and related narratives in Menander, for this character and play are the best preserved (although scarcely half of the play's script has been recovered, ancient visual representations provide unusually rich supplementation). The hallmarks of a Menandrian soldier are here: his desperate desire for marriage with a woman of unconventional social status, his urge to commit suicide, and his movement away from his military past toward accepting his new community's established norms for being a lawful husband in a settled domestic environment. Two other plays, more fragmentary, but with soldiers as protagonists, *Misoumenos* and *Sikyonios*, reveal analogous narratives when compared to *Perikeiromene*. Two further plays featuring soldiers in oblique ways, *Aspis*, with a soldier who has been presumed dead, and *Samia*, where a young man pretends to become a soldier, also benefit from comparison with soldier narratives. A survey of the remaining briefer fragments and references completes the chapter.

Chapter 4 "From Menander's Soldiers to the Miles Gloriosus on the Roman Stage," examines how the Latin plays of Plautus and Terence in the third and second centuries BCE, some of which were adaptations of Menander's plays, promoted not haunted mercenaries in love, but arrogant buffoons as the dominant type of soldier character in stage comedy. The Plautine examples of a true *miles gloriosus*, from *Curculio*, *Epidicus*, *Truculentus*, and the *Miles Gloriosus* itself, have no known links to Menander. By contrast, Menander's *Synaristosai* is adapted as Plautus' *Cistellaria*, which vestigially preserves dynamics of the sort of soldier's experience familiar from Menander, when the young man Alcesimarchus asks for military equipment and subsequently threatens to commit a warrior's suicide (cf. the soldier Cleomachus in *Bacchides*, whose role in Menander's original is unknown). Fundamental is Menander's *Kolax*, which featured the soldier Bias, the only soldier in Menander's corpus amenable to being reconfigured as a *miles gloriosus*, and who is interpolated as Thraso in Terence's adaptation of Menander's *Eunuch*. The reputation of Menander's soldiers being arrogant braggarts rests ultimately on this fraught and atypical example. Consequently the Roman playwrights deserve credit for originating and propelling the legacy of braggart soldiers on later stages in Europe and elsewhere.

The Epilogue will turn to some proposed pragmatics for utilizing Menander's scripts in the context of modern work with the dynamics of combat trauma. But for the moment, it is crucial to acknowledge that motives and consequences never translate seamlessly from communities so distant chronologically and culturally from global culture in the twenty-first century as classical or Hellenistic Greece are. At best, we can pull and shape dynamics from those communities that we might not have conceived of without the classical tradition. Inevitably, some of what I argue motivated Menander will repel some individuals who would otherwise be sympathetic, even energetic, about working with combat trauma and the many whose lives are affected by it. Aware of this, I choose intentionally to present a Menander as honestly as I think he can be understood, and I encourage those uncomfortable with that Menander not to forestall positive results from using his plays for noble ends today.

1

Menander in a Macedonian World (Revisited)

"Menander suffered the misfortune of living in interesting times."

WHEN I BEGAN AN ARTICLE more than two decades ago with those words, it was radical to argue that Menander's comedy had contours shaped by the shifting political and military tides of the age in which the playwright lived and composed. The standard scholarly position was that, if the tumult of the times defined New Comedy in any way, it was only as a painful backdrop from which the stage was an escape and a relief. A relief theater very likely was, but scholars now have more occasion to debate where Menander and Greek New Comedy best fit into the ideological landscape of early Hellenistic Athens than to claim that the landscape was hidden from view of the spectators.[1]

This chapter revisits and updates my original argument about Menander's political and cultural allegiances and how those allegiances shape the construction of his plays. The thrust of my argument remains fundamentally the same, but it is important to reiterate and reintegrate my position into the scholarly conversation that has evolved over the years. In addition, my study of soldiers in New Comedy hinges on Menander's ideological orientation in at least two ways. First, I argue that the characterization of the soldier in Menander's plays results substantially from the ideological anxiety, itself generated by a very real threat, about the role of soldiers, specifically mercenaries, in Greek communities as the political and military structures of the Greek world dissipated and re-formed continually in the first decades of Macedonian domination. Second, the famous stock character of the *miles gloriosus* took form as a matter of reconfiguring the cultural anxiety about soldiers in civilian domestic life, but on the available evidence this process took place subsequent to Menander. More precisely, Menander calibrated soldiers in his plays to soothe concerns about men who were militarized but lacked allegiances to polis-communities. Menander sets up a soldier's erotic desire to generate a preference for family and domestic life

---

[1] See most recently, for example, Heap 2019:27–35.

that overwhelms his dangerous impulses. Greek New Comedy, as it was adapted on Italian stages and spread across an increasingly Roman world, still responded to cultural and civilian anxiety about soldiers, but in a new form, the true *miles gloriosus*. Burying the damage a soldier or army can cause under manifestly delusional bragging about military exploits became the dominant mode of the soldier character in Roman New Comedy. Demonstrating that this characterization is best understood as tangential to Menander's corpus requires delineating the soldier in Menander's comedies as conceived distinctly in response to the pressures and anxieties of early Hellenistic Athens during the three decades of Menander's playwriting career. Even if it is clear now that, over the long arc of the Hellenistic period, Athens progressively became a prominent cultural center in a world of large imperial powers, Menander and his contemporary Athenian citizens had little access to such a vision of Athens' long-term future. For Menander and comedy on the Athenian stage during his career, it is productive to highlight three areas where, during Menander's lifetime, Athenians debated their city's identity and struggled to chart its course, at times with the city's very existence threatened.

First, Athenians continually had to make critical decisions about the amount of autonomy they would pursue in the shadow of various Macedonian kings and their proxies.[2] When Menander was born (ca. 342 BCE), Athenian citizens were already divided and debating how to respond to the Macedonian incursions into the Greek world under Philip II. Menander was a child when the Athenians spearheaded the showdown against Philip, culminating in Philip's decisive victory at the Battle of Chaeronea in 338 BCE. Athens' rebellion against the young Alexander the Great a few years later would also have been an event of Menander's youth. After Alexander died and Athens rebelled yet again in the Lamian War of 322 BCE, Menander was just barely too young to have been called for military action. Immediately afterwards his career as a playwright began, effectively simultaneous with the start of direct rule by Macedonian authorities, and continued productively for thirty years.[3] The early years of his adulthood saw a violent democratic rebellion (318 BCE). The next year began a decade which found Athens under the governance of one of their own, Demetrius of Phaleron, but still under Macedonian control. In 307 BCE, another Demetrius, this one a Macedonian earning the epithet the Besieger along the way, captured Athens and was heralded for returning democracy to Athens. This Demetrius lost the backing he had courtesy of the imperial power of his father (Antigonus the

---

[2]   Habicht 1997:36–123 remains a solid survey of early Hellenistic Athens; cf. Green 1990:1–134.

[3]   Hence there is ancient testimony about Menander as an ephebe but no hint that he subsequently took up military service, apparently launching immediately into his career as a playwright. See de Marcellus 1996 and Iversen 2011 on what might have been Menander's first play.

One-Eyed) in the east, when Antigonus was killed during the Battle of Ipsus in 301 BCE. In Athens, this brought on the tyranny of Lachares, a period about which very little is known and which is still poorly understood. When Menander was about fifty years old, Demetrius the Besieger recaptured Athens and his entrance was again heralded. Menander did not live to see the end of Demetrius' reign or Athens' subsequent independence, as he died just a few years into Demetrius' second reign, reportedly in a swimming accident.[4]

No single, coherent narrative of these years in Athens survives from antiquity, but patching together events from the variety of inconsistent sources available indicates both that the operation of the Athenian government changed to varying degrees with each political and military changeover and that the Athenians themselves were never unified about what form their government should have and by what principles they should strive for that form.[5] Insofar as Athens was solidly a democracy when Menander was born, the extent to which Athens remained democratic is one obvious way to characterize the variegated changes that ensued during the next six decades.[6] Political debate framed democracy and tyranny as opposing poles, so the idea of tyrannical rule inevitably also becomes part of the vocabulary for characterizing deviations from early governing structures. Thus the persistence of democracy and independence from imperial authority forms the second major ongoing debate about Athenian identity as Menander experienced it.

This debate had deep roots and was never settled during Menander's lifetime. In part, shifts in Athenian governance represent the manifestation of the beliefs or principles of assorted factions in Athens as they in turn enjoyed, lamented, or even resisted the varying tides of Macedonian influence in the city (Bayliss 2011). What Philip II's rising power could mean for Athens was already a subject of ongoing public maneuvering in the years just before and after Menander was born. Following victory at the Battle of Chaeronea in 338 BCE, Philip II began to establish a governing structure for Greece, including Athens, but his assassination cut short any meaningful implementation. His successor Alexander was lenient following Athens' rebellion but otherwise mostly too occupied with conquest elsewhere to direct the future governance of Athens within the context of Macedonian imperialism. In the years following his death, however, the assorted Successors corresponded to changes in Athenian governance with different consequences for the extent and way democratic power

---

[4] See de Marcellus 1996 and Schröder 1996 for somewhat differing views on Menander's dates.
[5] See Bayliss 2011 for a fresh assessment of democratic Athens during this period; for assessments of democracy in the Hellenistic world beyond Athens, see Mann and Scholtz 2011.
[6] On the ideological and political stability of Athens as a democracy from 403–322 BCE, see Ober 1989:299–304.

did or did not persist. Decisive Macedonian control in the year 322 BCE brought with it forced political reforms, including a financial requirement for citizenship that disenfranchised a reported third of the citizens who previously held franchise in the democracy.[7] Machinations by various Macedonians at higher levels allowed democratic forces to reclaim Athens in the spring of 318, but a year later the democracy found itself on the wrong side of the emerging Macedonian ruler of Greece, Cassander, who installed Demetrius of Phaleron as governor of Athens. While assessments of Demetrius' rule vary, his decade-long government prompted a "restoration" of the democracy under Demetrius the Besieger, but the personal aggrandizement that Demetrius demanded left Athens anything but independent and democratic. Little is known of the "tyranny" of Lachares that followed Demetrius' downfall, which proved to be an interim government before Demetrius stormed and again controlled the city. Upon returning to Athens, Demetrius publicly spoke of restoring the democracy, but there is little to suggest that Athenians of any stripe thought of the ensuing years as such, and Demetrius by this point was more devoted to being king of Macedon than a democratic reformer in Athens. Menander did not live to see the Athenians cast off Demetrius in 287 BCE and have something of an independent state for the next twenty-five years. Quite the contrary, for the years Menander was an active playwright, such a development could have seemed, and certainly did seem to some Athenians, quite improbable and undesirable.[8]

Equally crucial to Athenian identity in these same decades was the cultural and intellectual identity of the city. The proposal for state regulation of philosophical schools in 306 BCE, passed but soon revoked, gives but one example of a flashpoint in this third focus of civic debate.[9] While in the face of the growth of philosophical schools in Athens there could be a negative reaction to philosophical life in public arenas, there could be no such judgment against the most popular and influential manifestation of Athens' cultural significance, theater. That theater was a crucial expression of Athenian identity seems not to have been in question, but the shape and purpose of that expression evolved along with the broader shifting ideological landscape.

A complex matrix of factors constitutes the substantive forces that shaped the terrain on which Menander composed his distinct brand of stage comedy. It is only with recent generations of scholars that most of these factors have been given their due weight. Previously, characterizations of Menander were

---

[7] See Jones 1957:75–98 and Hanson 1986:36 for different ways of calculating the extent of this disenfranchisement and Casson 1976 and Owens 2011:356–357 for discussion of the relationship between financial franchise and characters in Menander's comedy.

[8] See Bayliss 2011:61–93 for analysis of this phenomenon.

[9] Habicht 1997:105–111; Nervegna 2013:43–44; and more broadly Börm and Luraghi 2018.

restricted by two factors external to direct and proper contextualization of his plays. First, until the twentieth century, little continuous text of Menander was available to modern scholars, so contextualization, such as it was, depended overwhelmingly on Roman adaptations of his plays and testimony from antiquity about Menander. Each category of information carries with it fundamental challenges for distinguishing Menander's own work from its reception. Such work is still critical and still problematic, but the availability of substantial chunks of Menander's scripts has allowed developments in this area that were simply beyond the grasp of even the most acute scholars of prior centuries.[10] Second, the primary, overarching narrative of ancient Greece was that the peak of Greek cultural achievement ended prior to Menander, i.e. during the "classical" period.[11] Moreover, Greek tragedy held distinct pride of place in the lionization of classical Athens, and much of the modern notion of the "tragic" stems from this conception (Billings 2014 and Leonard 2015). Greek New Comedy, and thus a fortiori Menander, was denigrated as a cultural failure compared to the achievements of fifth-century tragedy. Voices as prominent yet as different as Nietzsche and Wilamowitz offered resounding condemnations of New Comedy and Menander in accordance with these values (Gould 2009). Even as historians of the Hellenistic world began to rehabilitate the reputation of Greek culture and achievement in the postclassical years, New Comedy in general, and Menander as its leading exponent, continued to be dismissed as simplistic fare, unresponsive to the complex cultural and historical web of events of the Hellenistic era. The recovery and publication of papyrus fragments and eventually a complete play took (and takes) much energy and diligence just in terms of mechanics. Yet, throughout the process, the negative judgment persisted: Menander himself was a disappointment. Whatever fascination and lessons the Hellenistic world had to offer, Menander remained a diversion and dismissed. W. W. Tarn, in a much-quoted characterization, brushes off Menandrian New Comedy as "about the dreariest desert in literature" (1935:273). Cary considers Menander a hollow, unfunny playwright who "enjoyed a vogue" at Athens (1951:330). Welles hopes for more substance in the form of political allusions now obscure to us (1970:203). Green expanded on this view and mocks Menander's defenders as self-deluded critics clinging to their desperate admiration and professional standing (1990:77). Even recently Johnson judges the popularity of a Menander a result of "cultural dementia" (2018:96, cf. 103).

---

[10] See Ireland 2010:346–350 and Blanchard 2014 for surveys of the recovery of Menander.

[11] See Bayliss 2011:10–48 on the dismissive perspective of scholars toward democratic Athens in the postclassical period; for a less sanguine recapitulation of Athens during this period, see Harding 2015:53–74.

As generations of scholars arose who inherited a more positive narrative of Hellenistic Greece and could start working on Menander's scripts with some confidence, fresh perspectives, rehabilitation, and even spirited defenses have become more the norm. A key part of this rehabilitation involves articulating how Menander represented a continuation of Greek tragedy, primarily Euripides, at a time when the legacy of fifth-century tragedy was critical to the communal identity of Athens. Conversely, denigration of Menander as an author, or New Comedy as a genre, typically disparages it as a degraded deviation from the boisterousness of Old Comedy, effectively Aristophanes (e.g. Harding 2015:114–118). While the long-standing cross-pollination between tragedy and comedy in Athenian tradition means there are antecedents for New Comedy on the earlier comic stage, the thorough integration of Euripidean tragedy into Menandrian drama is critical to understanding Menander's style and success.[12] Recently in this context, Petrides has crafted a particularly forceful and detailed study of this dynamic. Challenging the notion that Menander is more "realistic" in his drama, Petrides counters that Menander stages a world that is every bit as fantastic as any staged by Aristophanes (2014a:47). By this he means, citing analogous work by Ian Ruffell (2011), that Menander deploys "possible worlds" on stage (2014a:42). In this model, Menander stages a world where divinities nudge or embody the direction of human events, where individual people act out emotions and typologies derived from analyses in philosophical schools, and, most importantly for understanding the integration of tragedy into Menander's plays, where these individuals, as they rub up against the plot patterns established by Euripidean tragedy, articulate and condense the broader principles that explain human life. In this last sense, Menander's stage world is thoroughly imbued with the world of Euripidean tragedy. In a broader sense, however, as Petrides rightly emphasizes, Menander's stage world is hardly "realistic" in the sense that events in human life outside the theater transpire as Menander dramatizes them.

Greek New Comedy can be "realistic" in the sense that the characters are "capsules of philosophical and political (in the widest sense) debate" (Petrides 2014a:18), i.e. the human actions dramatized are congruent with those articulated within an ideological framework. Praise of such dramatization equates

---

[12]   The scholarly work on this topic has grown vast. Katsouris 1975 and Cusset 2003 remain extensive studies that often serve as starting points for subsequent analysis. Hurst 2015:15–32 and 73–103 (the latter a reprint of Hurst 1990) and Carey 2015 are also rich and valuable. Cf. Nervegna 2013:9–10, 110–116 on the persistent pairing of Euripides and Menander in antiquity. See the next chapter for the more specific relevance of this line of scholarship for the current study. For fifth-century antecedents for the cross-pollination of stage tragedy and comedy, see now Jendza 2020.

with the resolution of such behavior in line with the desirability of this behavior according to the strictures of the critic's ideology.

Congruence with ideology and incorporating the language and cultural resonance of Euripidean tragedy could seem an esoteric activity, except that Menander's drama resonated so profoundly, and the stakes in invoking tragedy were particularly high during Menander's lifetime. Hanink has produced a rich portrait of fifth-century tragedy becoming "classical" in the last half of the fourth century. As she documents, this process surfaced in public dialogue in the various political arenas of the democracy. The discussion and the results are manifest now in the surviving political speeches and documentation from inscriptions, and embodied in the monumental expansion of the Theater of Dionysus. Much of this process took place as Menander was growing up, with the renovated theater debuting when Menander was a teenager.[13] By the time he had completed his ephebic training and debuted a play of his own, he was living in a city with a theater greatly enlarged for unprecedented capacity and a theatrical complex that monumentally showcased the Athenian legacy of Greek drama, not least in the portrait statues of Aeschylus, Sophocles, and Euripides, a group to which Menander himself would be added some decades later (Hanink 2014a and 2014b; Nervegna 2014).

The development and showcasing of the legacy of tragedy in the Lycurgan era (which is also effectively the era of Menander's youth) was also thoroughly enmeshed with Athens' identity as a democracy. As Hanink demonstrates, the value of "classical" tragedy rose in proportion to the political and military threat the democracy faced, primarily from Macedon.[14] As a result of these competing pressures, any way that Menander appropriated tragedy in his drama was fraught with political and cultural allegiances.

The continued tradition of stage comedy as such was also embedded in political and cultural allegiances. To return to the argument I posed two decades ago, it is no longer eccentric, as it was then, to point out that topical and political comedy in support of democracy in Athens persisted into Menander's day.[15] New Comedy came to dominate the stage, but it was far from the only mode

---

[13] See Papastamati-von Mook 2014 for recently recovered specifics about the features of the theater at this time.

[14] The democracy's close link to the public performance of tragedy was not in itself new, going back at least to the democratic restoration after the coup of 411 BCE (cf. Major 2013:133–162). On the other hand, the Macedonian elite had their own interest in Greek tragedy, as it facilitated their rule and strengthened their power, fostering a distinguishable stylistic preference for tragic performances in their own regional spaces (on which see Moloney 2014 and Duncan 2015).

[15] Major 1997; cf. Major 2013:16–17 for a summary of the debate about Aristophanes' political allegiances. For subsequent scholarly approaches to Aristophanes' politics, see Rosen and Foley 2020.

of comedy, even during Menander's lifetime. The remains of fourth-century comedy, fragmented and limited as they are, indicate a range of comic modes, so diverse that categorizing them remains complex and challenging even now (Hartwig 2014 and Scafuro 2014a).

This complex diversity of comic theatrical activity in the generation prior to and contemporary with Menander, fragmentary though the remains are, helps delineate how specific the traits of "New Comedy" are and can point to the choices embedded in this particular genre. In the long view of theater history, New Comedy seems to have taken no more than two generations to dominate the Greek comic stage and it remained the dominant mode of comic theater until the theatrical life of the communities where theater had prospered was gradually shuttered under the influence of Christianization. Rapid as the conquest by New Comedy was, with Menander its leading exponent, Menander's style of playwriting contrasted with much of what is documented about comic theater just before and during his lifetime.

Since Hellenistic times, Menander has been recognized as the leading exponent of so-called New Comedy and has been virtually synonymous with it, even when his works were known only in fragments and by reputation (Nesselrath 1990:180–187, Nervegna 2013:56–57). This identification of Menander with New Comedy and his long shadow over later comic drama have left critics dealing with the playwright who is shackled to dramatic and generic conventions so rigid that originality was possible only in details and subtle variations (e.g. Zagagi 199415–45). Menander is thus constrained by his own dramaturgy and that of his successors.

Menander's posthumous prestige should not, of course, automatically translate into dominance during his own day. Likewise, the ancient tradition that Menander was not appreciated during his lifetime should not be accepted uncritically, especially given the partisan debate over Menander's virtues and deficiencies (Hurst 2015:57–72; cf. T83–168 PCG). That only eight of Menander's more than a hundred plays won prizes—the evidence usually cited to prove Menander's struggle for popularity—reveals little.[16] Aristophanes, for example, did not win as many victories in his forty-year career as Menander in thirty years, yet no one challenges Aristophanes' popularity.[17]

---

[16] This figure from Apollodorus' *Chronicle* (Gellius *Noctes Atticae* 17.4) is appended to a certainly fictional anecdote about Philemon's shame at being more popular than Menander. Cf. Ireland 2010:334–336 and Scafuro 2014b:219–220.

[17] See Konstantakos 2008 for skepticism and analysis of the tradition about Menander's supposed lack of popularity in his own day. The greatest number of victories attributed to any comic poet is Magnes' eleven in the mid-fifth century (T3.5 PCG). Attempting to judge quality, influence, and popularity from the plethora of awards shows today would be comparable. In fact, Menander's

The extent of Menander's reputation from 322 to 292 does not confirm that he either dictated or obeyed comic conventions during this period. Indeed, contemporary evidence suggests he did neither. The fragments of fourth-century comedy, despite their paucity, give a sense of the range of comic drama but are not necessarily a reliable guide to trends and proportions of various types, devices, and characteristics. Still, the range of these devices and characteristics indicates from what possibilities and sources Menander had to choose when crafting his own plays. Considerable attention has been paid to precedents in fifth- and fourth-century plays for such staples of New Comedy as stock characters, plots revolving around domestic mishaps, and romantic endings.[18] These studies demonstrate that Menander and other poets of New Comedy reconfigure often familiar material from comedy and tragedy as much as they overhauled dramatic conventions to suit audiences after 322. New Comedy had deep roots, and in crucial respects represents the survival of vital strands of drama from the classical period. The disappearance of some fixtures from earlier drama not vital in Menander, on the other hand, can be overstated. Although it is a commonplace to observe the rarity of topical jokes and invective compared to Old Comedy and to try in this way to account for the change in taste, the remains of New Comedy do not suggest such a simple progression.[19]

The Athenian Timocles indicates some of the complexities. He debuted on the comic stage before Menander, and their careers overlapped somewhat. Although the remains of Timocles' plays include such comic fare as stock parasites (frr. 8–11, 20–21, 31), he did not keep silent about the political turmoil in Athens during the second half of the fourth century. His attacks on Demosthenes have real bite. One fragment emphasizes Demosthenes' greed in the context of the Harpalos affair (fr. 4). Another characterizes him as a hypocritical, smooth-talking warmonger (fr. 12; cf. fr. 41; *Adespota* 149). The venom here suggests a Macedonian partisan, but two other fragments give a different picture. Both pillory Aristodemos, son of Aristophon, as a vicious and pathological thief (frr. 14, 19; cf. Philemon fr. 41). Demosthenes likewise characterizes Aristodemos as a thief, but also as a supporter of Philip's cause (10.70–73). Inferences are speculative with such limited evidence, but Timocles may simply have had a distaste for

---

portrait statue erected after his death and the attention he garnered from authorities may point to considerable respect (Nervegna 2013:42–45 and 60–62; Fittschen 1991:273–279). On the Macedonian allegiances associated with this portrait, see Page 24]

[18] See Arnott 1981, Nesselrath 1993 with good discussion and further bibliography, and Ruffell 2014.

[19] Gomme and Sandbach 1973:23 is typical of assessments up to its time: "Comedy had in any case abandoned the political field for a generation or more before Menander began to write." Luraghi 2012 serves as a handy survey of politically tinged fragments from comedy during Menander's lifetime.

bribery, corruption, and hypocrisy in politics.[20] Whatever his political convictions, Timocles was still producing plays after Macedon conquered Athens, as his Jury Lover (Φιλοδικαστής) includes a swipe at Demetrius of Phaleron's sumptuary laws (fr. 34).

The most remarkable political satirist on the comic stage during the period—Philippides, son of Philokles from the deme Kephale—was active alongside Menander and, by all accounts, a vigorous Athenian patriot and formidable comic poet.[21] Philippides' active career, including a victory during Demetrius of Phaleron's reign and serving as *agonothetes* (284) for the official festivals, overlaps and extends beyond Menander's.[22] When Demetrius the Besieger had the rites of the Mysteries hurried and compressed for his own benefit, Philippides used the comic stage to skewer Stratokles, Demetrius' underling who facilitated the arrangements (fr. 25). In another fragment (26) an unidentified speaker, according to Plutarch, addresses Stratokles: "With her head turned away, you hardly kiss her" (ἀποστρεφομένης τὴν κορυφὴν φιλεῖς μόλις). This line even raises the possibility that Philippides caricatured his victim on stage. Plutarch draws a stirring portrait of Philippides as a successful comic poet of high character with a close connection to a bitter foe of Demetrius, Lysimachus of Thrace (*Demetrius* 12.5). Epigraphical evidence bears out Plutarch. *Didascaliae* testify to Philippides' success in dramatic competitions (T7). An inscription records an honorary decree detailing his public service, which included lobbying Lysimachus (T3). This is a unity of dramatic comedy and political activism unparalleled even among the poets of Old Comedy. A public decree from 283/2 BCE celebrates his benefactions on behalf of the Athenian democracy.[23]

Any claim that Menander knew comedy simply as domestic romances and stock routines must reckon with the success of Philippides. If Philippides cuts an extraordinary figure, he was not alone in pursuing both politics and comedy. Archedikos had comparable interests. Three of his four surviving fragments consist of typical comic fare, but Polybius records that Archedikos slandered Demochares, nephew of Demosthenes, by charging Demochares with sexual misconduct (12.13.7 = fr. 4). This attack aligns Archedikos generally with Macedon and Antipater. Habicht identified this Archedikos with the top-ranked registrar

---

[20] Webster 1970:45 argues that Timocles is a pro-Macedonian supporter who could not support Aristodemos because of scandal. Constantinides 1969:54–61 surveys the political content of Timocles' fragments in detail. Apostolakis 2014 finds Timocles emblematic of a late fourth-century resurgence of Old Comedy's ad hominem tradition.

[21] See Philipp 1973:497–509 for a thorough review of Philippides' career.

[22] Philippides' *Mystis* won in 313/312 (T8). T3.38–50 records his generous service in managing and sponsoring festival contests. Gellius (*Noctes Atticae* 3.15.2) records, for what it is worth, that he died at an advanced age after winning again in comic competition.

[23] IG II² 657 = Syll³ 374 = T3 PCG; for full discussion of the inscription, see Shear 1978.

(ἀναγραφεύς) in the early years of Macedon's control of Athens (Habicht 1993). Once again we find a partisan comic poet with an active and prominent role in politics—this time decidedly in the service of Macedonian overlords.

Other comic poets tossed in political barbs before, during, and after Menander's tenure on stage.[24] Alexis and Philemon engaged political satire throughout their long careers. Philemon refers to the notorious Harpalos in the mid-320s (fr. 15). He also joins Timocles in attacking Aristodemos (fr. 41). A fragment addressing a character named Kleon may refer to Stratokles (fr. 178), whose notoriety peaked under Demetrius the Besieger, since Plutarch (*Demetrius* 11.2) links Stratokles to the image of Kleon. A character in Alexis cheers Demetrius the Besieger for the bill casting philosophers out of Athens in 307/306 (fr. 99). Alexis sends up another cheer for Demetrius and Antigonus in fr. 116.[25] To Demetrius' ascendancy in the late 290s also belongs Apollodorus of Karystos' call for peace (fr. 5). The spirit of this long piece would suit Old Comedy well, except for the historical allusions to Demetrius' conquests and the markedly Hellenistic interest in Tyche (cf. Philemon fr. 74, a less stirring appeal). Even as late as the 270s political invective appears. A drunkard makes a disconcerting reference to the incestuous relationship of Ptolemy II with his sister Arsinoe (Alexis fr. 246).[26] As an example of wise restraint, Plutarch reports the reaction of King Magas of Cyrene to Philemon's insult in a comedy (*Moralia* 449e–f, 458a = Philemon fr. 132). After the play's performance, Magas happened to capture Philemon but ordered a soldier just to touch Philemon's neck with a sword. Heaping insult upon injury, Magas gave Philemon a dice and ball, "as if to a senseless child" (ὡς παιδαρίῳ νοῦν οὐκ ἔχοντι) and released him.[27] That Philemon, otherwise treated as a watered-down version of Menander in antiquity, and indeed in modern times, had a reputation for political engagement, in contrast to Menander, is notable.

This assemblage of politically tinged material from Menander's lifetime does not mean that political invective thrived as in Old Comedy. Plutarch's story about Philemon and King Magas indicates that by the 270s political authorities still noticed the remarks of a comic poet, but that retaliation was beneath them.[28] Even if the anecdote lacks a kernel of historical truth, it reflects an

---

[24] Webster 1970:37–56 surveys most of the topical references, political and otherwise, in comedy after Aristophanes.

[25] See Arnott 1996:259–265, 308–311, 324–328 for further details and analysis.

[26] See Arnott 1996:16–18, 686–691 for discussion. Even if Bergk is correct that the fragment was added by a hand other than Alexis', the date of the fragment still supports my argument.

[27] See Philipp 1973:495–496 on this fragment as political comedy.

[28] Nervegna 2013:37–42 further notes that from the fifth to the third century, non-Athenian playwrights increase among authors of comedy. Metics had a minimal voice in Athens and comic playwrights with political edge are consistently Athenian.

ancient perception about the earnestness of such political invective, its potential risk to the comic poets, and its ultimate futility in the face of the massive
empires under construction by the middle of the third century. Nonetheless,
in Menander's Athens, comedy included at least a strain of political engagement. When a prolific playwright like Menander consistently avoids political
and topical references, he does not do so from obedience to the narrow conventions of contemporary drama. Menander was not a passive recipient of a form
of comedy devoid of connection to the tumultuous changes sweeping the
Mediterranean world. He made a choice and actively pursued a type of drama
that avoided the bitterness of other contemporary poets.[29]

The rare historical and topical points of reference in Menander's plays indicate just how restrained his comedy is, compared with the more vigorous work
of rivals such as Philippides, Alexis, and even Philemon.[30] Such references differ
only in how they convey so little information. Without a context, some fragments are simply too slight to indicate the purpose of a given historical reference (e.g. a campaign with Aristoteles, fr. 258; the battle of Lamia, fr. 120). Others
are too vague or general to be of much interest. The references in *Perikeiromene*
to years of war and increasing Corinthian troubles (124) and to a crop of
misery all over Greece (532) need not be tied to a precise historical or political
circumstance. Schwartz's identification—often repeated—of an allusion to the
assassination of Alexander, son of Polyperchon, is tenuous at best (280–281).[31]
Adaptation and translation further obscure such vague references as Terence's
to Indian elephants in Strato's command (*Eunuch* 413) and to Pyrrhus (783), and
Plautus' to Clinia and Demetrius (*Bacchides* 912). When a specific name or event
can be securely identified, it is little more than a name. Alexander the Great, for
example, appears thus:

ὡς Ἀλεξανδρῶδες ἤδη τοῦτο. κἂν ζητῶ τινα,
αὐτόματος οὗτος παρέσται, κἂν διελθεῖν δηλαδὴ
διὰ θαλάττης δέῃ τόπον τιν', οὗτος ἔσται μοι βατός.

---

29 Henrichs 1993 emphasizes the general difficulty of orienting Menander in the context of
Hellenistic culture and literature. Philipp 1973 and Habicht 1997, each keenly aware of the
political dimension of comedy in the early Hellenistic period, both caution against generalizing
about Hellenistic comedy from Menander. Giglioni 1984:27–28 goes further: "La scelta di non
parlare di politica potrebbe gia essere una scelta politica."

30 Webster 1970:2–11 gleans as much historical information (and more) as can be squeezed from
Menander.

31 Schwartz 1929:3–4. Gomme and Sandbach rightly consider the basis for the identification
weak; attempts to identify the Androcles of *Samia* 606 are still more desperate. Cf. Gomme and
Sandbach 1973:615.

This is just plain Alexander! If I want someone, he'll be right here. And if there's some need for a way to pass clear through the sea, he'll be my path.

(fr. 598)

This passage contains an allusion to the reported miracle of the sea opening up for Alexander at the siege of Pamphylia, but it is not actually about Alexander, rather a comparison that uses his name.[32] At *Kolax* fr. 2, Strouthias uses Alexander's reputation for drinking to ridicule the intoxicated Bias. A reference to the fourth-century orator Callimedon uses a common pun on his nickname "crayfish" (fr. 224.14; cf. the same pun at Alexis fr. 198, and, with more bite, Theophilus fr. 4). Nothing is judgmental in any of this. Athenaeus (12.549c–d) preserves the harshest comments about any historical figure: three jokes at the expense of Dionysios of Herakleia for his notorious obesity and gluttony (fr. 25). Athenaeus downplays the force of these insults when he states that Dionysius' reputation for decadence did not impair his successful rule as a tyrant, so there is no reason to relate these jokes to a tradition of hostile invective. Rather, these are occasional witticisms about a renowned figure, like the remarks about Alexander and others. Athenaeus even adds—these jokes notwithstanding— that Menander was not at all prone to viciousness (ἥκιστά γ' ὢν λοίδορος). This comment from an author versed in a much more complete corpus than we have gives reason to believe that Menander's extant remains are indeed representative. The closest Menander ever comes to addressing a controversial topic is a reference to the *Gynaikonomoi* instituted by Demetrius of Phaleron (fr. 208), but once again the reference is utterly indifferent: just a detail in planning a banquet.

To a degree, then, the historical critics are correct: Menander's plays avoid all but a faint touch of political and topical precision. It does not necessarily follow, however, that Menander lived in a fantasy world and set his plays in an escapist environment with no bearing on the world his audience inhabited. If his audience recognized the world on Menander's stage at all—and ancient comments about Menander's realism suggest they did—they did not perceive a nonsense-world of fantasy and escapism. A fine line divides fantasy and escapism from idealism and representation. Determining on which side Menandrian drama belongs depends significantly on the world and expectations of the audience. Any generalizing is hazardous. To some members of the audience, the plays might indeed have been escapist. The political tumult of the

---

[32] Plutarch *Alexander* 17.6. Bosworth 1980 *ad* 1.26.1f discusses other sources and accounts of Pamphylia.

times, however, justifies inquiring how those embroiled in the political and military upheavals reacted to Menander. As it turns out, the inquiry reveals something about Menander individually and about the assumptions that went into formulating his distinct brand of comedy.

If Menander did not express partisan political views explicitly in his plays, he could nevertheless strike a nerve and provoke a decidedly political reaction. Ancient sources in fact document two such reactions. In chronicling the life of Demetrius of Phaleron, Diogenes Laertius (5.79) records a detail from Demetrius' retreat from Athens in the wake of Demetrius the Besieger's arrival: Μένανδρος ὁ κωμικὸς παρ' ὀλίγον ἦλθε κριθῆναι δι' οὐδὲν ἄλλο ἢ ὅτι φίλος ἦν αὐτῷ. ἀλλ' αὐτὸν παρητήσατο Τελεσφόρος ὁ ἀνεψιὸς τοῦ Δημητρίου, "Menander the comic poet was nearly sentenced for no other reason than he was a friend to him [Demetrius of Phaleron], but Demetrius' cousin Telesphoros interceded for him." This report contains valuable testimony about the company Menander kept. Although the quality and success of Demetrius of Phaleron's rule is still debated, he was certainly an authority who represented Macedonian domination over Athens. Demetrius the Besieger would soon disappoint Athenian democrats, but hope that he would restore the democracy had carried him into Athens with popular support. Diogenes minimizes the pretext for Menander's prosecution, but Menander's connection with the Macedonian overlord was nevertheless close enough and prominent enough to associate him with those of the ousted government brought to trial. Either something in his plays aside from overt political references or some activity aside from the plays drew attention to his link with Demetrius—a link specifically with Macedonian imperial domination. The amnesty granted Menander is unremarkable and may represent no more than Telesphoros' political opportunism.[33]

A few years later, in 301, Demetrius the Besieger was in retreat and his father Antigonus dead after the battle of Ipsus. Oligarchs soon took over Athens, but Menander was still on the wrong side. Most likely before the Dionysia in 300, the oligarch Lachares blocked production of Menander's *Imbroi*.[34] No reason is given, but Iversen's fresh analysis of the evidence concludes "it is entirely

---

[33] Philochorus (FGrHist 328F) states that many who stood trial after Demetrius' flight were, like Menander, not sentenced after all, a passage emphasized by Potter 1987:494, who also exposes the weakness in the often-repeated assumption that Telesphoros was kin to Demetrius the Besieger, as if Menander somehow had supporters on both sides of the fence. Potter raises the distinct possibility that Telesphoros is an Athenian relative of Demetrius of Phaleron.

[34] Reported in a papyrus fragment of the *Periochai* of Menander (P.Oxy. X 1235), partly printed at *Imbrioi* Ti. See Luppe 1993 for reconstructions of the text. On the chronology see Habicht 1997:82–87. O'Sullivan 2009 is justifiably skeptical about previous scholars' conclusions about the events hinted at here, but her suggestion that the incident in fact belongs to the controversy about Stratokles addressed in the fragments of Philippides is highly speculative.

plausible that in 302/1 Lachares, as a member of the Stratoclean wing of the democratic party, successfully censured [*sic*] Menander" (2010a). Imbros had been an Athenian colony until Antigonus took it while Cassander controlled Athens, but Antigonus returned it in 305/304. The plot of the play revolves around two poor refugees to Imbros. Only one fragment (191) of any substance remains:

οὐκ ἔστιν οὐδέν, πάτερ, ἐν ἀνθρώπου φύσει
μεῖζον λογισμοῦ, τῷ διαθέσθαι πράγματα
ἕκαστός ἐστι τῷ λογίσασθαι κατὰ τρόπον
ἄρχων, στρατηγός, ἡγεμὼν δήμου, πόλει
σύμβουλος· ὁ διαφέρων λογισμῷ πάντ' ἔχει.

There's nothing, father, in human nature better than reasoning; by analyzing situations everyone can reckon in their own way: the archon, general, leader of the people, advisor to the city. The man who decides by reasoning has it all.[35]

It is conceivable that Menander trod on a sensitive topic of the time, without making any more overt or specific political references than he ever does. Despite the great number of sententiae preserved from Menander, even such general remarks about politics and leadership as this are scarce.[36] In any case, he crossed the oligarchs in some fashion. The limited testimony, then, has Menander at odds with Athenian democrats and oligarchs alike, but linked to Macedonian

---

[35] See Major 1997:53n35 for Heimsoeth's conjecture of πόλει for πάλιν in line 4.
[36] Cf. fr. 769:

δεῖ τὸν πολιτῶν προστατεῖν αἱρούμενον
τὴν τοῦ λόγου μὲν δύναμιν οὐκ ἐπίφθονον,
ἤθει δὲ χρηστῷ συγκεκραμένην ἔχειν

One elected to lead the citizenry must have a capacity for speech that is not malicious but blended with good character.

See Major 1997:53-54n36 for discussion of Meineke's observation that this reads more like a tragedy than New Comedy and how Körte-Thierfelder points out that this is the only appearance of the word πολίτης in the Menandrian corpus, a fact striking in itself and increasing the likelihood that it is a tragic quotation, a misattribution, or a character in tragic mode. Cf. Knemon's brief vision of a political utopia (*Dyskolos* 743–746, quoted in the Introduction) and the range of people who are victims of flatterers at *Kolax* 87–92, discussed in Chapter 4.

authorities.[37] Eventually, a tradition will evolve around Ptolemy's attempts to bring Menander to his court, but it is of dubious historical value.[38]

Additional evidence supports Menander's ties to circles sympathetic to Macedon. Menander's closeness to Demetrius of Phaleron links him not only to Macedonian politics but to Peripatetic philosophy. Scholars have documented in detail passages that betray at least familiarity with, if not subscription to, Peripatetic doctrine.[39] Recent scholars have been increasingly assertive on this point. Nervegna (2013:45–54) is quite forceful about the link between Menander and Peripatetic philosophy and thence to Menander's ideological congruence with Macedonian imperialism. Petrides (2014a:5–7, 138, 143–7, 157, 169, 212, 214, 238) finds the Peripatetic doctrine of physiognomics critical to understanding New Comedy, its masks, and presentation of character on stage. These analyses find parallels principally with ethical and literary theory, but the Peripatetic school also had notable political leanings. As Lynch states flatly in his historical study of the institution, "Aristotle's school depended from the very first on Macedonian rule" (1972:94–95). Aristotle's family was connected to Macedonian elites. Aristotle's father had been a doctor in Macedon's royal court and Aristotle followed suit when he tutored the young Alexander. He continued

[37] It is worth noting that both events place Menander in Athens even during difficult times. Scholars have speculated about the influence of theatrical venues outside Athens. Habicht 1997:101 repeats a commonly held position when he attributes the lack of obscenity and political specificity to comic poets appealing to audiences beyond their local city-states. See Csapo and Wilson 2015 for the spread of theater in general in the fifth and fourth centuries BCE, but see Slater 1994:30–34 for a focus on comedy. Slater investigates the possible role of market forces across the Greek world in broadening the focus of stage comedy in the fourth century. For Menander to have produced over a hundred plays in thirty years would seem to require performances outside Athens, but this does not mean that it markedly affected his writing. Athens was still undeniably the center for such activity, and the occasional play set outside Attica does not mean these plays were performed there. Menander was a native Athenian and no testimony ever places him anywhere else. It could even be maintained (along the lines of the argument below) that if Menander did have his plays produced elsewhere in Greece, he did so relying on the stability and coherence of a Macedonian presence over the whole region.

[38] Cf. Pliny *Natural History* 7.30.111 (Menander refuses to go to Ptolemy's court) and Alciphron 4.18f (letters between Menander and Glykera celebrating the same refusal). Nervegna 2013:43 points out that these letters specifically put Menander in Piraeus, the stronghold of Macedonian control in Attica (cf. Funke 2016). To this tradition must also belong the lost epistles to Ptolemy listed among Menander's works in the *Suda*. Certainly Alciphron's letters indicate literary embellishment, if not outright creation. Phaedrus 5.1 works up a fable about Menander's first meeting with Demetrius of Phaleron, which Green 1990:72, 755n44 vainly attempts to read as historically plausible. Unlike the reports from Diogenes Laertius and the *Periochai* papyrus, Phaedrus is invoking and continuing a literary tradition, not even claiming to transmit historical information.

[39] Most thorough is Gaiser 1967. By contrast, efforts to find influence of the emerging Stoic and Epicurean philosophies have not proved fruitful: Barigazzi 1965:87–115 reviews and criticizes these attempts. Konstan 2014 surveys Hellenistic philosophical material in later Greek comedy.

a friendship with Antipater. After establishing the Peripatos, Aristotle in his last days had to flee Athens when anti-Macedonian sentiment swelled in the shadow of Antipater's approach. Demetrius of Phaleron was an active and prolific Peripatetic philosopher in his own right, which could only reinforce the connection for Athenians between the Peripatos and Macedon.[40]

Theophrastus, Aristotle's successor, also has strong ties with Macedon in ways that are pertinent for understanding Menander. The tradition that Theophrastus taught both Menander and Demetrius of Phaleron is quite plausible.[41] Theophrastus kept up direct ties with Macedon. He had an audience with Cassander and at least an invitation from Ptolemy. He may have composed a work on kingship (βασιλεία) for Cassander (Diogenes Laertius 5.47; cf Athenaeus 4.144e = fr. 603 F). As Cassander's appointee, Demetrius of Phaleron was in a position to help Theophrastus obtain property for the Peripatos (Diogenes Laertius 5.39). Agnonides, very likely the same man who brought charges against Phokion (leader of the anti-Macedonian faction in Athens), unsuccessfully brought him up on a charge of impiety.[42] When Athenian nationalists came to power and Demetrius of Phaleron was cast out, anti-Macedonian sentiment led to a bill to expel the heads of the philosophical schools, of which the Peripatos was easily the most prominent. Although Menander ultimately avoided penalty in this wave of resentment, Theophrastus suffered exile until the law was declared unconstitutional the next year and he could return.[43]

Theophrastus' own brand of Peripatetic philosophy provides some useful parameters for understanding Menander as a comic poet. The debate about the degree to which Menander can be reckoned a Peripatetic has tended by necessity to rely on Aristotelian doctrine.[44] Except for comparison with Theophrastus' *Characters*, Theophrastean theory has played little role in studying Menander's debt to the Peripatos.[45] The fragmentary works of Theophrastus will not settle the issue of Menander's debt, but a few observations can help explain a paradox that emerges in Menander's biography. Menander moves among the Macedonian

---

[40] Williams 1997 extensively documents the relationship between Demetrius' philosophy and political activities.

[41] Diogenes Laertius 5.36. See Gaiser 1967 for an overview of the possible iconographic tradition linking the three. On the other hand, the report in the *Suda* that the comic poet Alexis was Menander's uncle expresses more literary than biological pedigree, on which see Arnott 1996:11–13, 26–28.

[42] See Ditadi 2005:91–96 for a review of this incident.

[43] See Diogenes Laertius 5.37 for the events and Lynch 1972:98, 103–104, 152–53 for the politics of Macedon's support of the Peripatos.

[44] Traill 2008:171–174 finds Menander un-Aristotelian.

[45] Nervegna 2013:45–54, esp. 49, makes more extensive use than most. On *Characters* and Menander, see Pertsinidis 2018:53–58 and Heap 2019:29–30.

elite and Macedonian sympathizers prominently enough to cause friction with opposing political camps, yet Menander's plays reduce political content to an absolute minimum. Theophrastus enjoyed similar, probably greater, elite connections, while his writings on politics and comedy have a dichotomy similar to that in Menander. Particularly striking in view of Menandrian New Comedy is Theophrastus' definition of comedy as "a story of private affairs involving no danger" (ἰδιωτικῶν πραγμάτων ἀκίνδυνος περιοχή, fr. 708.9f F).[46]

That comedy defined this way is staunchly apolitical is confirmed by Theophrastus' sharp distinction between the domestic and political spheres.[47] The first-century BCE Epicurean Philodemus protests against the way Theophrastus circumscribes the field of managing domestic affairs (οἰκονομική); for Theophrastus, Philodemus charges, claims that οἰκονομική is different from politics, πολιτική, and that the two are in no way analogous (μήποτε ἀναλογοῦντ' εἶναι περὶ ἐκετέραν, fr. 659 F). Philodemus responds that this is irrelevant and false, and goes on to insist that because establishing a household is logically prior to establishing a city, so, too, household management is logically prior to politics (καὶ ταῦτ' ἐναργέστατον ὑπάρχον, καὶ τὸ πρότερον οἰκίαν πόλεως συστῆναι, διὰ καὶ τὴν οἰκηνομικὴν τῆς πολιτικῆς). By this refutation Philodemus implies that Theophrastus had posited the reverse order, with politics having priority over domestic management.

A rigidly confined domestic world with no apparent analog in the political arena accurately describes the setting for Menandrian drama. The restriction to the domestic realm is so strict that institutions and concepts associated with the public realm must be filtered and reconstituted in order not to disrupt the household setting of a play. For example, Menander shapes a dispute as pretrial arbitration in *Epitrepontes* but recasts every component to keep it a household event. The scene for which the play is named features a trial about custody of a foundling's tokens. The defendant, a shepherd named Daos, found the child and retains the objects left with the infant. The plaintiff, a charcoal burner on the estate named Syros, adopted the baby from Daos. To decide who has rights to these objects, Syros and Daos select a passerby to serve as arbiter. This judge, Smikrines, unknown to all present, is the child's grandfather and remarks on the informality of the scenario, "You worthless garbage, you're wandering around presenting cases in overalls?" (ὦ κάκιστ' ἀπολούμενοι,/ δίκας λέγοντες περιπατεῖτε, διφθέρας/ ἔχοντες; 228–230). As it turns out, Syros, incongruously for his occupation, is adept at court procedure; as Daos notes with alarm, "I've

---

[46] See Fortenbaugh 1981, esp. 258 for Theophrastus on comedy, although he focuses on character in particular.

[47] Henderson 2014:190–195 surveys topics under the rubric of domesticity in fourth-century comedy.

gotten myself mixed up with something of an orator" (μετρίῳ γε συμπέπληγμαι ῥήτορι, 236). This humble charcoal burner uses sharp rhetorical questions (313), elevated diction (320–326), sententious remarks (343–345), and, in a perfect blending of a domestic backdrop and public performance, Syros brings his wife and newly adopted child to "court," going so far as to claim that he is merely speaking on behalf of the child, who is the true plaintiff in the case (303–307). Moreover, a tragic motif overlays the proceedings when Syros cites tragic exempla (325–330). He invokes conventions from stage tragedy when nobles recover their identities by means of tokens. Syros actually comes close to accusing Daos of larceny, a crime with a heavy penalty in a public court, but the seriousness of such a charge is allowed to pass here (312).[48] In many ways, the scene encapsulates Petrides's model of "realism" in Menander: "His verisimilitude is the disguise of, or the vehicle for, a discursive intent, and his ethical types, 'realistic' as they may be in their external accoutrements, are eventually capsules of philosophical and political (in the widest sense) debate ... 'a genre of political inquiry' (τοῦ πολιτικοῦ ζητήματος γένος)" (2014a:18). The use of tragedy is also integral: "Tragedy, then, can be anywhere and everywhere in Menander, even behind the most mundane, that is, seemingly 'realistic' situations" (2014a:79). Menander is willing to put the world of the tragic stage on an equal footing with comedy, but the consequences of public and political life are entirely excluded. Theophrastus defines comedy as a story of private affairs. This episode, like all others in Menander, concerns strictly private events. Theophrastus further requires that the story of a comedy involves no danger. In this scene and others, Menander has bypassed or ignored the potential danger that could arise were these events to take place in a truly public, political setting (cf. the discussion of Agnoia's speech in *Perikeiromene* in Chapter 3). Moreover, Theophrastus insisted on a sharp demarcation between the domestic realm and the political environment in which it is couched, a separation Menander also maintains.

Theophrastus' brand of Peripatetic philosophy, then, provides something of a framework that accounts for the sharp exclusion of political activity from Menander's plays. If the analogy with Theophrastus' life and thought holds thus far, one possible additional parallel may be valid. Despite the elite connections Theophrastus maintained and the enormous amount of research he undertook on political topics, he was notoriously ignorant or at least naïve about his own political environment. Philodemus in fact chastises Theophrastus for spending

---

[48] See Gomme and Sandbach 1973:313, Hurst 2015:105–114, and Heap 2019:81–89. Scafuro 1997:154–161 analyzes *Epitrepontes* against the backdrop of what she argues is a social paradigm of dispute settlement by means of pretrial arbitration.

his whole life in private (ἰδιωτείᾳ) and in ignorance of regal affairs (βασιλικῶν, fr. 27 F). Citations from Theophrastus' political writings tend to be of historical and legal details and betray an interest mainly in the theoretical problem of critical moments (καιροί).[49] Aelian and Proclus both speak of an occasion when Theophrastus was dismally unsuccessful before the Areopagus. Aelian reports that Theophrastus lost his nerve and that Demochares, a prominent and virulently anti-Macedonian democrat, mocked him for it (*Varia Historia* 8.12 = fr. 32a F).[50] Proclus explains Theophrastus' utter failure on this occasion by saying that the Athenians were not persuaded about topics of which Theophrastus had no experience (ἐν οἷς ἀπείρως εἶχεν, fr. 32b F). In short, Theophrastus enjoyed the company and support of the Macedonian elite at Athens but was ignorant of the broader political scene to the degree that he was unable to conduct himself adequately before a political body such as the Areopagus. He lived in private and considered the private, domestic realm distinct from the political arena, even if he believed that public government was logically prior to the domestic realm. And he assigned comedy to this domestic field.

No known ancient source asserts that Menander was equally at a loss about politics, unless there is a kernel of historical truth in the tradition of Menander rejecting Ptolemy's overtures. Menander did share with Theophrastus Macedonian support and wrote plays congruent with Theophrastus' conception of comedy by setting his dramas in a specifically domestic sphere. In so doing, Menander implicitly manipulates his comedies within a domestic realm that—continuing with Theophrastus—presupposes some sort of political establishment. This implied political establishment can only have been Macedonian.

In staking and standing by this claim, I am remaining on a side of a debate in which scholars have yet to reach consensus. While scholars increasingly acknowledge that understanding Menander's plays involves orienting the playwright in the ideological grid of early Hellenistic Athens, individual scholars differ about where to place him. Most prominently among scholars who would have Menander on the other side of the political spectrum is Lape, who in her 2004 book *Reproducing Athens* articulated an argument that Menander's plays reiterate and support democratic ideology when it was under attack from Macedonian and oligarchic forces. Lape invokes especially the Periclean citizenship law of 451 BCE, which effectively closed the democratic citizen body of Athens. She suggests that when citizen couples in New Comedy finally receive sanction to marry, they are enacting the renewal of democratic culture. In

---

[49] See frr. 589–665 F, esp. fr. 590 F (= Cicero *De finibus* 5.11), with Podlecki 1985.
[50] See Marasco 1984:23–84 on Demochares' politics, esp. 42–46 on his involvement with the charges against Theophrastus.

the context of Macedonian repression of the democracy, such performances become acts of dissent. Lape extends her case: "Menandrian comedy not only depicts and champions fundamental precepts of Athenian democratic ideology but ... also, in certain cases, offers reactions to and commentaries on immediate political events" (10), although "comedy's family romances are often subversive of the democratic cultural order they instantiate" (12).

While no one can prudently claim certainty in this debate given the evidence, I argue that an argument like Lape's requires claiming for democratic ideology associations that are in some cases dubious and even contradictory. For example, Lape accepts a supplement ὕβριν in *Dyskolos* 298 and emphasizes the importance of hubris for her democratic interpretation (117). In part, however, scholars have proposed and accepted the supplement because it fits Aristotelian doctrine so closely. Aristotle says young, wealthy men (such as Sostratos in the relevant scene) are especially prone to hubris (*Rhetoric* 1378b26) and says so in the context of anger, specifically the anger a superior feels for his inferior. This is hardly a democratic, egalitarian conception of hubris. And herein lies the problem: Lape claims for democratic ideology terms and contexts that can just as easily invoke elite, decidedly non-democratic doctrine.[51]

On balance, what is known about Menander's biography and his links to the philosophical positions of the Peripatetic school are most consistent with Macedonian oligarchic ideology. As Nervegna summarizes, "Menander did not 'feel' like a democrat," and adds, "nor perhaps did he look like one," given the features of the portrait statue that joined the Athenian tragedians that were erected in Menander's childhood (2013:44), which scholars have increasingly recognized as invoking elite Macedonian status in contrast to the visual emblems associated with Athenian democratic culture.[52]

To recapitulate, Menander pursues a narrowly focused brand of New Comedy, which steadfastly avoids the topical and political content found in contemporary comic poets. In view of Menander's attested associations with the Macedonian elite and with the Macedonian-backed Peripatos, and given the views of Theophrastus, the rigidly domestic world of Menander's comedies presupposes the stability of the Macedonian establishment. His comedy is thus produced from so deep within one political structure that the plays do not reach beyond this context. To see the effect of this origin on the literary form of Menander's plays, we need to locate Menandrian comedy in a field that tracks the boundaries of a play's theatrical space as it encroaches on political space.

---

[51] For further analysis of the strengths and weaknesses of Lape's volume, see Major 2004, Iversen 2010b, Owens 2011:351–356, and Nervegna 2013:42–45, all of which trend toward Menander's plays being congruent with Macedonian oligarchic ideology.

[52] Zanker 1995:78–93, Palagia 2005, Papastamati-von Mook 2007, and Bassett 2008:212–214.

For a mechanism to map this field, this study capitalizes on work modeling theater as a community's ritual to reiterate and probe its identity. For the democratic ideology that dominated the political landscape of Athens in Menander's youth, Ober has analyzed political authority as it was defined, maintained, and stabilized in democratic Athens during the first three quarters of the fourth century. Using principles of political sociology to study how political ideology is expressed via semiology, especially in rhetorical texts, he finds that from the ouster of the Thirty in 403 until the reconfiguration of Athens' citizenship by the Macedonians in 322, the *demos* maintained the integrity and stability of the democracy by wielding the authority to determine what signs constitute its ideological identity. According to Ober, this authority defines political power and cohesion more than constitutional authority (1989:22–23, 299–304). Rather, the *demos* exerted power through collective judgment, and "in the ongoing dialectical give and take of public oratory, audience response, and demotic judgement, a set of common attitudes and social rules was hammered out."[53] Although Ober focuses principally on rhetorical and political texts, he has, with Strauss, expanded the application of these sociological models to include performances in the public theater (Ober and Strauss 1990). Strauss borrows the concept of "social drama" from cultural anthropology: "a public episode that passes through ritualized stages of tension, crisis, redress, and reintegration" (Ober and Strauss 1990:245). Thus defined, social drama embraces a variety of public events, from a religious rite to a court trial, from the installation of a public official to a play in the theater. More importantly, episodes from different venues may cross-pollinate. An orator may quote or otherwise evoke a tragedy. A play may appropriate a scenario from public life, as Old Comedy did often. Religious ritual in turn permeates many episodes of Athenian communal life. All these episodes of social drama are united in so far as they employ symbolic action and interaction (Ober and Strauss 1990:249). This model is developed primarily to study the interaction of oratorical and dramatic texts of the classical period, where the uneven distribution of remaining texts (a preponderance of dramatic texts from the fifth century and of rhetorical texts from the fourth) make such studies difficult.

After 322 BCE, Ober's scenario of a stably maintained democracy no longer holds. Still, the model and observations of Ober and Strauss are useful for orienting Menandrian New Comedy in the new political environment. Without denying the very real material and personal losses during the period, we may legitimately characterize the five decades or so after 322 as a time of ideological crisis for Athens, as surveyed earlier in this chapter. If in the eighty years after

---

[53] Ober 1994:89. This article is a useful summary of Ober 1989.

the Peloponnesian War the Athenian *demos* enjoyed the power to manipulate civic symbols in order to construct its own ideological image, democrats over the next several decades struggled to regain that power. Likewise, Athenian oligarchs, if not dominant in the construction of popular ideology in those same eighty years, were always an active participant and a force to be reckoned with in the game of symbolically establishing civic identity. Now they faced loss of even this role to the Macedonian elite. Macedonian encroachment meant a new ideological force, and a new type at that. Alexander and the Successors initiated a process of empire building unlike the tentative and short-lived previous attempts by various Greek city-states. With this process came new methods and types of ideology formation (Bulloch 1993). Already in Menander's youth, under the impact of Macedonian incursions spearheaded by Philip II, democracy was a rallying cry. As Habicht puts it, a "strongly nationalistic mood was matched by an equally strong emphasis on democracy in the political thought of the time" (1997:28). The topography of Athens was but one field where this mood materialized, with notable visual depictions of the Demos and Democracy (Raubitschek 1962). In contrast, under Macedonian rule, verbal and visual propaganda of individuals flourished and increased in sophistication. At stake was the identity of Athens as an independent democracy, a part of a Macedonian empire, or something in between.

The new Macedonian methods of promoting ideology affected civic dramas as well. When Demetrius the Besieger entered Athens in 291 with a procession and was hailed in an ithyphallic hymn as a divinity, the whole travesty stood as a prominent example of recasting one civic drama, a religious procession, as a different civic drama better suited to serve Macedonian imperial ends (Green 1990:55, 126; Habicht 1997:92). The civic drama of comic performances was one battleground for rival ideological imagery. Historically, comic drama had a tradition of articulating the character and force of the democratic *demos*.[54] Controlling the imagery of comedy, therefore, meant controlling a portion of the civic ideology of Athens. The politically active comic poet Philippides addressed this issue when Demetrius the Besieger in 302 BCE had another prominent civic drama, the rites of the Eleusinian mysteries, reworked for his own benefit (cf. Habicht 1997:78–79). Philippides (fr. 25) attacks Stratokles, the flatterer who facilitated the arrangement:

Δι' ὃν ἀπέκαυσεν ἡ πάχνη τὰς ἀμπέλους,
ὁ τὸν ἐνιαυτὸν συντεμὼν εἰς μῆν' ἕνα,

---

[54] The outright personification of Demos in Aristophanes' *Knights* illustrates this function. See Henderson 1990 and Major 2013:64–82.

ὁ τὴν Ἀκρόπολιν πανδοκεῖον ὑπολαβὼν
καὶ τὰς ἑταίρας εἰσαγαγὼν τῇ παρθένῳ.
δι᾽ ὃν ἀσεβοῦντα δ᾽ ὁ πέπλος ἐρράγη μέσος,
τὰς τῶν θεῶν τιμὰς ποιοῦντ᾽ ἀνθρωπίνας.
ταῦτα καταλύει δῆμον, οὐ κωμῳδία.

The man cut the year down to a month, managed the Acropolis like
a motel, and introduced whores to the Virgin. By him rime froze on
the vines. By his unholiness was the middle of the robe torn when he
dedicated human honors to the gods. This ruins the democracy, not
a comedy.

The health of the *demos* is at stake. Allowing a Macedonian imperialist to subvert
so precious a social drama as initiation into the Eleusinian mysteries compro-
mises the ideological identity of the *demos*. Apparently in response to some
charge that comedy could harm the *demos*, Philippides adds emphatically that it
does not do so.[55] But could comedy in fact undermine the ideological identity of
the *demos*? Did it? To a democrat like Philippides desiring to restore the integrity
of the *demos* or to an Athenian oligarch intent upon warding off the intrusion of
the Macedonian elite, the narrow domestic setting of Menandrian comedy does
nothing to advance their cause. It may even be a hindrance if it originates from
within the Macedonian establishment and represents a settled society where
the mass of the population has no interest in the political concerns of parties,
factions, and empires.

That Menander wrote plays thus compatible with pro-Macedonian ideology
does not make him a conscious propagandist for the Macedonian cause nor
reduce him to a mere pamphleteer. Rather, for someone in Menander's position
to write the plays he did, he had to take certain things for granted and make
certain a priori assumptions, which include the existence (but not the explicitly spotlighted presence) of communal political stability, so that household
and family members can make their primary concern the conjugal, financial,
and emotional rectitude of their homes. Any external forces that interrupt the
proper function of the home can be addressed and rectified entirely by action
within the home (perhaps with the participation of a neighboring household).
External circumstances are such that household members feel no compulsion to
mix political with domestic concerns. Neither democratic nor oligarchic ideology
called for this isolation of the domestic sphere, especially when the proponents

---

[55] Harding 2015:24–27 looks at this fragment from the perspective of politics and censorship.

of these ideologies had been knocked on their heels in 322. Macedonian presence is once again implicit.

Too often studies of Menander and Athenian audiences suppose a certain homogeneity in their mores, social rank, material status, and political aspirations (if any).[56] Some scholars have reacted against this generalization by aligning Menander with some class or faction, and still others have responded by promoting Menander as a playwright who undermines class distinctions (Giglioni 1984:39–43; Konstan 1995:166–167). However, in terms of the image projected on stage—an image that contributes to the ideological vision expressed in the plays—Casson makes a salient point: the lead characters in Menander have means and finances (or are attached to households of such means) at a level found only among the extremely rich in Athenian society.[57]

Households not politically engaged but materially prosperous thus form the core of the Menandrian world. Family structure, occupation, and personality are allowed to vary appreciably within certain parameters. This variation consumes the interest of most literary critics (Zagagi 1994 and Heap 2019). Konstan has mapped this literary variation onto an ideological plane, but his interests lie almost exclusively with these internal differences, not with the boundaries of the ideological vision of the play or what lies beyond them.[58] Menander sharpens the execution of his craft to the point where no element in the play threatens to pass beyond the ideological boundaries of Menandrian comedy. Here theatrical technique and political ideology meet and interact; here Welles hopes to find political allegory, and here Wiles claims that such an allegory operates in the *Dyskolos*, with Knemon representing the oligarchic leader Phokion.[59] Both Welles and Wiles seek a way for politics to become visible on stage, when in fact Menander works for anything but. When an event or character might stray beyond the confines of the apolitical domestic realm of eventual prosperity, Menander imposes a clear limit.

As an illustration, Menander's *Sikyonios* contains several such potentially disruptive points. Each reveals Menander's determination to keep everything

---

[56] Zagagi 1995 speaks as if there were a monolithic spectator perception and reception in Menander's comedy.

[57] Casson 1976; cf. the brief summary and critique at Giglioni 1984:21n17 and Owens 2011:355–356.

[58] Konstan's focus on the internal dynamic of ideological tension may explain the relative homogeneity of his approach and readings, whether he discusses Aristophanes, Menander, Plautus, Terence, or Moliere. His collaboration with Matthew Dillon on Aristophanes' *Wealth* comes closest to considering the intrusion of ideological forces from beyond the play (1995:75–90, a slight revision of Konstan and Dillon 1981).

[59] Welles 1970:203 and Wiles 1984, the latter of which should be consulted with Owens 2011, who more plausibly finds Sostratos imbued with recognizable characteristics of Demetrius of Phaleron.

within his range of vision. A snatch of heated dialogue introduces some of the hazards, as well as Menander's absolute control (150–161):

—ὄχλος εἶ φλυάρου μεστός, ὦ πόνηρε σύ,
δίκαια τὸν κλάοντα προσδοκῶν λέγειν
καὶ τὸν δεόμενον· τοῦ δὲ μηδὲ ἓν ποεῖν
ὑγιὲς σχεδὸν ταῦτ' ἐστι νῦν τεκμήριον·
οὐ κρίνεθ' ἀλήθεια τοῦτον τὸν τρόπον,
ἀλλ' ἐν ὀλίγῳ πολλῷ γε μᾶλλον συνεδρίῳ.
—ὀλιγαρχικός γ' εἶ καὶ πονηρός, Σμικρίνη,

...

—ὦ Ἡράκλεις, ἀπολεῖτέ μ' οἱ σφοδροὶ πανύ[60]
ὑμεῖς. τί γάρ μοι λοιδορεῖ βαρυ...
—μισῶ σε καὶ τοὺς τὰς ὀφρῦς ἐπηκότας
ἅπαντας· ὄχλος ὢν δ'...

You're a mob full of rubbish, you fool, expecting a man who cries and begs to be right. These days it's practically a sign of being up to no good. Don't judge the truth that way. It's far better with a small, elite committee.

—You're a real oligarch and a fool ...
—By Heracles, you're absolutely ruining me! Why are you picking on me?
—I hate you and all your arrogant kind. Even if I am just a mob ...

In a political context, the terminology of ὄχλος, ὀλίγος, and ὀλιγαρχικός would be provocative and potentially divisive. Here it is mere generic banter between two characters at home. The anger and bitterness is between two individuals.[61] Whereas Philippides took on a Macedonian overlord and stood up for the sanctity of the Athenian democracy, the cause of the dispute in this passage is much more modest. The exact incident cannot be pinpointed, but the "mob" character goes on in the ensuing fragmentary lines to accuse the "oligarch" of theft (163–166). Then either the "mob" character or another messenger reports to the "oligarch" about a trial, which took place at Eleusis. Like the trial staged in *Epitrepontes*, this reported trial is about custody. Philippides invoked the *demos* in face of Demetrius the Besieger profaning the rites of the Eleusinian mysteries.

---

[60] I follow Kassel's supplement to line 158, but see Arnott 1997:24.
[61] The identity of the two speakers is not completely certain. The "oligarch" is very likely Smikrines. who may be Stratophanes' father. The "mob" may be Blepes, who delivers the speech about the trial. See Chapter 3 for fuller discussion of this play.

Menander has a jury in Eleusis preside over a case about child custody, citizenship, and right to marriage. In the *Epitrepontes*, Menander narrows the trial's topic but also casts the litigants as characters far removed from urban political life. Critical in the testimony of the plaintiff Syros is the self-conscious use of tragic exempla. Menander smothers the trial in *Sikyonios*, a much more public event, with more tragic coloring. The entire report is modeled on a tragic messenger speech, specifically that of Euripides' *Orestes*.[62] Within the trial, the plaintiff, this time the young man Moschion, once again brings up tragedy when he complains that his opponent uses a tragic story (τραγῳδία 262) to sway the jury. The more public the setting and potentially political the events, the more Menander suffuses the scene with a theatrical, tragic tradition.

Stratophanes, Moschion's opponent and the girl's surprise advocate in the trial, represents another volatile element in Menandrian comedy: the soldier. The character carries with him an inherent risk of crossing the boundaries of Menander's ideological vision of the comic stage. By his very existence, a soldier threatens to disrupt Menander's ideological continuity in two basic ways. First, the soldier's military occupation serves political ends, so the soldier's identity does not bind him to a private household (cf. Rop 2019). Second, unless the play is set in a military environment, which would be utterly incompatible with a domestic setting, the soldier cannot pursue his occupation except outside the home and beyond his local community. In both space and function, then, the soldier is a difficult character to keep integrated in the rigidly domestic culture of Menandrian comedy. When a soldier's identity and occupation play a role, Menander keeps very tight artistic control so that ideological consistency is maintained. Just how Menander manages these soldier characters will be the core subject of this study. For now suffice it to say that, at these critical moments, the juncture between Menander's craft and ideological vision is once again revealed.

Positing such an ideological orientation for Menander's plays does not, it must be emphasized, reduce Menander to a pamphleteer for the Macedonian cause or his plays to Macedonian propaganda. Menander's ideology had its roots in his experience of his own times. The world depicted in his plays operates within his ideological perception of the world, not outside it. Displaying this world to the spectators of the theater required faith in the relevance of his vision. For Menander to believe that his narrowly focused comedies had any relevance and that the strict resolution of domestic conflict was at all intelligible, he had to take for granted that the citizenry of Athens and other city-states would prosper best if they considered it their civic duty to maintain a

---

[62] For analysis, see Belardinelli 1994:145–157, Petrides 2014a:273–274, and Chapter 3.

strong household. Insurrection and revolution can only weaken the underpinnings of the community and cause more disruptions for individual households. Leave the politics of governing and empire to the elite and the professionals. Relying on such a belief, then, Menander put plays before the public that show the people how best to serve themselves and their communities by channeling their energies toward the *oikos* and away from the *polis*. By doing so, Menander participates in the struggle to form a dominant, coherent popular ideology. He dramatizes that particular ideology operating successfully and yielding prosperity. In this ideological vision, Greek families care for themselves, each other, and their homes, homes in a Macedonian world.

2

Setting the Stage for Menander's Soldiers

"It was neither the quality nor the quantity ... It was the mixture. Grasp that and you have the root of the matter."

—Evelyn Waugh, *Brideshead Revisited.*

THIS CHAPTER AIMS TO CHART a specific area of conceptual space where Menander reached into theatrical traditions to dramatize a character who embodied political and cultural tension in his community: the soldier. Whereas the previous chapter argued that Menander's priorities included an ultimate goal of private, domestic lives settled within a Greek world stabilized by Macedonian imperial control, this chapter seeks to outline issues and tensions that shape Menander's soldier characters. Toward this end this chapter has four components: (1) a survey of the anxiety about mercenary soldiers in the Greek world during Menander's lifetime; (2) a survey of soldier characters on the comic stage prior to and during Menander's career, which indicates that the braggart soldier was one possible option for such characters on the stage, not yet the default expectation; (3) an analysis of cooks as true braggart characters, to discern how Menander deploys them in contrast to the way his soldier characters function; and (4) a focused look at tragic antecedents for soldier characters, a tradition that contributes more to the expectations of Menander's soldier characters than does the idea of a braggart soldier.

All these analyses involve a substantial and novel reorientation of the traditional historical and literary context given for Menander's soldier characters. Traditionally Menander is said to be working with the established "stock" character of the braggart soldier, the *miles gloriosus*, but this chapter argues on two counts that this is incorrect. First, Menander's soldier characters are not just generic soldiers but specifically mercenaries, constructed in response to cultural apprehension about mercenary soldiers in the Greek world during Menander's lifetime. Second, the *miles gloriosus* came to dominate the soldier character on stage only after Menander's career. Soldier characters were not standardized as braggarts at the end of the fourth century, so Menander could, and did, choose the qualities of his staged soldiers to meet his ideological criteria and dramatic ends. The specifics of this process will be the focus of Chapter 3, but establishing the sociopolitical context and theatrical options from which Menander constructed and manipulated his characters is the focus here.

Mercenaries in Menander's World

This will not be just a negative argument, i.e. the lack of a central *miles gloriosus* in Menandrian comedy, but a positive claim that the central dynamic of a soldier character is the integration of a veteran lacking a commitment to his community, a figure labeled here a "mercenary," into the community as a citizen, specifically a civilian husband. It is necessary to delineate what the label "mercenary" conveys in the context of Menander and this study, as there is something of a disconnect between modern terms for this character and the Greek terminology available to Menander. Menander's soldiers are mercenaries in the sense that they participate in military campaigns and receive financial remuneration, but their contingent is not an army maintained by a government of a polis. The Greek of Menander's day had no single, specific term for mercenaries. The term *xenos* is the word used most often in Menander, a pregnant choice that simultaneously evokes broader issues about the soldier's identity and status as outsider.[1] As scholars have documented, however, this does not make them the romanticized amoral freebooters that the term easily conjures up today.[2] Rop's recent study of Greek mercenaries in the ancient Near East during the fourth century argues that Greek mercenary armies were always political agents embedded in the ongoing imperial strategic games among the Greek poleis, various components of the Persian Empire, Egypt, and other players (Rop 2019:19–26). As with all political agents in these events, unpacking and specifying the political motives of these armies and individuals within them is never straightforward. Indeed masking or misrepresenting the political agenda of these agents was a typical part of their effectiveness (or a way to undercut their effectiveness).

Rop's study covers the period to 330 BCE, hence including the years of Menander's youth, but his characterization holds true for the early Hellenistic

---

[1] See the analyses in Chapter 3. Cf. Avramović 2015 on ancient Greek mercenaries having outsider status more broadly. Scholarship on ancient Greek mercenaries overwhelmingly concentrates on the classical period and earlier. See Trundle 2013:330–350 for a basic survey and Bettali 2013 for a more extensive look down to the end of the classical era. Less helpful are English 2012 and Boulay 2014:105–111. For the Hellenistic era, Griffith 1935 remains the most extensive survey. For ancient moral qualms about mercenaries, see Beek 2020.

[2] See Trundle 2004:21–24 for discussion. Also for this reason, in the performance script in the Appendix I find "Private Military Contractor" actually a better modern analogue (see note there).

era too, and thus the years of Menander's career as a playwright. Consistent with Menander's ideological priority of dramatizing settled, domestic life within a tacitly established, stable imperial environment, his plays never acknowledge the political agency of the soldier characters or their campaigns. Menander does, on the other hand, implicitly address the ideological anxiety that the Greeks—or at least Athenians—expressed about mercenary agents. While Rop makes a legitimate argument that mercenary armies were in fact political agents, sometimes even serving the political agenda of the polis from which they might seem independent or even estranged, the anxiety that Athenians express about mercenary soldiers revolves around their lack of loyalty and commitment to a polis or Greeks in general (Trundle 1998). It is this particular anxiety that Menander constructs his soldier characters to address.

Both democratic and aristocratic voices in Athens expressed anxiety about the many mercenary soldiers in the fourth century. Isocrates, for example, urges Philip II of Macedon to conquer vast swaths of territory and therein settle the many men who are roving in poverty and mugging those they meet (κτίσαι πόλεις ἐπὶ τούτῳ τῷ τόπῳ, καὶ κατοικίσαι τοὺς νῦν πλανωμένους δι' ἔνδειαν τῶν καθ' ἡμέραν καὶ λυμαινομένους οἷς ἂν ἐντύχωσιν, 5.120).[3] These rovers without a polis Isocrates considers a fearful and growing threat to Greek life (μηδὲν ἧττον αὐτοὺς εἶναι φοβεροὺς τοῖς Ἕλλησιν ἢ τοῖς βαρβάροις ... κοινὸν φόβον καὶ κίνδυνον ἅπασιν ἡμῖν αὐξανόμενον). He then specifies that Philip should assemble mercenaries serving abroad in this group (ξενιτευομένους) to defend new cities as border states to an expanded version of Greece (ἀπαλλάξαι τε τοὺς ξενιτευομένους τῶν κακῶν ὧν αὐτοί τ' ἔχουσι καὶ τοῖς ἄλλοις παρέχουσι, καὶ πόλεις ἐξ αὐτῶν συστῆσαι, καὶ ταύταις ὁρίσαι τὴν Ἑλλάδα καὶ προβαλέσθαι πρὸ ἁπάντων ἡμῶν, 5.122). Thus Isocrates explicitly lays out the tension and threat embedded in mercenary identity: that these militarized men are not bound to any polis and thus fundamentally threaten civilized Greek life. His proposal would group these men in new cities outside Greece (at least Greece as Isocrates conceives of it) and direct their military potential to border defense. Menander, by contrast, will dramatize the same threat, a militarized man not bound to a polis, but the resolution of his plays will have the mercenary abandon his military identify in favor of communally approved domestic life within a Greek polis. Such a resolution is, to emphasize the point again, consistent with Menander's ideology supporting stable Macedonian rule, rather than a vision like that of Isocrates, which promotes Hellenic, and specifically Athenian, hegemony.

---

[3] See Taylor 2017:149–194, esp. 152 on how Isocrates' proposal fits into broader anxiety about poverty in the fourth century BCE. Economic status will be an explicit factor in the way Menander identifies his mercenary soldier characters.

Additionally, the increasing number of rootless mercenaries within the Greek world in Menander's day is an anxiety that Isocrates also addresses, frustrated that the Athenians do not take this situation seriously:

... πολλοὺς δὲ δι' ἔνδειαν τῶν καθ' ἡμέραν ἐπικουρεῖν ἀναγκαζομένους ὑπὲρ τῶν ἐχθρῶν τοῖς φίλοις μαχομένους ἀποθνήσκειν. ὑπὲρ ὧν οὐδεὶς πώποτ' ἠγανάκτησεν, ἀλλ' ἐπὶ μὲν ταῖς συμφοραῖς ταῖς ὑπὸ τῶν ποιητῶν συγκειμέναις δακρύειν ἀξιοῦσιν, ἀληθινὰ δὲ πάθη πολλὰ καὶ δεινὰ γιγνόμενα διὰ τὸν πόλεμον ἐφορῶντες τοσούτου δέουσιν ἐλεεῖν, ὥστε καὶ μᾶλλον χαίρουσιν ἐπὶ τοῖς ἀλλήλων κακοῖς ἢ τοῖς αὐτῶν ἰδίοις ἀγαθοῖς.

... many, from lack of basic needs, are driven to serve [as mercenaries] and die fighting for their enemies against their friends, but no one has ever protested these developments. Meanwhile people are content to weep over the calamities which have been concocted by the poets, while they view the real suffering, the many terrible sufferings which result from war, and they are so far from feeling pity that they celebrate each other's sorrows more than their own blessings.

4.168[4]

Isocrates' anxiety was a consequence, at least in part, of the explosion of mercenary service in the fourth century. This phenomenon, or at least the perception of it, even led Isocrates to an ironic potential upside to the problem: he suggested to Philip II that in Greece it was easier to build an army from exiled mercenaries than from citizens (5.96). On the other side of the debate about how to respond to Philip's incursions, Demosthenes disparaged the use of mercenaries when calling for Athens to mount an expedition to fight Philip II (4.4.19, 23–24; cf. 4.46).[5] The debate, and the trend toward increased use of mercenaries, only accelerated in the early years of the Successors, that is, the decades of Menander's career.[6] The accuracy of Isocrates' assessment of the situation

---

[4] See also 8.24, 9.9 and a similar fear at Plato *Laws* 697e. Aristotle reasons that mercenary soldiers (στρατιῶται) are more prone to emotional decisions (πάθος) in a crisis than operating on the courage (ἀνδρεία) of those bound to a polis (πολιτικά) at *Nicomachean Ethics* 1116b5–18 and 1117b17–22. Aeneas Tacticus 12-13 addresses the reliability of mercenaries in sieges (see Roy 2017 for analysis).

[5] See Rop 2019:136–140 for analysis of the "Mercenaries Decree" extrapolated from the scholiast on this speech, which finds the decree fundamentally mischaracterized in the passage.

[6] Miller 1984 is a good starting point for analysis of the reasons for the mercenary "explosion" of the fourth century. See also Marinovič 1992. There is a crucial debate about the social status of and economic pressures on those who pursued mercenary work. Whitehead 1991 and McKechnie 1994 use the issue of who supplies equipment to explore these issues. Iapichino 1999 supports

and the Athenian response to it is debatable and in many ways beyond certain determination on available evidence.[7] Whether or not Isocrates was right that Athenians did not take sufficient action in response to the expanding presence of mercenaries, other sources do indicate that there was at least an ideological frustration about the phenomenon. As has been long observed, oratory, derived from courtroom cases under the fourth-century Athenian democracy, preserves the ideological preferences and flashpoints of potential jurors (Ober 1989; cf. Chapter 1), insofar as elite speakers before juries shaped their rhetorical presentations to make their situations more ideologically appealing (or at least less unappealing). A pair of extant documents derived from fourth-century inheritance cases thus provides simultaneously real-world instances of Athenian citizens who did embark on mercenary service and the concomitant anxiety that such activity was not popular or easily sanctioned among Athenian democrats.

A legal contest over an estate, this one belonging to the Athenian Nikostratos, who had been a mercenary abroad for eleven years (Isaeus 4), shows how one court opponent cast aspersions on mercenary experience. The speaker is supporting claimants to the estate against a man who had a will created while Nikostratos was employed for mercenary service abroad. The speaker emphasizes that the rival claimant never served with the jurors in the military, καὶ ὑπὲρ μὲν ὑμῶν οὔτε στρατείαν οὐδεμίαν ἐστράτευται ("He did not serve with you on any military service," 4.29; cf. 4.1 which emphasizes that the speaker's clients never even visited where Nikostratos served, and 4.18–19). Thus Nikostratos would be doubly isolated from many of the jurors' ideology of being local and loyal to Athens, for he served in geographically distant territory and, it is implied, not in service to Athens. The tensions embedded in this scenario also have resonances in Menander's drama. The soldier Stratophanes in *Sikyonios*, for example, has been a mercenary abroad in distant Karia (cf. *Samia* for Karia as part of a contrasting pair with Bactria in the context of mercenary service). Controversy and uncertainty about Stratophanes' citizenship, financial responsibilities, and reliability/loyalty derive both from this service and the will of his foster parents at Sikyon, i.e. outside of Athens.[8]

Whitehead. Luraghi 2006 probes the underlying assumptions of the debate; cf. McKechnie 1989:85–95, Loman 2006, Hale 2013, and Avramović 2015.

[7] See Trundle 2004:146–147 and Rop 2019:121 for more positive assessments of mercenaries in this period. This current study is not concerned directly with whether these assessments are accurate, but rather that the ancient testimony testifies to anxiety about the perception of the risks inherent in mercenaries and how Menander dramatized his characters around this anxiety.

[8] Cf. Chapter 3 for detailed discussion. In the model of Rop 2019, it is very likely that Nikostratos' service and the contingent with which he operated did play some role affecting Athens in the larger scale of multinational maneuvering, but the speaker in this case is not interested in allowing for such possibilities, even if they were applicable. The speaker is playing on the

The congruence of geographic and political distance from Athens of citizens who embarked on mercenary service was already established by the time of Nikostratos' case. In analyzing the narrative of the most famous Greek mercenaries, Xenophon's Ten Thousand on their journey from the Persian interior back to Greece, Ma (2004) focuses on the troubled relationship between location and identity (cf. Trundle 1999, Roy 2004, and Baragwanath 2019). Xenophon is himself and will remain an exile from his home Athens. The traveling collection of mercenaries brushes with the prospect of staying or founding a location in order to become a true community, but it never happens, leaving the story with a sense of displacement and lack of complete identity. As Ma further documents, and Xenophon is explicitly aware, Greek culture had long had an embedded awareness of the tension between a soldier returning from campaign and being settled at home, going back at least to the *Odyssey*. The legacy of the *Odyssey* becomes explicit when Xenophon compares the Ten Thousand lingering at Babylon to the lotus eaters (*Anabasis* 3.2.25). This broad and deep cultural background also surfaces in drama, as will be argued below for tragedy's influence on Menander.

In the mid-fourth century (roughly the period of Menander's youth) comes another inheritance case preserved in Isaeus and one which resonates specifically with a comedy of Menander. In Menander's *Aspis*, a young man named Kleostratos goes abroad on mercenary service in order to provide a substantial enough dowry to support an advantageous marriage for his younger sister. When he instead goes missing and is presumed dead in combat, however, his estate and sister fall into danger for plucking by an unscrupulous uncle.

Parallels can be found in Isaeus 2 (*On the Estate of Menekles*), a case involving a pair of Athenian brothers who have two sisters. After their father died, the brothers arranged marriages for their sisters to Athenian husbands and then became soldiers abroad. When they returned, the younger sister, married to Menekles, was still childless, so at Menekles' urging she was remarried to another man. Menekles subsequently adopted one of the two brothers to ensure an heir for his estate. When Menekles died, however, Menekles' own brother laid claim to the estate, asserting that the sister had undue influence over the adoption and will. Such an outline reads like part of a hypothesis to a play by Menander. Indeed, here an uncle files suit to claim a contested estate left by a former mercenary who had taken care of one of his sisters. In Menander's *Aspis*, an uncle (Smikrines) hopes to marry the sister of a deceased mercenary in order to claim her estate, and frets that the case could end up in court (line 272). That

---

expected anxieties of the jurors at hand. Thus this example does not invalidate Rop's larger argument, but it does provide a particular perspective on it.

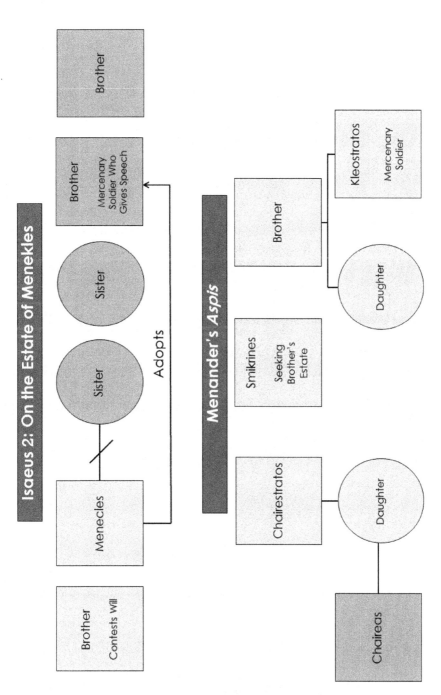

Figure 1: Family trees for Menander's *Aspis* and *Isaeus* 2
(*On the Estate of Menekles*).

Isaeus 2 preserves an outline of individuals and events from an actual legal case from the mid-fourth century BCE is telling for the modern reader of Menander. How elements of this scenario were presented to a jury is thus of interest and relevance for understanding how and why Menander dramatizes comparable scenarios on stage a generation after this case. Of particular interest here is the brothers' time as mercenaries abroad. The speaker of the extant speech is the brother adopted as heir, defending his right to the estate. He mentions his soldiering but is oblique about having been a mercenary. He is careful to say that he and his brother took care of their sisters' marriages first (cf. *Aspis* 35 and 82–83 about Kleostratos' motives for his mercenary service), so as not to appear to have gone adventuring at the expense of family responsibilities. The brothers were of appropriate military age and went abroad to Thrace under the celebrated general Iphikrates (ἐκδόντες τοίνυν τὰς ἀδελφάς, ὦ ἄνδρες, καὶ ὄντες αὐτοὶ ἐν ἡλικίᾳ ἐπὶ τὸ στρατεύεσθαι ἐτραπόμεθα, καὶ ἀπεδημήσαμεν μετὰ Ἰφικράτους εἰς Θράκην, 2.6). They served worthily, built up some money, and returned "here" to Athens (ἐκεῖ δὲ δόξαντές του εἶναι ἄξιοι περιποιησάμενοί τι κατεπλεύσαμεν δεῦρο).[9] Only then did they learn of their sister's childlessness, which sets in motion the events that led to the speaker becoming heir. The speaker is cautious in several ways when referring to his mercenary work. While Iphikrates was prominent and successful as an Athenian commander and general, his mission in Thrace, and its mercenary character, was and remains controversial.[10] The speaker does not say how long they were abroad, but it was enough for one sister to bear two children, and he never refers to his mercenary expedition again in the speech.[11] As such, in Menander's cultural milieu, mercenary activity was widespread but a source of anxiety.[12]

---

[9]   Schaps 1979:74–81 analyzes the brothers' wealth vis-à-vis their sister's need.

[10] See Demosthenes 23.130–132 for an ancient hostile portrayal of Iphikrates' mission to Thrace; cf. Trundle 2004:150–151 and, on Iphikrates' later use of mercenaries, Rop 2019:100–107.

[11] Miller 1984:153 and Parke 1933:232 take the diminutive reference to mercenary activity to mean that service is ordinary. Perhaps, but for the speaker, the more pressing issue is the jurors' evaluation. Even if such service is common, why not emphasize it if the reaction is expected to be positive? Quite the contrary: since jurors are not likely to respond favorably, the reference is kept to a minimum. Later in the speech (12), when the speaker asserts that the other brother would not be a good heir because he travels abroad, it might be a gentle allowance that this brother continued on as a mercenary soldier. The obliqueness of the acknowledgment again suggests caution against signaling his career as a mercenary.

[12] See also Marinovič 1989 for mercenaries in the Lamian War, just as Menander's career was beginning.

Soldiers on the Comic Stage: Antecedents and Progeny

As a playwright, Menander inherited and continued theatrical traditions, so it is crucial to investigate what were Menander's precedents in dramatizing soldiers and what dramatic tools he inherited to explore the distinct cultural pressures of his own day. It remains standard in accounts of Greek stage comedy to assert that Menander worked with the stock character of the braggart soldier (*alazon*). Since Menander's soldier characters do not fit this mold, it is also standard to assert that Menander works against and adds nuance to the blunt stock character.[13] This disjunction should lead to fresh investigation of just what the experience and expectations of Menander and his spectators would have been. Evidence is frightfully fragmentary, but it is still fair to ask whether the available fragments are consistent with the literary-historical narrative scholars are promulgating. Instead, the fragments are consistent with soldier characters appearing on stage without there being an expectation of them being braggarts, and that the centrality of the *miles gloriosus* is a post-Menander development. In this scenario, Menander engaged with the theatrical and cultural heritage of the soldier and shaped his own soldier characters according to his own dramaturgical and ideological priorities. Accordingly Chapter 3 will analyze the mercenary soldiers in Menander in a different and, I argue, more accurate way, and Chapter 4 turns to the ramifications of this revised perspective for understanding soldier characters in Roman comedy. But now it is imperative to review what is known about soldiers on the Athenian stage prior to Menander, a survey that reveals there is minimal evidence for the *miles gloriosus* on earlier comic stages.

In current scholarship, it remains standard to analyze soldier characters in Menander with the idea that military figures in Greek comedy as early as the 420s BCE are early examples of what will become standardized in New Comedy.[14] In fact, however, Lamachos in Aristophanes' *Acharnians* ends up standing in for the entire supposed tradition in Old Comedy.[15] Moreover, it is mere assertion that Lamachos or hypothetical other *alazones* soldiers like him were reference points for playwrights of subsequent comedy, as no specific parallels or ancient testimony link later soldier characters to fifth-century forebears.[16] It is a major argument of the current study, however, that positing such reference points

---

[13] Ruffell 2014 is a representative recent example.

[14] MacCary 1972 is the standard reference survey. See also Konstantakos 2015b and 2016.

[15] Konstantakos 2016. Storey 2003:246–260, esp. 257–260 would add Phormio of Eupolis' *Taxiarchoi* to this tradition, on which see also Bowie 1988 and Olson 2015.

[16] For the development of the term *alazon* in general, see MacDowell 1990 and Major 2006.

critically misrepresents soldier characters in the first generation of Greek New Comedy.

This leaves the murky era of fourth-century comedy for the development of the character. In assorted surveys of the braggart soldier, several of some two dozen or so fragments are cited as glimpses into the development of the stereotype in the decades prior to Menander and contemporary with his career.[17] Upon inspection, these examples suffer from one of two problems: either the role or presence of a soldier goes beyond the evidence, or a reference to a soldier does not corroborate his character as a braggart.

As an example of the first problem, consider Ephippus fr. 5.18–21:

περιαγγέλλειν τί οὐχ ὑποκαίεις,
Λυκίων πρύτανι· ψυχρὸν τουτί·
παύου φυσῶν, Μακεδὼν ἄρχων·
σβέννυ, Κελθ' ὡς μὴ προσκαύσῃς.

... and they gave orders: "Why aren't you kindling the fire,
O Lycian leader? This part is cold.
Stop fanning the fire, leader of Macedon.
Quench the fire, O Celt, so you don't burn it."

Trans. Slater

Athenaeus quotes this fragment from *Geryones* because of its account of an extraordinary fish dish prepared for the mythical creature Geryon. Among those called upon to help out with the cooking are a Lycian and Macedonian leader, as well as a Celt. Arnott puts this passage in the mouth of a braggart soldier, who boasts of his exotic experiences in faraway lands, reasoning from what Athenaeus says next, that the same lines were repeated in another play of Ephippus, *Peltast*, with an additional five lines (fr. 19). There is nothing, however, in the context, the text itself, or other information about these fragments or plays to indicate that a peltast or any soldier character is involved. Rather, as Konstantakos (2011) proposes, *Geryones*, this scene in particular, has more to do with recontextualizing mythology to the world of an Athenian cook (see next

---

[17] Arnott 2010:324–325, Ruffell 2014:147–156, Blume 2001. Hunter 1985:66 serves as a representative example of speculative reasoning that has long underpinned the assumptions about the development of the character: "Although the most extreme examples are found in Roman comedy, it is a reasonable supposition that this character was fully developed as a stock type in the period of Greek Middle Comedy. It was during the fourth century that a large growth in the use of Greek mercenary soldiers would have made such professional warriors with their marvellous tales of exotic places a familiar phenomenon." In fact, as this survey indicates, available evidence for this supposition ranges from lacking to inconsistent.

section for the cook as *alazon*). Another dozen or so fragments that have been cited as involving braggart soldiers likewise lack any evidence of soldiers. Like the Ephippus fragments, Alexis fr. 63 describes a marvelous event, this time an elaborate pigeon shower, but it is speculative that a soldier is bragging about it (see below for Antiphanes fr. 200 about a similar pigeon shower, a report that seems closer to the ambassador's bragging in Aristophanes' *Acharnians* 61–122). Indeed, a cook is an equally likely speaker. The same is true of the elaborate meals of Alexis frr. 135–137 and Eriphus fr. 6, where cooks are more likely candidates for speakers than soldiers. Alexis fr. 96 comes from his *Thrason*, the title character of which could well be a soldier, but the fragment itself, in which someone complains to a woman of her garrulousness, gives no indication of any involvement of a soldier. While it is sensible to expect that Alexis' Στρατιώτης (*Soldier*) included soldiers, fr. 212 from the play, a dialogue about a baby foundling, does not indicate what role the one or more soldiers played nor any information about their character. Philemon also wrote a play titled Στρατιώτης (*Soldier*), but fr. 82, about the successful cooking of fish, gives no indication of what role or character any soldier might have had.[18] Another fragment of Philemon (fr. 124) charges someone with cowardice, which could be spoken to or by a soldier, but there is no context to help.[19] The story that Philemon insulted Magas, half-brother to Ptolemy II, in a play (fr. 132) hints at a political or even military dimension rarely found in New Comedy, but nothing about soldiers. Finally, the term ἀλαζών can refer to a braggart soldier, but it also applies to other types of characters, as in Theopompus fr. 44, which applies a synonym ῥαχίστης to a Demophon, who, based on his name, was most likely an old man.

Other fragments do involve soldiers but not braggarts. A line from Apollodorus (fr. 10), for example, says to someone that they are a soldier rather than a free man, but this is an isolated quote from Stobaeus, so it comes with no context and does not provide evidence that a soldier or any other character was a braggart. Another fragment, ascribed to Diphilus (fr. 55), says a character does not look like a soldier because he is equipped with household implements. Perhaps this is someone trying to look like a soldier, or who was a soldier, but in his attempt to make some sort of domestic siege, fails (cf. Barsby 1999:228–239 on such scenes in Menander's *Perikeiromene* and *Kolax*). Anyway, there is a ridiculous parody of a soldier, but nothing requires a bragging soldier character. An intriguing fragment is Alexis fr. 236 (*Wounded Man*):

---

[18] The topic again favors a cook. Cf. Wilkins 2000:387 and 391 on this fragment.
[19] *Adespota* fr. 152, another fragment about someone's cowardice, likewise lacks context.

τίς οὐχὶ φήσει τοὺς ἐρῶντας ζῆν μόνους;
εἰ δεῖ γε πρῶτον μὲν στρατευτικωτάτους
εἶναι, πονεῖν τε δυναμένους τοῖς σώμασιν
μάλιστα, προσεδρεύειν τ’ ἀρίστους τῷ πόθῳ,
ποιητικούς, ἰταμούς, προθύμους, εὐπόρους
ἐν τοῖς ἀπόροις, βλέποντας ἀθλιωτάτους.

Who wouldn't say that lovers alone are really alive?
First, they have to be soldiers through and through,
Able to endure great bodily suffering,
The best at persevering in their desire,
Clever, hasty, eager, inventive
When there's no way out, looking utterly wretched.

Trans. Slater

Here someone, very likely a desperate lover, says that lovers are very much like soldiers when measured by their endurance, resourcefulness, and so on.[20] I want to highlight here that this equation of lover and soldier resonates broadly in Greek New Comedy. In the scheme of characters and masks preserved in Pollux, for example, the soldier is but a variation of the young man in love.[21] This can easily make military motifs a focus of comedy and ridicule but not, without additional evidence, a braggart soldier.

Once again, a number of other fragments have been cited as examples of the braggart soldier, passages that have something to do with soldiers but nothing that requires or is in any way predicated on them being arrogant braggarts. In Alexis fr. 120, someone sees a character drinking in a bar, with his στρωματέα and γύλιον near him, and he may be a soldier, but this gives no hint about his character. In *Adespota* fr. 1018, a slave jokes about a soldier's life to the annoyance of the soldier, but nothing indicates that the soldier is a braggart. Another bit from Alexis (fr. 181) mentions a type of cup possibly linked to soldiers, but even so, this gives no hint about the soldier's character. A line from Antiphanes (fr. 136) says to a character, "You have fasting gray mullets [= honest people] but not soldiers," but the context is unknown and there need not even be any soldier character in the play. Antiphanes' play Στρατιώτης (*Soldier*), a.k.a. *Tychon*, likely involved at least one soldier, but the fragments—fr. 200 = Olson C13 (a soldier

---

[20] Alexis' lengthy career began before Menander was even born and continued on after his death, and no information indicates where this play or passage might belong chronologically. Cf. Arnott 1996:664–668 and chapter 4 for his *Karchedonios*, Menander's and Plautus' *Poenulus*.

[21] Petrides 2014a:213–216. As it happens, Plautus' adaptations of Philemon tend to preserve this motif. See Chapter 4 and Fraenkel 2007:161.

asked to tell about doves fanning a king of Cyprus), fr. 202 (about the transience of possessions), and fr. 203 (peacocks reproduce but honest men do not)—do not indicate any characteristics of the soldiers.[22] Diphilus wrote a play *Airesiteiches* which sometimes included Στρατιώτης (*Soldier*) in the title (*Airesiteiches*; *Eunouchos* or *Stratiotes*) but the remains—fr. 5 refers to drinking, fr. 6 refers to a useless torch, and the other three fragments are even more meager—do not explain how soldiers might have played a role or what character they had. The speaker of Hipparchus fr. 1 asks if the listener is paying attention to a soldier, but the corrupt sequence following lists luxuries, and the relationship of this snatch of dialogue to the soldier mentioned is obscure. Two sententious remarks from Philemon involve soldiers but do not even mean that the plays had soldier characters (fr. 122 says doctors do not want to see their friends healthy and soldiers do not want to see a city without smoke; fr. 142 likens a soldier to a beast to be sacrificed). Apollodorus (of Carystus or Gela) *Aphanizomenos* fr. 2 is an aphorism from Stobaeus about a soldier's lot, but, yet again, with no context. Theopompus fr. 56 contrasts a soldier's pay with what it costs to support a wife or woman, and the play, based on its title (Στρατιωτίδης [*Little Soldier*]) likely involved one or more soldiers, but again, nothing about a soldier's role or character is known. *Adespota* fr. 1096 (= Arnott 2000 *Fabula Incerta* 7; lines 10–27 + 83–88 = Sandbach pp. 354–355; cf. discussion in Chapter 3) has a character whose name is abbreviated Thras- (Thrasyleon?), presumably a soldier, but there is nothing helpful beyond his name. *Adespota* 1018 features scraps of a slave talking about life in a military camp but the context is unknown. Plutarch (*Moralia* 62e = *Adespota* fr. 712) quotes a snatch of dialogue where someone brags about being able to fight a soldier, but Plutarch himself argues that the braggart is a flatterer (and note that the speaker is the braggart, not the soldier, who does not participate in the conversation).

There is but a single fragment from comedy after the fifth century that is predicated on a braggart soldier character, Phoenicides fr. 4.4–11:

εὐθὺς ἐπιχειρήσασα φίλον ἔσχον τινὰ
στρατιωτικόν· διαπαντὸς οὗτος τὰς μάχας
ἔλεγεν, ἐδείκνυ’ ἅμα λέγων τὰ τραύματα,
εἰσέφερε δ’ οὐδέν. δωρεὰν ἔφη τινὰ
παρὰ τοῦ βασιλέως λαμβάνειν, καὶ ταῦτ’ ἀεὶ
ἔλεγεν· διὰ ταύτην ἣν λέγω τὴν δωρεὰν
ἐνιαυτὸν ἔσχε μ’ ὁ κακοδαίμων δωρεάν.
ἀφῆκα τοῦτον ...

---

[22] Note especially that the soldier of fr. 200 is asked to tell about the marvel of another king, not that the soldier is bragging about himself. Cf. the discussion above about Alexis fr. 63.

... I had a lover who was a soldier. He was constantly talking about his battles and showing off his scars as he talked. But he didn't produce any income. He claimed he was getting a grant of some sort from the king, and he was always talking about it. And because of this grant I'm describing, the bastard was granted me as a gift for a year. I got rid of him ... (trans. Olson).

Here a *hetaira* complains about her life and the miserable clients she has endured. The first of these clients was a soldier who kept talking about his battle exploits, showing his wounds, and had some sort of stipend from a king. The *hetaira* says that this stipend was what bound her to him, but he in fact produced no income and she moved on to her next client, a doctor. This image of the bragging but fraudulent soldier comes closest to the character found in Plautus and Terence: the soldier shacked up with a prostitute drawn to his wealth, who is vaguely attached to a distant Hellenistic monarch.[23]

Although the precise date of this crucial fragment cannot be determined, all available evidence points to it falling later than Menander. Only five fragments of Phoenicides are preserved and this one is not attributed to a particular play. One fragment (fr. 1) is preserved by Hesychius, who says that Phoenicides was from Megara but competed in Athens at the City Dionysia. The fragment quoted by Hesychius alludes to a treaty between Antigonus and Pyrrhus, which would have been in the mid-280s BCE. Inscriptions indicate that Phoenicides did compete in Athens, as Hesychius says, at the Lenaea in the 280s (IG II² 2319.56, IG II² 2319.65 = T4–5 PCG) and victoriously at the Dionysia in the 270s (IG II² 2325.76 = T3 PCG). All this puts his known career later than that of Menander, whose death was at the end of the 290s (Olson 2007:415). Whether Phoenicides' career extended earlier into the 290s or later beyond the 270s cannot now be determined, but broadly he seems to have been a playwright a half generation or full generation later than Menander, and in turn two to three generations earlier than Plautus, thus squarely in the pool of the authors of Greek New Comedy whose plays early Roman comic playwrights adapted, although no specific testimony says that they used Phoenicides' plays.[24] Last and least, Athenaeus, quoting a Nicostratus (fr. 8), says a braggart soldier (ἀλαζὼν στρατιώτης) boasts about his dishes, a passage that probably postdates Menander, for the better-known

---

[23] *Adespota* fr. 934 might provide a parallel. Syrianos quotes a reference to commanders under whom a soldier in comedy served, but he is interested mostly in the Doric pronunciation of the names and leaves his source vague (τῶν κομικῶν τις περὶ τινος ἀλάζονος στρατιώτου φησί...) so the source, date, and even accuracy of the citation are obscure.

[24] I am also tempted to speculate that his play Μισουμένη (*A Hated Woman*) was inspired as a response to Menander's Μισούμενος (*A Hated Man*).

Nicostratus was a son of Aristophanes, but this is more likely a later playwright of the same name (see Nicostratus II and III in PCG and IG II² 2325.4.13). To be clear, the claim here is not that there were absolutely no pompous soldiers on the Greek stage prior to or contemporary with Menander. Although there is no direct evidence among the fragments, it is unlikely that the example from Phoenicides was the first or only. Given the evidence in Menander's day, however, pompous bragging was just one of multiple characteristics with which a soldier character could be imbued.

The rest of this chapter, then, turns to the two separate components of the braggart soldier. First, we look at a character type that really was a stereotypical and expected braggart, the cook, in order to see how Menander deploys this type, in contrast to how his soldier characters operate. This analysis also spotlights how Menander brings, sends away, and generally calibrates the presence of characters in his theatrical space. Then we will return to soldiers with an eye toward the theatrical tradition that Menander did decidedly draw upon to shape his soldier characters: tragedy.

Cooks as *Alazones* and Barometers of Domestic Tension

Within the fragmentary and uneven evidence regarding the fourth-century Greek stage, the character of the cook has bequeathed the most extensive and explicit testimony about being a braggart, an *alazon*, not least because Athenaeus, who preserves the lion's share of the preserved fragments of fourth-century comedy, was particularly interested in dining experiences.[25] While this situation skews the preserved texts and makes them generally unrepresentative of fourth-century comedy, these same texts do provide helpfully rich and specific testimony about the tradition of cooks and *alazoneia* that Menander inherited as a comic playwright. While the main subject of this study is the soldier character in Menander's plays, analyzing how cooks were dramatized will enhance the analysis of soldier characters in two ways: (1) The examples of and testimony for the character of the cook as an arrogant braggart throw into sharper relief the examples of soldiers surveyed in the previous section. (2) Scenes featuring cooks, even fragmentary ones, reveal a sophisticated technique deployed by Menander for calibrating their appearance to the emotional dynamic of a scene. Isolating this technique will be helpful for the full analysis of soldier scenes in

---

[25] See Jacob 2013 [Please add to the bibliography.] for a deep analysis of Athenaeus, including the role of sympotic traditions in his writing.

the next chapter, even when Menander's handling of soldiers stands in contrast to his deployment of cooks.

Athenaeus not only preserves examples that confirm the stereotype of the bragging cook but editorializes that the race of cooks consists of nothing but *alazones* (ἀλαζονικὸν δ' ἐστὶ πᾶν τὸ τῶν μαγείρων φῦλον).[26] One of Athenaeus' examples brings together several tropes central to the current study:

> ...ἅπας γάρ ἐστιν οἰκεῖος τόπος
> ὑπὲρ τέχνης λαλεῖν τι· τῶν ἡδυσμάτων
> πάντων κράτιστόν ἐστιν ἐν μαγειρικῇ
> ἀλαζονεία· τὸ καθ' ὅλου δὲ τῶν τεχνῶν
> ὄψει σχεδόν τι τοῦθ' ἡγούμενον.
> ξεναγὸς οὗτος, ὅστις ἂν θώρακ' ἔχῃ
> φολιδωτὸν ἢ δράκοντα σεσιδηρωμένον
> ἐφάνη Βριάρεως, ἂν τύχῃ δ' ἐστὶν λαγώς.

Everywhere is a prime opportunity for saying something about the profession. Of all the seasonings in the culinary profession, the most potent is *alazoneia*. You will see it thoroughly in the lead among the professional pursuits. Here is a commander of mercenaries in his fancily intricate breastplate or iron dragon shield of Briareos, if he meets up with a bunny.

Posidippus fr. 28.2–9

This extract includes the explicit comment, played for laughs, that bragging is integral to the cook's profession, at least on the comic stage. The bragging cook moves on to a military metaphor, in this case, a commander of mercenaries (ξεναγός). Posidippus' reference to mercenaries takes on added weight in the context of the anxiety about mercenaries discussed in the first section of this chapter. In the wake of such anxiety, it makes sense that the cook reveals how this leader of mercenaries may look like Briareos, the fearsome hundred-handed monster from the Titanomachy, but in fact is really a cowardly rabbit. This is a succinct way to imbue the cook with military pretensions and release tensions embedded in the image of a contingent of mercenary soldiers. Such military imagery is not unusual in a cook's declamation on the Greek stage, nor is the concomitant puncturing of pretension with an eye toward relieving the

---

[26] Athenaeus 7.290b; cf. *Adespota* 1093.221–232 = Sandbach p. 337, in which a cook named Libys feels sorry for cooks in comedies, a metatheatrical awareness of the sort Plautus later expresses about soldiers, for which, see Chapter 4. See Konstantakos 2015a on the metatheatrical tradition imbued in a cook as well as cooks in later Hellenistic stage traditions that bypass New Comedy.

theatergoers' angst about military might. Thus in Dionysius fr. 2, a commander (ἡγεμών) who pulls off a military coup and becomes a general (στρατηγός) is on par with a chef (μάγειρος, rather than an ὀψοποιός, an underling associated with specialties like fish; cf. Wilkins 2000:363, 396). Such motifs are common enough that they run through an entire section in Athenaeus.[27] Wilkins situates this type of appropriation within a broad spectrum of areas of professional expertise (τέχναι), from scholarly language and philosophy to transforming human civilization and raising the dead (Wilkins 2000:387–412). Vogue for these elaborate speeches by cooks seems to be operative at least a generation prior to Menander, in the 370s–350s (e.g. Dionysius, quoted above) and to have continued after him (e.g. Posidippus, quoted earlier). The wide-ranging plethora of examples of such *alazoneia* should be enough to caution against attributing bragging to a soldier in a comic fragment without context. Indeed, it was suggested more than once above that cooks are preferable candidates for speakers in some fragments that scholars have associated with braggart soldiers (see the discussions of Alexis frr. 135–137, Ephippus fr. 5, Eriphus fr. 6, and Philemon fr. 82).

Athenaeus also includes examples from Menander (e.g. frr. 351 and 409, *Kolax* fr. 1), which testify that Menander did know and make use of the tradition of boastful chefs. But Wilkins has pointed out that, unless this testimony and the recovered scripts are misleading, Menander "appears not to have favoured the extended speeches of the boastful cook full of his own learning, but to have presented the *mageiros* as the caterer for weddings and other social occasions" (Wilkins 2000:413). This is consistent not only with the larger arc, across the history of Greek theater, of *mageiroi* moving from an identity subsumed by a play's protagonist to being a vehicle for giving voice to disputed areas of cultural change, including professionalism, sympotic culture, ritual, pleasure and desire. It also suggests that there is more to be unpacked in the ways Meander refocuses and situates the cook characters in his plays, and consequently one perspective on how he foregrounds and circumscribes *alazoneia* in his characters more broadly.

In delimiting the braggart cook as a functionary in comedy's communal ritual practices, Menander actually manages to oppose the prestigious legacy of a *mageiros* against a community's or household's need or hope for his presence and expertise. Along these lines, scholars have cataloged and surveyed the critical roles cooks play in stage comedy (Dohm 1964, Berthaume 1982, Wilkins 2000, Arnott 2010:319–322). Such studies establish that the *mageiros* is an expert professional who has the critical task of slaughtering and butchering animals for

---

[27] Wilkins 2009:409, analyzes the section in book 9 on the pig, also featuring Athenaeus' own *mageiros* for the *Deipnosophistae*, "the elements picked out in particular are *alazoneia* based on military bravado..." and analyzes Dionysius fr. 2 in particular.

sacrifice, then preparing the meat for consumption. Such work had to be done carefully, precisely, and reliably. The role of *mageiros* in sacrifices and meals integrates him, indeed makes him fundamental, to the many rituals and sacrifices which establish, maintain, and solidify a Greek community. Consequently, his role in the preparation of food for a wedding allows him to stand as a symbol of the most critical ritual which marks the successful resolution of a Greek comedy. Scodel has deepened the study of comic cooks by integrating this authority of the *mageiros* with the coarser elements of the stereotype. "The cook is always an *alazon*," Scodel writes, "yet within the dramatic tradition, his task as sacrificer and cook justifies his claims" (1993:173). She speculates that the gravity of sacrifice would overwhelm the atmosphere of comedy so the comic *alazon* arose to obviate the tension between such seriousness and the humorous environment of the comic stage. Scodel may be correct, and if she is, this could parallel the development of the true *miles gloriosus* on the Roman comic stage (cf. Chapter 4), but a Greek comic playwright still faces difficulties in utilizing the character of the cook. The character of the *alazon* is unpleasant in his own right, and his repugnance as an *alazon* creates tension with the need for the *mageiros* to complete the wedding ritual and celebrate at the end of the play. The question then becomes, how does a comic playwright prevent traditional authority from clashing with the buffoonery? Menander addresses these tensions by limiting the cook's role as an *alazon* to scenes where domestic tension is already high. In this way, the obnoxiousness of the cook correlates to the degree of disruption in the household. Conversely, the presence and actions of the cook in his rudest comic form can serve as a barometer of the domestic tension Menander intends to convey. A settled household does not suffer at the hands of a cook, but a home in turmoil can expect the worst.

Absence of the *mageiros* as a character in extant Aristophanes and the loss of continuous portions of other comic playwrights make it impossible to compare Menander's technique with that of others. The different social status and responsibilities of Roman cooks also mean that Latin versions of the plays do not preserve *mageiroi* in a way which we can reliably analyze for Greek practice (Lowe 1985). In some cases in Menander, too, scenes with cooks are too fragmentary to speak with confidence about his modus operandi. At *Misoumenos* 270–275 (= 671–676 Arnott), for example, the young man Kleinias is fretting over dinner arrangements with a cook, but the scene seems to depend on a subplot in the play now all but unrecoverable. Kleinias' anxiety, however, is consistent with the cook operating as an *alazon* at a moment of high tension in the *oikos* (cf. fr. 409, whose speaker is exasperated with a cook, but the context is unknown). The remains of the *Phasma* contain a similar scene (57–74). The slave Syros says something about a wedding in the house and gets into an argument with the cook, who delivers an encomium of his profession. The lines are too tattered to determine anything more. *Epitrepontes* features at least two scenes with a cook named Karion, but both are scantily preserved. In one, Karion is gossiping with the slave Onesimos, at least in part about the scandal of Onesimos' master, Charisios, shacking up with the harp-girl Habrotonon shortly after getting married (fr. 1). The cook is thus immediately associated with the disruption of the household. In a later scene (603–631 Arnott), the few remaining words indicate Karion is reporting the turmoil that ensued inside the house when Habrotonon presented a ring and implied that Charisios had earlier raped her and gotten her pregnant. While this incident will in fact turn out to be a step toward restoring propriety to Charisios' marriage, at the moment of the revelation, as the cook reports it, it has the appearance of totally wrecking any opportunity for repairing this particular marriage. In both scenes, then, the cook's presence matches harsh scandal in the *oikos*.[28]

The remains of the conclusion of *Perikeiromene* show a scene where the cook is prevented from disrupting the proper resolution of the crisis. The soldier Polemon is nervously getting ready to receive back Glykera, the women he loves but who has lately spurned him for attacking her early in the play and violently cutting her hair. His slave Doris tells him he should be involved in a celebratory sacrifice when Glykera and her father come. Polemon first says he has a cook inside who should get the sacrifice started, but then he changes his mind and decides it would be better to engage in the sacrifice himself (995–1001). By doing so, he will be more persuasive, says Doris supportively (πιθανώτερος / πολλῷ φανεῖ γοῦν, 1000–1001). Within a few lines Glykera is betrothed and freely reconciled to Polemon. While the final few lines of the play are lost, nothing suggests the cook would have an opportunity to be disruptive or put on one of his virtuoso showpieces. In this case, then, the reformed lover Polemon, after reconciliation has been delicately negotiated during the course of the play, can proceed with the appropriate sacrifice and keep the cook under control.

Better-preserved scenes show the same principle in action, but more clearly. An early scene in *Aspis* has a cook marking a spike in the troubles of an *oikos*. A young man, Kleostratos, is reported dead on a military campaign. Because the youth had gone on the campaign to make enough money for his sister to secure a good marriage, his sister's wedding plans are now in jeopardy. One of their uncles had stepped in earlier, guaranteed the girl's dowry, and set up a marriage. However, another uncle, Smikrines, out of greed intends to step

---

[28] Cf. *Adespota* 1007, where a young man is rejecting his slave's advice to confess about his sexual impropriety when a cook arrives. Fraenkel 2007:166 cites lines 29–41 of this fragment as a contrast to Plautus, who would characteristically expand the underplayed military motifs in the slave's monologue (on which see Chapter 4).

in and marry the girl himself to gain control of the dowry. The plot of the play becomes the scheme to thwart the greedy Smikrines. The cook appears immediately following the scene in which Smikrines declares his intent to marry the girl despite the resistance and criticism he faces. Because of Smikrines' declaration, the girl's original wedding plans collapse. Accordingly, the cook hired for the wedding feast is fired. He emerges from the house furious at the cancellation, which has cost him his fee. He and his assistant *trapezopoios* make their appearance on stage at this critical juncture to vent their frustration. The *mageiros* is angry and rebukes his assistant for not even stealing anything while they had the chance. The *trapezopoios* trades barbs with the household slave Daos and departs with the cook (217–249). This rather standard scene of a cook's fury flows directly from the chaotic situation in the house. It would be unsurprising for this cook to return for the double wedding mentioned in the few remains of the last act of the play (521), but the script is too fragmentary at this point for this to be anything but hypothetical.

The *Samia* features two cook scenes, similar to ones seen in other plays and parallel to each other. The young man Moschion is scheduled to marry the girl next door, who has already had his baby. Out of fear of his foster father, Demeas, he is trying to cover up the existence of the baby until after the marriage. Demeas' mistress, Chrysis, is nursing the infant, pretending it is one she was supposed to expose. Troubles mount as Demeas learns part of the plot, concluding incorrectly that his son Moschion has fathered the baby by Chrysis. The cook appears twice, each time immediately following a monologue by Demeas, during which Demeas reveals what he has just learned and, drawing hasty and incorrect conclusions, grows increasingly angry and impulsive.

The trouble begins when Demeas overhears that the baby Chrysis is nursing is actually Moschion's baby (without hearing that Chrysis is not the mother herself). At this critical juncture, the cook swaggers in to begin his preparations for the feast to accompany Moschion's wedding to the girl next door, the true mother of the child. The cook crosses words with a household slave as a typically arrogant and annoying cook does, and goes inside (283–295). This is the usual pattern of the cook's *alazon* routine accompanying the rise of a crisis in the household.

Following the cook's return inside, Demeas interrogates a slave to confirm what he has overheard. Upon confirmation, Demeas bursts into a full rage, mistakenly believing his mistress Chrysis seduced Moschion and has his baby. The cook returns to the stage just in time to watch Demeas throw Chrysis and the baby out of the house (357–382). As Demeas explodes with greater and greater fury, Menander uses the cook to demonstrate the degree of Demeas' virulent anger. The cook actually tries to settle Demeas down but retreats

(383–90), indicating that Demeas seethes with an anger and outrage beyond that associated with a character who is normally angry and outraged. The fury which Demeas exhibits is so extreme that in the final sequence of the play, his own (adopted) son, Moschion, feels obligated to stage a scene in order to teach Demeas a lesson about his anger (cf. the discussion in Chapter 3 of Moschion's use of soldier motifs in this scene).

The *Dyskolos* uses these same techniques and involves the character of the cook even more. This time, it will be the anger and antisocial behavior of the old misanthrope Knemon which will find definition opposite the character of the cook. The introduction of the cook Sikon to the play follows a pattern we have seen several times. Just as tension in the house rises to its first crisis, the cook appears. In this case, the young man, Sostratos, has fallen in love at first sight with the old grouch's daughter and hopes to win his blessing to marry her. On advice from Knemon's stepson, Sostratos has just gone to work the fields in the hope of winning the old man over. The cook enters, hired to assist Sostratos' mother with a sacrifice (393–402). She has had a disturbing dream about Sostratos doing manual labor on another's land and plans the sacrifice so that the dream will have a good end. As so often in Menander, what initially provokes anxiety will develop into a happy resolution, but at this point in the play, trouble is brewing. The cook bosses a slave around while he learns of the troubling dream, simultaneously arriving at a sign of trouble and acting as his stock annoying self. At the conclusion of their dialogue, the slave Getas opines that the cook is praiseworthy but untrustworthy (425–426).

Sikon goes inside and after he reemerges a little later in the play, his role runs analogous to that of the cook in *Samia*. Like the cook in *Samia*, Sikon will serve as a foil to the old grouch Knemon, demonstrating the hyperbolic extent of Knemon's anger and hatred. After a slave has failed to secure some cooking implements from the old man, Sikon steps in, declaring he can handle this properly, typical of an arrogant cook (487–521; cf. Wilkins 2000:396–397, 412–414). In confronting Knemon, he confronts the true source of the domestic crisis. Knemon violently blows Sikon back. Menander shows that a character's anger goes beyond the pale by having him intimidate a character known for intimidation.

Interestingly enough, while the cook still has the power to irritate a household slave (546–551), the sacrifice for Sostratos' mother at which Sikon performs seems to go without incident (555). The contrast is significant, for it indicates that Sostratos comes from a stable household where a cook is kept under control, compared with the chaos of his encounter with Knemon.

Sikon's next appearance solidifies the contrast and emphasizes the disaster of the whole situation. When Knemon is reported to have fallen into a well,

Sikon rejoices bitterly (620–665). He encourages Knemon's slave woman to kill him while she can. He reckons Knemon's fate is divine justice for having dared to abuse the noble race of cooks (οὐδὲ εἷς / μάγειρον ἀδικήσας ἀθῷος διέφυγεν 644–645). While intentionally and humorously absurd, Sikon's rejoicing serves to reinforce the judgment of Knemon as spectacularly excessive in his antisocial fury.

The correlation between Sikon's attitude and the disarray of Knemon's house in part drives the final scene of the play, where Sikon and a household slave torture the crippled Knemon until he consents to attend the wedding festivities. Several scholars have well analyzed how Sikon participates in a procedure of compelling Knemon to reintegrate himself into the human community, beginning with a ritual, in this case a feast, with his family as they prepare to join another family via the communally sanctioned ritual of marriage (Lowe 1987 and O'Bryhim 2001). As with Demeas in the *Samia*, the scales are still out of balance for the anger and hostility manifested early in the play. Since Demeas' own son teaches the lesson in *Samia*, it may seem odd for Sikon to be involved in resocializing Knemon, rather than someone integrally involved in one of the households. but if Sikon operates as a barometer of domestic tension, then he can serve as a dramatically appropriate agent for signaling that Knemon still requires reform. In the end, then, the cook as *alazon* can serve paradoxically as a facilitator of domestic reconciliation. Despite Sikon's role as a facilitator, however, cooks are never, and never become, members of an *oikos*; they serve only as agents of the community's will toward sanctifying the results of an approved ritual activity.

The ways that cooks behave as *alazones* and serve as ancillary characters align them more with the *miles gloriosus* on the Roman stage, where soldiers bluster as futile impediments to the erotic hopes of the young protagonist (see Chapter 4) than with Menander's soldier characters. In Menander, the soldier himself is consistently the youthful protagonist whose erotic desire will ultimately result in a communally approved marriage. Braggadocio of the sort demonstrated for cook characters, even in their more curtailed form in Menander, is conspicuously absent, every bit as much as it is lacking in the fragments before and during his career.

From Tragic Warriors to Comic Mercenaries

Unlike braggart cooks, Menander's soldiers by contrast are desperately in love, violent, distracted, and suicidal. Since Menander did not draw these troubled figures from the comic tradition, I suggest that Menander drew theatrical paradigms for his soldier characters from a well that he plumbed often and deeply:

tragedy. As scholars have analyzed Menander's tools and techniques with increasing sophistication in recent decades, they have documented Menander's pervasive recourse to tragedy both as a source and precedent for theatrical activity and to tragedy's body of mytho-historical narrative as a resource for cultural knowledge and expectations. With regard to soldier characters retiring to a domestic life, as in Menander, tragedy in turn contains a large-scale ancient Greek cultural dialogue about warriors after combat experience on the battlefield.

In recent years, scholarship has increasingly recognized culturally driven patterns in soldiers' behavior on the battlefield and, more directly relevant for the current discussion, their reintegration into civilian life. As Kurt Raaflaub has demonstrated in a brief but powerful survey, the vicious consequences of war played out broadly and deeply, not just on the battlefields but in Greek communities throughout antiquity (2014, esp. 30–32 on mercenaries). Rural or civic life without the disruption of war and its consequences appears only as a utopian vision, one articulated in large part explicitly by the absence of war's effects, but even then only sporadically.[29] Otherwise, any analysis of communal life had to reckon it not in isolation but as the intersection of battlefield consequences and the ongoing community.

Performance art in the Greek world could and did articulate this intersection in a wide array of ways. Tyrtaeus composed hymns that promoted the courage of Spartan warriors as essential to communal prosperity (e.g. fr. 11). Heraclitus describes war as the "father and king of all" (πόλεμος πάντων μὲν πατήρ ἐστι, πάντων δὲ βασιλεύς), responsible for the division between humans and superhumans (τοὺς μὲν θεοὺς ἔδειξε τοὺς δὲ ἀνθρώπους) and slave and free (τοὺς μὲν δούλους ἐποίησε τοὺς δὲ ἐλευθέρους, 22 B53 DK = Laks-Most D64). In the epic tradition, the entire Trojan War could be a divine scourge to depopulate the human race (*Cypria* fr. 1). In stage comedy, Aristophanes' *Acharnians*, *Peace*, and *Lysistrata* all showcase how war impacts the lives of individuals in Athens and beyond. In many cases, of course, analysis of this intersection is more nuanced. The performance art that loomed largest in Greek antiquity as a meditation on the consequences of battle for an individual and in turn for the health of their community is, to be sure, the *Odyssey*. As noted earlier in this chapter, as an exiled mercenary trapped in non-Greek territory, Xenophon naturally elided the disaffection of his soldiers to those of Odysseus in the land of the Lotus Eaters. And no doubt the *Odyssey* looms somewhere in the background of any soldier whenever Menander depicts him as moving toward

---

[29] Lauriola 2009 provides a survey; Race 2014 analyzes the Phaeacians in the *Odyssey* in this context, to which should be added the peaceful world on the shield of Achilles in *Iliad* 18.490–508.

domestic life, but Menander's more immediate points of reference were perhaps not buffoons from the comic stage but the haunted figures on the tragic stage. As Hanink has surveyed and analyzed, tragedy, and in particular the three tragedians Aeschylus, Sophocles, and Euripides, were being valorized and canonized during Menander's lifetime (2014a and 2014b; cf. discussion in Chapter 1).

Relevant here, then, are the ways scholars explore the dynamics of soldiers' lives on and off the battlefield. These scholars have been devoting more attention to tragedy as a community's occasion and mechanism for identifying and articulating how soldiers' battlefield traumas could, do, or should play out.[30] Peter Meineck (2012 and 2016) has broadly outlined how Athenian tragedy offered "cultural therapy" for combat veterans, their families, and the society to which they belonged. Following the lead of Jonathan Shay (1994 and 2002), much scholarly exploration of soldiers on the tragic stage involves merging the experiences and perspectives in the ancient scripts with the experiences and accounts of combat veterans in modern times. Sherman (2014) finds Sophocles' *Philoktetes* showcasing, in terms immediate in the twenty-first century, the difficulties of building trust for victims of moral injury in warfare. Using not just *Philoktetes* but also Sophocles' *Ajax* and Euripides' *Herakles*, the Theater of War project has been probing how the Athenian tragic stage dramatized actions and places where the combat veteran no longer fits into his community and the catastrophic results for veterans and those around them (Doerries 2015).

To date, similar work on stage comedy has not been as comprehensive, and Alan Sommerstein has even put forth a case that comedy was culpably negligent in addressing the community's needs in this area (2014b). To what degree it is fair to consider comedy's engagement deficient I will leave aside but in Chapter 3 I hope to make the case that Menander's plays do dramatize issues germane to this tension in a distinctive way and to a degree greater than has been recognized.

Before analyzing Menander's scripts and methods, however, more analytical tools are needed. Scholars like Petrides are increasingly recognizing how tragedy is as vital a starting point for Menandrian comedy as his comic forebears and specifying how Menander deploys these reference points (Hurst 1990, Ireland 2010:357–360, Petrides 2014a:49–59). These are points of reference and sociocultural frameworks, however. Menander was predominantly a practicing playwright who wrote scripts that came to life on Greek stages. As scholars have come to recognize and explore with ever-increasing skill and appreciation, dramatic meaning is incomplete without adequate consideration of what was communicated via live performances.

---

[30] See Carter 2011, esp. 1–7, for studies of tragedy's roles in broader cultural discourse.

Petrides has compellingly argued that Menander's reputation for "realism" in antiquity was in large part an appreciation of Menander's ability to harness the exalted world of tragedy within an urban, domestic world on stage. He writes, "Menander's plots 'urbanise' (put into an urban context) narrative patterns drawn from tragic myth; in other words, they are not so much mirrors of life, as mirrors of stories. As a set of narrative and performative precedents, tragedy for Menander is not an extraneous theatrical mode to be deconstructed, debunked or antagonised ... but is an inherent mode, a constituent of New Comic theatrical medium, deeply ingrained in the genome of Menander's hybrid world" (4; cf. 79–81). In this mode, Menander can insert tragic language (meaning tragic in diction or meter), structure family dynamics, follow and diverge from plot patterns, and have characters live in a world suffused with the experience of tragic theater. Indeed scholars have cataloged all this activity (Petrides 2014:10–83, with 58–59 and esp. 103 providing a good guide to scholarship in this area).

Menander's spectators attended the theater with anxieties about real soldiers, especially mercenaries, but he used the traditions and techniques from tragedy to dramatize and resolve those tensions. In tragedy he found narratives of militarized men ostracized from their communities, who confronted and explored the angst that resulted from conflicting commitments, one to their military identity and another to civilian life incompatible with military behavior. Unfortunately, the near-total obliteration of the remains of tragic theater in Menander's day severely limits the specific points of contact that we can now establish, but as far as soldier narratives from tragedy, that of Ajax is richly suggestive. In Menander's lifetime, tragic Ajax narratives were iconic enough that Aristotle could cite them to epitomize one of the four strands of tragedy, the emotional (τραγῳδίας δὲ εἴδη εἰσὶ τέσσαρα ... ἡ δὲ παθητική, οἷον οἵ τε Αἴαντες, *Poetics* 1455b.31–34). The emotional turmoil of Menander's soldiers finds parallels in the emotional life of Ajax, primarily his last days tormented by betrayal, dishonor, confusion, and death by suicide. Menander takes the specter of a former mercenary—violent, conflicted, and unwelcome at home—and expresses it with theatrical dynamics from tragedy, but resolves the conflict, both on stage and to the community of the spectators, by having the soldier forgo his military prerogative and settle down happily with the woman he loves in a ritual with his new civilian community's approval, i.e. a wedding.

Within this process, Menander composed comedies, but he knew that laughter could originate in pain and suffering. One way to refer to such laughter in ancient Greek was Αἰάντειος γέλως, "Ajax laughter." An explanation of the phrase survives in a second-century CE collection of explanations of proverbs. The explanation reads:

Αἰάντειος γέλως· ἐπὶ τῶν παραφρόνως γελώντων. ὁ Αἴας γὰρ παραφροσύνην νοσήσας καὶ μανεὶς διὰ τὸ προτιμηθῆναι τὸν Ὀδυσσέα εἰς τὴν τῶν Ἀχιλλείων ὅπλων κατοχήν, κατὰ τῶν Ἑλλήνων ξιφήρης ὥρμησε καὶ κατὰ τῶν βοσκημάτων προνοίᾳ θεῶν τραπεὶς ὡς Ἀχαιοὺς ταῦτα φονεύει. δύο δὲ μεγίστους κριοὺς κατασχὼν ὡς Ἀγαμέμνονα καὶ Μενέλαον δέσμευσας ἐμάστιξε καὶ κατεγέλα τούτων μαινόμενος. ὕστερον δὲ σωφρονήσας ἑαυτὸν κτείνει.

"Ajax Laughter" refers to deranged laughing. Ajax, diseased with a mental derangement, driven insane because he was passed over in favor of Odysseus to possess the soldier's equipment of Achilles, sword in hand, swore against the Greeks and, by the will of the gods, turned on cattle and slaughtered them as if they were Achaeans. He caught and bound two enormous rams, thinking that they were Agamemnon and Menelaus, and then whipped them and laughed at them madly. Later he came to his senses and committed suicide.

Zenobius 1.43

Thus Zenobius explains this type of laughter as manically vengeful and deranged. But a later version of this collection of proverbs provides a somewhat different context for the occasion when Menander deployed the phrase:

Αἰάντειος γέλως· μέμνηται ταύτης Μένανδρος ἐν τῇ Περινθίᾳ τῇ πρώτῃ· λέγουσι δὲ ὅτι Πλεισθένης ὁ ὑποκριτὴς τὸν Καρκίνον Αἴαντα ὑποκρινόμενος εὐκαίρως ἐγέλασε· τοῦ γὰρ Ὀδυσσέως εἰπόντος ὅτι τὰ δίκαια χρὴ ποιεῖν, μετὰ εἰρωνείας ὁ Αἴας τῷ γέλωτι ἐχρήσατο.

"Ajax Laughter" Menander uses this saying in his first *Woman of Perinthos*. They say that the actor Pleisthenes, when performing the *Ajax* of Karkinos, laughed opportunely, because when Odysseus said that it was necessary to do the right thing, Ajax used his laughter ironically.[31]

Unfortunately, none of the other fragmentary remains of Menander's *Perinthia* (nor anything in Terence's *Andria*, which interpolated part of play), help us understand where Menander deployed the phrase. Nevertheless, the explanation is illuminating for how Menander understood the proverb and presumably

---

[31] Emmanuel Miller, *Mélanges de littérature grecque* (Paris 1868) 1.60, p. 355 = TGrF I2.70 (Carcinus II) fr. 1a, p. 211 [erroneously listed as 1.61] = Menander fr. 9 Körte, also quoted in part as fr. 9 Sandbach, p. 288; *Perinthia* not included in PCG.

conveyed the context of the phrase. Menander alluded not to the myth of Ajax generally, but a specific theatrical performance of the character. Indeed he referred to a specific performance of a specific tragedy about Ajax.[32] Moreover, in this performance the moment of Ajax laughing came not at the point in the story where explanations of the proverb typically place it, at the height of Ajax's delusional slaughtering of animals, but in bitter irony when Odysseus speaks of justice, when he already had been, or was going to be, anything but just to Ajax.[33] This is a laughter of knowing irony, not irrational insanity.

The *Perinthia*, if Terence's comment that it and Menander's *Andria* were in some way interchangeable is to be trusted (9–14; see Germany 2013:229–230 for analysis of this statement), abounded with elements commonly associated with Menander's plays and of stage comedy of his era: romances, angry fathers, the identification and legitimizing of infants, and miscommunication about all of the above. Yet, at some point in the play, one or more characters invoked a moment from a tragic performance. Furthermore, in the context of this study, the reference to a scene with Ajax and Odysseus in particular, one a Greek warrior facing betrayal, humiliation, and ultimately suicide brought down by the other, who was himself to be haunted and troubled, is not random or accidental, but consistent with an important pattern of characters and references in Menander's plays about the pain and suffering of troubled militarized men.

Menander's performances included elements and action beyond the verbal. Mueller's work on objects on the tragic stage helps further unpack theatrical elements that link the staging of Ajax with Menander's soldier characters. Mueller analyzes not so much objects as props, tools that facilitate dramatization on stage, as much as the use of objects in tragedy within the broader social context where such objects communicate a range of voices, choices, authorities, and actions resulting from their associations with, and presence at, activities that can be distant from the characters currently on stage. While Mueller makes use of a number of theoretical models to delineate the communicative agency of an object on the tragic stage, the concept of "distributed personhood" from anthropologist Alfred Gell proves especially fruitful for Ajax as performed in Sophocles' *Ajax*. Gell's model essentially says that an object by its presence

---

[32] The dates of Karkinus' career are uncertain, but Menander has a character in *Aspis* quote him at 416–417.

[33] No other testimony or fragment survives from Karkinos' play, so the exact occasion of the laughter remains undetermined. An obvious surmise is that Karkinos' play staged the debate between Ajax and Odysseus as they each made their claim to Achilles' panoply, but it is possible that the play staged another exchange between the two that occurred at some other occasion. Cf. Grossman (1968), who explores how the idea of laughter runs through the epic tradition and in particular in Sophocles' *Ajax*, but his focus is not on the proverb in particular and he does not address Menander's use of the phrase.

can communicate a host of decisions and consequences of those decisions by a variety of members of the community prior to and distant from a particular occasion and bring the authority of those absent voices to bear on immediate proceedings. Thus a soldier's implement such as sword or shield can carry with it not just its functionality or potential, but its history and legacy, uniquely configured and authorized by the people whose deliberations and authority led to the object currently being in the soldier's possession and bolstering the meaning of that possession for a community where the soldier wields it.[34]

In Sophocles' play, Ajax's sword and shield thus become richly evocative participants in the staged action. As Mueller elucidates, the sword is recognized and used as a critical agent in every phase of the play, from the violent carnage Ajax inflicts on animals just prior to the stage action, through the entire process of Ajax contemplating, debating, and eventually committing suicide on stage, to the controversy afterwards, when characters debate what will become of Ajax's body, even as it remains on stage fatally impaled by the same sword (Mueller 2016:15–38). Additionally, that Ajax acquired the sword in his duel with Hector in the *Iliad* compresses and infuses the stage narrative with Ajax's epic martial success, as much as the absence of the weapons of Achilles, possession of which Ajax reckons a fundamental component of full recognition of his warrior prestige. Thus, Ajax's interaction with the sword brings together all these phases and forces, with tragic results. Ajax's iconic shield brings its own set of associations, both as the hallmark of his identity as a premiere warrior on the battlefield at Troy and as a bequest to his infant son, in whom Ajax hopes to pass on the noble and successful portions of his life experience (Mueller 2016:134–154; cf. Weiberg 2018). While there is no specifically documented point of contact between Menander and Sophocles' play, Menander clearly knew such tragedies and the script of Sophocles' play, along with much evidence about earlier traditions of Ajax. As such, Ajax is most helpful for charting examples of theatrical activity that easily lend themselves to recognition in Menander's "urbanization" of tragic warrior narratives into those of citizens trying to transition from being mercenaries abroad to a settled domestic life in a stable community. Menander's soldiers not only have comparable weapons, but their weapons are fraught with entanglements and opportunities. It is the positive opportunities that are most emblematic of New Comedy, where "tokens" rewrite a character's known past and facilitate their path to domestic stability, freedom, and citizenship. Soldiers in Menander, such as Stratophanes in *Sikyonios*, may experience such recognition via tokens, but objects like their sword and shield are more

---

[34] Mueller 2016:15–38; cf. Powers 2014 for cautions about scholarly methods used to read ancient tragic performance. See Tordoff 2013:105–109 for a list of props called for in Menander's scripts.

likely to be complications. In *Misoumenos*, the recovery of a sword simultaneously (and erroneously) communicates the death of one citizen and implicates the soldier in his killing. In *Aspis*, the shield both disguises and represents a lost soldier, who will have to return to the stage to prove he is alive and able to avert crisis in the household for whose benefit he initially went on campaign. In *Perikeiromene*, Polemon's sword, as a marker of his military identity, hobbles his efforts to reach safety and stability in the home he yearns to have (especially if he used it to cut his girlfriend's hair). Menander's ability to integrate the history and associations of objects, now "urbanized" and repurposed, is a byproduct of his constant and thorough engagement with tragic theatrical practice.

The broader ramifications of a play like Sophocles' *Ajax* may well also have been "urbanized" and redirected. Scholars have explored the play as an arena for analysis and debate about the very principles of practicing democracy.[35] I have argued that Menander's political and ideological goals would have been quite different from those of tragic playwrights in the fifth century, but there is no reason that would have impeded him from reconfiguring those sorts of capacities in tragic precedent for his own new purposes, as he did in virtually every area of the drama he spearheaded.

Finally, at this point it is worthwhile to declare limits of my claims for the impact of Greek tragedy on Menander's dramatization of soldiers. For the most part, scholars have documented Menander's redeployment of tragedy in terms of quotations from tragedy, metatheatrical references to tragedy, and dramatic structures that parallel scenes known from tragedy. The evidence and testimony that survive for soldiers in Menander and tragedy do not include many parallels of these types. The reference to Karkinos' *Ajax* is crucial but limited. The stage props called for in the scripts of Sophocles' *Ajax* and Menander's plays are suggestive but again limited. I will not be arguing, for example, that any of Menander's soldier protagonists participate in scenes that specifically invoke analogous scenes in Sophocles' *Ajax*, along the lines of what Petrides has argued for Menander's invocation of scenes from Sophocles' *Oedipus Tyrannos*, Euripides' *Bacchae* and *Orestes* (2014a:55, 76–78, 274). That Menander constructed scenes involving soldiers along these same lines is quite possible, and I would expect indeed likely, but the haphazard survival of scripts and other evidence so far does not present an example of such a parallel in detail. Within these limitations, in the analyses to follow in the next chapter on soldiers in Menander's plays, I will note specific points of contact but mostly invoke narrative patterns and expectations where the surviving narrative does imply that Menander and

---

[35] See Anhalt 2018:115–148 for an overview of these approaches to Sophocles' *Ajax* that dissect it as a critique of democratic deliberation.

his audiences would have experience of the robust performance tradition of tragedy, even when the surviving scripts of tragedies are not the direct source for these narratives. My hope is that the honest presentation of these points of contact and the invocation of narrative expectations from indirect sources will validate the resulting picture.

Conclusion

To recapitulate, we now come armed with several categories of tools and support to analyze soldier characters in Menander's plays. Menander has ideological priorities that call for neutralizing a soldier with military capabilities that could destabilize a settled domestic community. His community comes to the theater with anxiety about the increase of former mercenaries, who are at least perceived to lack bonds to Greek communities, a tension that Menander's ideological priorities need to neutralize. In terms of theatrical referents to shape and put soldier characters into action, Menander has vignettes of soldiers and military life, but they are not restricted to, even dominated by, the stock character of the braggart. Indeed, Menander is as likely to reach to the traditions and techniques on the tragic stage, where troubled soldiers struggle, even fail, to reintegrate with their community away from the battlefield. This theatrical tradition includes a rich array of not just narratives, but visual and aural techniques to signal adherence to and departure from the cultural narratives that Menander and his Athenian theatergoers knew about how and whether soldiers can become demilitarized husbands and citizens. Finally, perhaps drawing on theatrical precedent, but perhaps distinct to Menander's dramatic technique, he deploys true braggarts, notably cooks, in ways that correlate to the distance from the domestic stability that is the ultimate goal of his comedy's resolution.

The next chapter brings all these techniques together, to illuminate how Menander introduces a militarized man, a former mercenary, in conflict with the ideological goal of being a responsible domesticated citizen, and uses a specific range of theatrical tradition and technique to bring about a reassuring conclusion.

3

Love in the Age of War
Soldiers in Menander

Let man's petty nations tear themselves apart.
My land's only borders lie around my heart.

"Anthem" from the musical Chess, lyrics by Tim Rice

BECAUSE MENANDER'S PLAYS WITH soldiers as protagonists ranked among the more popular and familiar of his plays, ancient references to these plays and their soldier characters are relatively plentiful and all the more revealing because the scripts of these same plays are today incomplete. Indeed, the impact of Greek New Comedy and Menander on the ancient Greek world remains broadly visible in a host of venues where motifs from the Greek comic stage appear, from visual emblems to verbal cues to character types, making New Comedy a matrix of cultural tropes as much as it was a theatrical phenomenon. As Nervegna has cataloged, Menander's legacy in the ancient world consisted in substantial part in his remaining a fixture in theaters, symposia, and schools. Menander and New Comedy suffused a full range of literary expression as well.[1] Except for praising the quality of Menander's language, language which might ironically have made him expendable to medieval readers,[2] ancient Greek authors did not, and perhaps could not, articulate what made his plays resonate so broadly and deeply with them centuries after his death. "New Comedy" was decidedly a revolution in comic theater and there was never any question that Menander's plays were its embodiment and best specimens. From a modern perspective, not counting those who discount New Comedy as

---

[1] Nervegna 2013, Funke 2016, cf. Peterson 2019 for a parallel study of the ancient reception of pre-Menandrian comedy.

[2] Blanchard 2014:239–241. For an example of ancient criticism of Menander's language in late Antiquity, see Phrynichus *Epitome* 418 = Menander T 119 PCG, who expresses exasperation at the popularity of Menander, and then pedantically focuses on how Menander falls short of proper Atticism.

a phenomenon to be lamented and criticized,[3] the resonance of Menander's plays resulted in part from their synthesis of so many defining *topoi* of Greek culture: polis-identity, one's social role in a community, economic status, the role of the divine in human life, Greece's mytho-historical past especially as conveyed in tragedy, and the consequences of military activity in the broader Hellenistic world (in ways that resonated differently, but still meaningfully, in that same world when dominated by Rome, on which see Chapter 4). All these elements have their place in Menander's drama as a vehicle of Greek culture, its constituent elements coming into conflict in a variety of configurations and ultimately resulting in harmony. One such area where culturally Greek communities felt a need for harmony, both in Menander's day but also in subsequent centuries under Macedonian and Roman hegemony, was between the desire for settled domestic life accepted by a local community and the prerogatives of a militarized life without being rooted to any community beyond a specific campaign. That Menander made this conflict central to several of his most resonant comedies, and achieved the yearned-for resolution to this tension, was one component of Menander's persistent appeal in the Greek world.

More than eight hundred years after Menander's career, in a cultural environment where theater was increasingly derided as a locus of barbaric behavior and gradually to be marginalized and eliminated, the Byzantine poet and historian Agathias ("Scholasticus") made wry use of Menander's enduring impact on the Greek-speaking world. Weaving in motifs from Menander's plays into a scurrilous poem about forbidden erotic desire, Agathias invokes one of Menander's most recognizable soldiers:

> τὸν σοβαρὸν Πολέμωνα, τὸν ἐν θυμέλῃσι Μενάνδρου
> κείραντα Γλυκέρας τῆς ἀλόχου πλοκάμους,
> ὁπλότερος Πολέμων μιμήσατο, καὶ τὰ Ῥοδάνθης
> βόστρυχα παντόλμοις χερσὶν ἐλήσατο,
> καὶ τραγικοῖς ἀχέεσσι τὸ κωμικὸν ἔργον ἀμείψας,
> μάστιξεν ῥαδινῆς ἅψεα θηλυτέρης.
> ζηλομανὲς τὸ κόλασμα. τί γὰρ τόσον ἤλιτε κούρη,
> εἴ με κατοικτείρειν ἤθελε τειρόμενον;
> σχέτλιος· ἀμφοτέρους δὲ διέτμαγε, μέχρι καὶ αὐτοῦ
> βλέμματος ἐνστήσας αἴθοπα βασκανίην.
> ἀλλ' ἔμπης τελέθει "Μισούμενος" αὐτὰρ ἔγωγε
> "Δύσκολος," οὐχ ὁρόων τὴν "Περικειρομένην."

---

[3] Cf. Chapter 1.

That violent Polemon, who on Menander's stage cut off the hair of his wife Glykera, has an imitator in a younger Polemon, who with audacious hands plundered Rhodanthe of her curls, even changing the comic deed to tragic aches, whipped the limbs of the slender female, an act of punitive jealousy, for what did the girl do so wrong if she decided to take pity on my frustration? The villain has separated us, going so far as to block even a jealous glimpse. But he ends up "A Man in Hatred," while I am a "Grouch" when I don't see my "Girl with Her Hair Cut."

Greek Anthology 5.218

Agathias does more than include specific vocabulary and name-check play titles.[4] While theater was certainly deprecated in Agathias' day, it was alive enough to be the site of scandalous activity.[5] Agathias also made use of pagan traditions, which would include theater, to a surprising degree in his day, so much that the devotion of his Christianity has been questioned by modern scholars.[6] Just what Agathias would have read of Menander cannot be determined precisely, but his use of σοβαρόν (line 1) in the same metrical position as σοβαρός in *Perikeiromene* 172 suggests that he had at least more than titles and summaries. He invokes the jealous anger of Menander's soldier Polemon from the *Perikeiromene* and transforms his rival into another anguished soldier, Thrasonides from *Misoumenos*. For Agathias, these soldier characters and their tragicomic behaviors communicate jealousy, anger, and violence. Nothing invokes the bluster of the braggart soldier, for that is not how Agathias reads these characters and scenarios.

Another manifestation of New Comedy's impact in the form of a soldier appears in a poem of Theocritus, whose floruit places him roughly in the generation immediately after Menander. This poem features Aeschines, a young man who in name, disposition, and experience resembles many a youthful protagonist of Greek New Comedy. He is a young man desperate in love, jealous, and drunkenly abusive to the object of his affection at a party, all of which can be paralleled in New Comedy.[7] In his misery recalling another young man suffering from love who found solace in military life, Aeschines ponders whether such a move would heal his own emotional wounds. He further opines, ...οὔτε κάκιστος / οὔτε πρᾶτος ἴσως, ὁμαλὸς δέ τις ὁ στρατιώτας ("It's not the worst, maybe not

---

[4]   Contrast *Greek Anthology* 12.233 by Fronto, which does little more than patch in a number of titles of Menander plays.

[5]   See Puchner 2017:62–74, esp. 69 on terms and attitudes toward theater in this period.

[6]   Cameron 1970:57–88 and Kaldellis 1999. For how Agathias' epigrams fit into the cultural context of the sixth century, see Smith 2019:1–32.

[7]   See Hunter 2003:110–115 on the comic motifs in this poem with valuable observations in Kyriakou 2018:12–18.

the best either, but being a soldier is stable enough," *Idyll* 14.55–56). Aeschines' evaluation of a soldier's life comes as he contemplates becoming a mercenary soldier in particular. As documented in Chapter 2, the motif of a young male lover likening his plight to that of a soldier had precedent, and this particular conceit of escaping to mercenary life to avoid the pitfalls of love and marriage is also attested in Menander.[8] Theocritus is playing with a host of poetic genres, especially the revolution in stage comedy, but nonetheless Aeschines is no braggart soldier. He does not boast of fanciful military accomplishments. He is perhaps a fraud, and certainly hapless in his aspirations, but this does not make him a *miles gloriosus*.[9] Rather, the opposition he articulates between a successful and stable romantic relationship with a woman and a military life abroad reflects the core tension that propels the actions of and around soldier characters in Menander's plays.

With regard to this tension, the previous chapters have built up the case that soldier characters in Menander's plays represent an especially sensitive area where Menander must deploy considerable dramaturgical skill to make the hazards of his characters lead to a culturally desirable and reassuring conclusion. In Menander's drama, a soldier's citizenship in a polis is typically unstable, while his commitment to his domestic community stands in conflict with his behavior as a militarized man. His erotic desires diverge from the norms and laws of his community, and the culturally recognized patterns for a soldier's life after a war do not tend to stabilize in the form of harmonious domestic life. Menander dramatizes all these tensions and yet steers his plays to a domestic harmony that is novel compared to long-established cultural patterns.

This chapter presents and analyzes the remains of Menander's drama where these tensions play out and are resolved. It is necessary, and traditional, at this point to spotlight the fact that the plays involved are all incomplete and fragmentary to different degrees. Soldier characters were protagonists in some of the more popular and recognizable of Menander's works in antiquity, but as it happens today, the script that is the closest to complete, that of *Dyskolos*, has no soldier character, and that which is next nearest to completion, that of *Samia*, makes use of a soldier character in only a single scene, an oblique use of the character's narrative expectations that will be analyzed and discussed in this chapter once the normative dynamics have been established. Of another two dozen or more plays which contain at least some part of a scene that can be reconstructed, has a scene preserved in visual art, or otherwise exists beyond the barest of citations, at least half a dozen feature prominent soldier characters,

---

[8] See the discussion of *Samia* below.
[9] Chapter 4 will elaborate on the characteristics of developed braggart soldiers.

and these will be the principal focus of analysis in this chapter. These plays vary considerably in their degrees of completeness and to what extent the remains are conducive to extrapolation.

Despite these limitations, the goal here is to begin with one particular play, *Perikeiromene*, which includes nearly all the tensions outlined above, that will serve as a point of reference for comprehending and analyzing other fragmentary plays with militarized men.

Perikeiromene: Her Hair Cut

The soldier characters that Menander dramatizes are dynamic, in the sense that a crucial development in the action of any given play lies in the soldier successfully choosing to pursue a settled, domestic life while leaving behind military prerogatives. As this study continually argues and emphasizes, Menander's soldiers do not come equipped with the expectation that they are static, fumbling braggarts. Instead Menander sets up a tension in the soldier's situation, and the gradual resolution of that tension is a significant driver of a play's action. Accordingly, analyzing this trajectory effectively calls for tracking how Menander initializes and then transforms the behavior of the soldier and of other characters reacting to him. In many discussions of Menander's fragmentary plays, it is standard, for pragmatic reasons of clarity, to outline and summarize the plot of a given play and then steer toward a particular analysis. Given the goals of the analysis here, and since plentiful outlines and summaries are available for the plays in this chapter, the discussion here will proceed somewhat differently. As far as evidence permits, the following analyses will proceed through a play in performance order, with particular attention paid to the soldier characters, to build up and modify what Menander's audiences hear and his spectators see of soldiers as a live performance begins, continues, and concludes. As far as is practical, information will be relayed out of sequence only to explain why sometimes we know how to correctly interpret fragmentary information that would have been comprehensible to an ancient audience at a specific point in performance. Even for plays with complete scripts, such an approach cannot yield definitive conclusions about the experience of ancient theatergoers, but for Menander's soldier figures in particular, such readings serve as a counterpoint to studies where so much about soldier characters is assumed at the expense of what Menander presents dynamically across scenes and entire plays. The fragmentary state of all these plays, of course, brings significant limitations to this approach and the synthesis of the plays. The soldier protagonist of *Perikeiromene*, Polemon, because of the distinct remains of the play that are available and because of his pronounced character, will provide a valuable template for making sense of the comparatively more fragmentary remains pertaining to soldier characters in other plays.

To begin at the beginning, the first act of *Perikeiromene* survives in both a surprisingly rich and frustratingly deficient array of sources. Generally for Menander, the growing collection of identified visual representations of scenes from Menander plays has brought equal parts fresh information and interpretive challenges. Broadly speaking, I follow the lead of Csapo and others who reckon that these images derive from a Hellenistic master collection of images made approximately in the generation after Menander's death.[10] Multiple surviving versions of the same image demonstrate that orientation, proportions, background details, and the arrangement—even presence—of characters can vary according to the needs of the artist and setting, so a precise sense of the early Hellenistic model, to say nothing of that model's correspondence to any live performance of Menander's plays, is limited.[11] Still, where these images and a play's script can be compared, there are meaningful points of contact, so, as with any ancient reception of Menander's plays by people who could have experienced Menander's plays more fully than is possible now, whether expressed via quotations, epigram, essay, or the visual arts, I will treat ancient visual representations as products that instantiate a moment of such reception and thus likely to communicate correspondences with ancient performances that reinforce and extend what survives of the plays' scripts.

For *Perikeiromene*, the excavation and publication of a mosaic from a suburb of ancient Antioch, Daphne, has improved our ability to make sense of the other illustrations, although critical questions remain. The Daphne mosaic (Figure 2) is explicitly labeled "*Perikeiromene*, act 1" (περικειρομενης με α'), a section of the play whose script is only partially recovered. Of the first act, only the last 145 lines or so survive now, with some gaps, and the scene in the mosaic matches nothing in these lines, so the mosaic must represent dramatic action from the lost lines prior to the extant text, a loss reckoned at approximately 120 lines. The surviving text starts during a speech by the divinity Ignorance (Ἄγνοια), providing background for the events in the earlier scene.[12] Fortunately, between this speech and other surviving parts of the script, we can securely identify the characters in the mosaic and something of the action transpiring. Prominently included among the three characters in the mosaic is the protagonist soldier, so the current analysis of soldier characters in Menander begins with the visualization of this particular character, which will require teasing out what these

---

[10] Csapo 1999.

[11] Csapo 2010:140–167 and Dunbabin 2016:62–77.

[12] An ancient illustration of Agnoia herself has also been recovered, in a crude pen and ink drawing on papyrus, Gutzwiller and Çelik 2012 figure 8.

visualizations imply about what the scene in performance conveyed to ancient spectators.

The tableau in the Daphne mosaic depicts three characters, with the soldier central (Figure 2). A badly damaged and fading wall painting in Ephesus features roughly the same scene (Gutzwiller and Çelik 2012 figure 14), and in fact the recovery of the Daphne mosaic has assisted comprehension of this painting. A frieze from Delos might also depict this scene, but this identification is problematic (Gutzwiller and Çelik figure 15). A fragment of a mosaic in Chania shows a soldier character who has been identified with Polemon of *Perikeiromene*, a possible but still speculative assignation (Gutzwiller and Çelik figure 7). Finally, a rough ink drawing on a torn bit of papyrus appears to represent Polemon as well (Figure 3).

Following the fundamental publication and analysis of the Daphne mosaics by Gutzwiller and Çelik (2012), the most sophisticated analysis of these depictions of Polemon has been by Petrides.[13] While my analysis will differ in significant ways, Petrides's thoughtful and detailed study will serve as a rich and valuable arena for the discussion here.

Figure 2: Mosaic of *Perikeiromene*, Act 1 from Daphne
(drawing based on Gutzwiller and Çelik 2012 figure 10).

---

[13] Petrides 2014a:84–91, 213–16.

As the Daphne mosaic is the best preserved and most detailed of the five potential visual representations of Polemon, it will be most productive to focus on it initially, analyze the other representations in comparison, and proceed from there to the extant portions of the play's script. Gutzwiller and Çelik describe Polemon in the Daphne mosaic this way:

> ... holding a staff in his right hand and looking toward Sosias ... He has a strong, handsome face, light in complexion, a long, straight nose, a small mouth, blue eyes, and even blond/light brown eyebrows slanting downward to the sides. His tousled blond hair, made of cream and brown tints, falls over his forehead and frames his face around the ears. This hairstyle, called "ἐπίσειστος" (tossed over the forehead), is characteristic of soldiers in both tragedy and comedy. Polemon's naturalistic mask is in all likelihood a late version of the second ἐπίσειστος (Mask 16), said by Pollux (Onom. 4.147) to be a fair-haired, more delicate version of the first ἐπίσειστος, who is a braggart soldier, dark in hair and complexion. He wears on his head a light blue πῖλος ... , a soldier's cap without a brim, pillbox in shape ... His look is distressed rather than angry, not unlike the youth in the Ephesos painting. Polemon is dressed in a generously cut white chiton with broad deep blue clavi and wide sleeves. The tight sleeve of an undergarment can be clearly seen on his right arm. A brilliant red military cloak (with orange highlights), decorated with a large emblem, hangs over his left shoulder and is fastened by a brick-red strap; it is pulled up from behind on his right side and rests on his leg. His damaged officer's emblem, called a *scutula* or *orbiculus*, displays a Gorgoneion (it seems) in orange and yellow, with forehead and nose highlighted in white on a square background, of which only a few blue and green tesserae remain. His right hand reaches across to hold his cloak, and in his left hand he holds a blue staff with a crook. In the Mytilene mosaics and elsewhere, the staff is part of the costume of old men who are authority figures; here, it marks the chiliarch Polemon as a mature youth (labeled "*neaniskos*" in Men., *Pk.* 129) with his own household and military command. The text rather demands a sword (cf. 355), and the odd circular fold of Polemon's chiton below his right hand seems to outline a hilt with the blade continuing over the left knee. His hands are white with brick-red contours, suggesting a skin color appropriate for a fair-skinned man with an active lifestyle. The border of his chiton is visible above his sandals, indicating that if he should stand, the garment would fall to midcalf length. The white legging visible on his left leg shows that he

wears a full-body undergarment, ... His sandals are made of deep blue tesserae...

Gutzwiller and Çelik 2012:586–587 and figure 12

Several features combine to indicate not merely that Polemon is a soldier but more about his military prerogatives. The object conveying his military identity most visible to spectators in the theater is the red cloak (specifically a *chlamys*), a vivid and distinct marker of a military man. Two other objects convey that Polemon is an accomplished military man, not just a rank-and-file soldier. His *chlamys* has an emblem, though it is unfortunately damaged such as to prevent precise identification. As noted by Gutzwiller and Çelik (n. 59), there are analogous iconographic examples of emblems on cloaks. An historical occasion known from Kallixeinus of Rhodes (FGrH 627 F 2), preserved by Athenaeus (5.196f), mentions military cloaks (ἐφαπτίδες, see the discussion below on line 179 for more on this garment) which were displayed with woven images at the time of Ptolemy II's grand procession (ἐφαπτίδες τε κάλλισται, τινὲς μὲν εἰκόνας ἔχουσαι τῶν βασιλέων ἐνυφασμένας, αἱ δὲ μυθικὰς διαθέσεις, "and beautiful military top coats, some with royal portraits woven in, others with mythological subjects," trans. modified from Olson). This procession would have occurred generally around Csapo's time frame for the creation of the master set of Menander images that lie behind this and other mosaics. This gives some idea from an occasion close to Menander's lifetime of the dignity a military cloak with an emblem could represent, and opens up the possibility that the mosaic's representation of Polemon's cloak derives from Hellenistic times close to Menander. In any case, the emblem certainly indicates prestige and authority. The staff held by Polemon also conveys authority, another object which is known to be associated with a warrior's authority, though in stage comedy it is often elders who carry staffs as emblematic of their seniority (Gutzwiller and Çelik n. 60). Together, however, these cues communicate that Polemon is not just militarized, but accomplished and authoritative. This is consistent with a reference in the script of *Perikeiromene* that Polemon is in fact a chiliarch, that is, a commander over hundreds of infantry soldiers (line 294).

At this juncture it is worth noting, indeed emphasizing, that there is nothing in the images of Polemon or in the script to suggest that these signs of military achievement and recognition are anything but legitimate. If the assumption remains that soldiers are by default *alazones*, then such symbols would automatically conflict with Polemon's character. Such a conflict is often assumed and sometimes explored by scholars regarding another component of Polemon's visualization, his mask.

Petrides provides the most elaborate and productive analysis of Polemon's mask along these lines. Like Gutzwiller and Çelik, he finds the mask of Polemon consistent with a description in Pollux (Mask 16, 4.147): τῷ δ' ἐπισείστῳ, στρατιώτῃ ὄντι καὶ ἀλαζόνι καὶ τὴν χροιὰν μέλανι καὶ μελαγκόμῃ, ἐπισείονται αἱ τρίχες, ὥσπερ καὶ τῷ δευτέρῳ ἐπισείστῳ, ἀπαλωτέρῳ ὄντι καὶ ξανθῷ τὴν κόμην ("The Tossover [ἐπίσειστος], being a braggart soldier, has dark skin and hair. The hair is tossed over [the forehead], as also on the second Tossover which, being gentler, has light hair"). Scholars, including notably Wiles, have taken Pollux's catalog of mask descriptions as a roughly coherent semiotic system, though other scholars have expressed skepticism that such coherence is inherent in Pollux's writings.[14]

Petrides, however, argues that Menander and New Comedy broadly employed a complex system of visual symbols that conveyed a great deal of meaning in performance, especially in comprehending the dynamics of individual characters. While it will become evident in what follows that I find a number of specifics of Petrides's system untenable, overall he has made a hugely important and positive contribution toward an invaluable holistic understanding of the dynamics of New Comedy. For a long time to come there will be much critical work for modern scholars and spectators to understand the ancient experience of these plays. Petrides is a pioneer in working in a sophisticated manner to build a model for this experience, and he deserves much credit for it.

Petrides's system in particular consists of the interplay of three principal components: a matrix of binary associations embedded in the system of masks, a physiognomic system of conveying and "reading" character extrapolated from Peripatetic philosophy, and a use of the tradition of spectacle built up in the theater over the many generations prior to Menander. Fundamentally I agree with Petrides that playwrights and spectators of New Comedy engaged in an ongoing process of using oral delivery, visual cues, and meaning through spectacle and movement in ways that articulated the meaning of performance, but I expect that this dynamic was more fluid and less precise than what Petrides describes. Petrides's most detailed example of his system is the messenger speech in the *Sikyonios*, which prominently features the soldier Stratophanes, and I will engage with Petrides's account when looking at that play, but he also offers a rich account of the *Perikeiromene*, especially the opening tableau.

In Petrides's system, the specific mask is critical to decoding a character, because the mask has a matrix of components, each of which communicates some character trait. The playwright and spectators can use, follow, or work

---

[14] Wiles 1991, but see the reservations expressed about reckoning Pollux's descriptions as systematic in Poe 1996.

against what these components communicate. In the case of the *episeistos* masks, the difference between the skin tones and hair color (dark or light) are opposing pairs not just in tone but also opposing character traits. In this case, darker skin is more masculine, while light hair is "leonine" and cowardly. As this example indicates, the same mask can thus have divergent components when "read" as a guide to character, a guide which in turn the action of the play and words of the script can further refine or "rewrite" for a variety of nuanced results. Petrides finds Polemon wearing the second *episeistos* mask surprising, since the first mask is the one that explicitly belongs to a braggart soldier and the script of *Sikyonios* seems to support the soldier in that play, Stratophanes, wearing this first type. Petrides probes the idea that two kinds of *episeistoi* are variable masks for braggart soldiers, an option he never seems comfortable with, and a position, as he himself notes, at odds with his earlier work.[15]

Part of Petrides's struggle with Polemon and his mask is the a fortiori assumption that a soldier is a braggart, although he acknowledges it is in Roman palliata where this type is actually attested. As Chapter 2 demonstrated, however, for Menander and his age, there is insufficient reason for this default expectation, and hence Chapter 4 will return to Petrides's analysis of Plautus' *Miles Gloriosus*, where he finds dynamics more consistent with his system. Chapter 2 argued that withdrawing the expectation of the braggart soldier better fits the known evidence for Greek comedy before and during Menander's career.

So, jettisoning the expectation that Polemon should be an *alazon*, we return to the visualization of Polemon in the Daphne mosaic. The staff and red cloak with its emblem indicate that Polemon is, or has been, an accomplished military man. The mosaic has a subtle indication that Polemon also carries a sword, another object, in tandem with the cloak, that is a distinctive visual marker of a soldier (see discussion of the *Samia* below for use of this prop). The cap he wears, the pileus, is also part and parcel of the soldier's equipment, also evident in other depictions of the character. The papyrus drawing clearly shows this cap and it is evident enough in the fragment of the Chania mosaic.

His face, or rather the face of the mask, is where features can separate the Polemon in the Daphne mosaic from the other depictions. "Distressed rather than angry," as Gutzwiller and Çelik describe him, with curly blond hair and distinct eyebrows that lead them sensibly to link the mask with Pollux's second *episeistos*. The ink drawing on papyrus has a wavy line beneath the cap that could outline a similar hairstyle, and the eyebrows, again crude, are consistent with those of the Daphne mosaic (Figure 2).

---

[15] Petrides 2014a:96 contra Petrides 2005.

The features on the Ephesus wall painting (Gutzwiller and Çelik figure 14) are less distinct because of fading and damage, but seem consistent with the features of the mosaic, although his expression is, if anything, even more distressed, with an open mouth and a gaze staring vaguely to the viewer's left, rather than rightward toward Sosias as in the Daphne mosaic. The depictions conjecturally linked to the *Perikeiromene* stand as outliers by comparison. The Chania fragment does seem to depict a soldier, for he sports a cap and cloak with a deep red portion (Gutzwiller and Çelik figure 7).

His extended right hand might have held an object like a sword, but the fragment breaks off well above his wrist, and his left arm and hand seem mostly obscured by the cloak. His pose (leaning or moving toward his right) and position within the frame (stage left rather than center) do not match those of the Daphne mosaic or Ephesus wall painting, both of which are labeled *Perikeiromene*.[16] He has black hair and seemingly knit eyebrows (in contrast to the eyebrows in the ink figure and the Daphne mosaic, which are separated

Figure 3: Ink drawing probably of Polemon on P.Oxy 2653
(drawing based on Gutzwiller and Çelik 2012 figure 9).

---

[16] The ink drawing (Figure 3) survives only from near the top of the cap to the top of the chest, which tells us little about his overall pose, but it is not angled as the figure in the Chania mosaic is.

and even tend toward the temples). At least two different tones are used for his skin, and while these are evidently dark compared to those used in the Daphne mosaic, they are comparable to those used for the figures the *Plokion* mosaic by the same artist (Gutzwiller and Çelik figure 6), so it does not seem to indicate markedly dark skin. Even so, there are so many more divergences than parallels that it seems hard to identify this figure with Polemon unless it is a radically different visualization. More likely, since by its location there are good grounds for the fragment belonging to a tableau of Menander, it is a soldier from another play. Popular plays like *Misoumenos* (less likely since a Mytilene mosaic has another scene from the play) and *Kolax* thus become legitimate candidates, but this remains speculative.[17]

The central figure in the Delos frieze (Gutzwiller and Çelik figure 15), meanwhile, need not even be a soldier, to say nothing of Polemon. His cloak is less evidently a military chlamys and it is only the general arrangement of figures that suggests the tableau of *Perikeiromene*.

In the fuller tableau of the Daphne mosaic and the Ephesus painting, Polemon is but one figure. He is flanked by two characters in strikingly different modes. In the Daphne mosaic he looks stage left to his attendant Sosias, who is moving toward him, aggressive in both appearance and gesture. Based on the remains of the play's script and what can be reconstructed of the plot, this aggressiveness derives from the belief that he has witnessed Polemon's beloved being unfaithful. Sosias had witnessed the girl in an apparently amorous exchange with a young man who lives nearby. In the surviving portions of the script, the personified Ignorance describes this meeting in an expository monologue (153–162), which implies that the spectators had not in fact witnessed it. Very likely Sosias had referred to or described what he had seen, however. Thus the Daphne mosaic seems to show Sosias speaking to Polemon about the matter. Since Polemon appears upset, it is also possible that Sosias is addressing Polemon's emotional state. Polemon's stance with respect to Sosias differs in the Daphne mosaic from the analogous scene in the Ephesus wall painting. In the Daphne mosaic he looks toward Sosias, but in the wall painting he looks downstage and away. In both cases, his distress stands in marked contrast to Sosias' posture, a contrast which could well be fueling Sosias' aggressiveness, whether he is berating the girl, Polemon, both, or even attempting to console Polemon (this last seems least likely).

Let us pause to consider what this says of Polemon's character to those in the theater. Visually he comes across as an accomplished military man, and the initial scene between Polemon and Sosias could well have referred to his

---

[17] Cf. below (p.40), where Nervegna 2013:fig17c links this image with Stratophanes of *Sikyonios*.

accomplishments, status as such, or both. He is also emotionally wounded, thinking that he has been betrayed by the woman he loves. And he is young, explicitly confirmed later in the script (νεανίσκου, line 129) and by his mask, both in its appearance and its type, for the *episeistos* is but one of a number of variations cataloged by Pollux for the young man in love. The conflict at this point, then, resides in the opposition between Polemon's military success and the despair in his love life. None of this requires or expects Polemon being a braggart. The characterization of Polemon as a braggart relies on nothing but the external assumption that soldier characters in New Comedy are by default braggarts. In this case, importing this assumption changes the dynamic of Polemon's character significantly without justification. If Polemon is a braggart, then he promotes himself as militarily accomplished beyond his legitimate success, if any. Polemon's despair would then move closer to failure warranted by his arrogance, something approaching the comeuppance that is standard for such characters on Roman stages (on which, see Chapter 4). Instead, Polemon is failing as a lover, to his distress, in spite of being a success in the military. But of course there is a sharper dramatization of this contrast between his military ability and erotic misery.

Glykera, the woman with whom Polemon is in love (ἐραστοῦ γενομένου, line 128) was also on stage, for Ignorance explicitly reminds the spectators that they saw her (ἣν νῦν εἴδετε ὑμεῖς 127–128). The Daphne mosaic and Ephesus wall painting feature Glykera prominently and thus suggest that she was on stage with either (or both) Polemon and Sosias during the opening sequence of the play. She is a striking figure and scholars have offered strong readings of her effect on the tableau. She stands stage right, looking off further stage right, thus away from both Polemon and Sosias. She is veiled and wearing a striking blue himation, which she has pulled up to cover much of her head, in a pose recognized as one communicating a distressed emotional state (Figure 2; cf. Gutzwiller and Çelik figure 11).

And, of course, she is the *perikeiromene*, the girl with her hair cut. The famous title refers to Polemon's response to learning of what he thinks is Glykera's infidelity: he forcibly cuts her hair. That Glykera has her head wrapped in the Ephesus wall painting (Gutzwiller and Çelik figure 14) led previous scholars, at that point uncertain where in the play the tableau was supposed to belong, to conclude that the wrapping hides her shorn hair. Hair is visible beneath this wrapping on the Daphne mosaic, however, leading Gutzwiller and Çelik to conclude that at this point in the play Polemon has not yet cut her hair. While not impossible, this is far from likely. Such a conclusion means that the tableau shown in these illustrations represents the characters before the shocking event. If these three characters played out a scene, it would practically require that Polemon cut her hair on stage and she flee the stage before Ignorance arrives to address the audience. It would then also remain a mystery how different Glykera would appear later in the play when she returns with her hair cut. It would be an odd artistic choice to illustrate the brief opening scene where Glykera still retains her locks at the expense of a shocking event and what must have been her more memorable appearance afterwards.

Moreover, there is no requirement that Glykera be deprived of hair to the point that none appears in her hooded state. The covering itself can indicate the haircut is sufficiently degrading that she must cover it. And there was theatrical precedent for such a haircut. In Euripides' *Electra*, Electra herself sports a slave's haircut as part of her degradation. It is distinctive enough that Orestes remarks on it when he first notices her (ἐν κεκαρμένῳ κάρᾳ, 110), before he even approaches her.[18]

Figure 4: Electra as a *perikeiromene*
(drawing based on Geneva, HR 29, ca. 370 BCE).

[18] See Figure 4, an early Paestan neck amphora (Geneva, HR 29, ca. 370 BCE), which shows a mourning Electra uniquely with no head covering and her hair cut short. LIMC Electra 19a Geneva, HR 29, illustration in Cambitoglou et al. 1986. Louvre MNB 167 (K 544), Naples Mus. Nat. 81841 (H 2858), Naples Mus. Nat. 81843 (H 2856), Munich Antikenslg. 3266 (J. 814), all ca. 350 BCE and all illustrating Aeschylus' *Choephoroe*, have visual analogues to the depictions of Glykera

The long scene to follow, where brother and sister meet and engage in cautious dialogue, sustains tension as Electra, much like Penelope in the *Odyssey*, seems to realize that the stranger can be her long-lost brother, but it takes the decisive evidence adduced by the pedagogue before she is willing to acknowledge him.[19] With increased awareness of Menander's absorption and redeployment of tragedy, it seems reasonable to suggest that Menander is characteristically redeploying elements from an already classic scene in the Theater of Dionysus, the reunion of Orestes and Electra.[20] Menander evokes the brother-sister reunion with some twists. In an inversion of which sibling knows the other, only the sister, Glykera, knows the identity of the brother, Moschion, although the two must have had a full recognition later in the play (finally staging the encounter that the spectators only hear about in the first act). It is similarly inverted that Moschion/Orestes is the wealthy, elite, and settled sibling (142–143), while the sister Glykera/Electra is the unrecognized visitor from out of town. The sister Glykera/Electra is traditionally unmarried or, in the case of Euripides, married to a poor local farmer and trapped in a hostile home. Glykera is attached to the soldier, who will prove to be local and is responsible for the degrading haircut, and the prospect of marriage is troubled and problematic. As so often, all these dynamics with tragic antecedents are couched and resolved in a domestic setting.

As Ferrari, May, and Petrides have further articulated, the shorn Glykera is an especially evocative image, for her cut hair can project associations with crisis, mourning, looming nuptials, and more.[21] Petrides also finds Aeschylus' staging of the embodiment of grief, Niobe, behind the iconic Glykera, but there seems to be too little known of both scenes for this to be more than speculative (it expects that Glykera was silent for a significant portion of the scene, for example, which goes beyond our evidence since the script is deficient here).

To return to Polemon, Glykera's degradation, no matter how staged, is a powerful theatrical statement about Polemon's capacity and ability to use his military power.[22] This is not the action of a braggart, for the essence of the braggart is that he boasts of achievement and ability which other characters expose and the audience recognizes as false (for elaboration of this idea and examples from Roman comedy, see Chapter 4). Polemon's power is real. Menander starts

---

(LIMC Electra 7–10). Less certain depictions of Electra but with similarities are British Museum F 57, Berlin Staatl. Mus. 30042, and New York MMA 29.54 (LIMC Electra 56, 66–67).

[19] See May 2005:277–280 on the parallels in the haircuts. For recent analysis of the emotional dynamics in this sequence, see Dunn 2020.

[20] Traill 2008:33–46 provides a strong analysis of Glykera, along with 133–134 on comparisons with Euripides' *Electra* and *Iphigenia in Tauris* and 155–156, 175.

[21] Ferrari 1996:235, May 2005, Petrides 2014a:88–90.

[22] Traill 2008:147–149.

the play by signaling Polemon's military credentials, showcasing the very real danger that the skills inherent in those credentials pose to settled domestic life, but he also has Polemon recoil from his very power and its realization. The resolution of this conflict will take the entire play, but for the moment, having thrust all these conflicting dynamics in front of the spectators, Menander brings on stage a figure to reorient the audience's understanding of those events, literally the very embodiment of inadequate knowledge.[23]

For the modern scholar working to reconstruct as much of the play as possible, Ignorance's speech conveys valuable information, but for an audience at a performance, it is a mix of helpful background, surprising information, and murky foreshadowing. It is some lines into this speech that the first lines of the recovered script become available. At this point the audience does not know the identity of the speaker who has emerged to address them. In the first lines to survive, she is already explaining the backstory of Glykera and Moschion. Their mother had died in childbirth. Moschion is now living under the auspices of a foster mother, Myrrhine, whose home is on stage. As a result of war and "Corinthian troubles" (125), the old woman who raised Glykera separately from Moschion gave her to Polemon, who had fallen very much in love with her (ἐραστοῦ γενομένου, 128). Polemon is of Corinthian stock and "extreme" (σφοδροῦ, 128). When the foster mother was elderly and dying, she informed Glykera about the twin brother, Moschion. It is here that Ignorance slyly reveals her own identity, saying that the old woman wanted to prevent "ignorance" from allowing unintended consequences for Glykera and Moschion (140–142). Polemon has recently moved into the neighborhood, bringing Glykera into proximity of her brother, although the brother is unaware that such a sister even exists, for Glykera has maintained the secret so as not to hamper Moschion's prosperity. But Moschion is, emphasizes Ignorance, "rather bold" (θρασυτέρου, 151) and characteristically takes hold of Glykera, which for him constitutes boldly pursuing the pretty girl next door, while for her this is the long-delayed reunion with her brother. As a witness to this emotional reunion, Sosias sees and reports what he saw to Polemon, says Ignorance, a statement that again suggests that the spectators had not in fact earlier witnessed Sosias give this report (so the earlier scene with Polemon and Sosias probably included only general or elliptical references to Glykera's betrayal). Ignorance then adds that it sparked (ἐξεκάετο, 162) what was going to happen and explains (163–167):

... εἰς ὀργήν θ' ἵνα
οὗτος ἀφίκητ'—ἐγὼ γὰρ ἦγον οὐ φύσει

---

[23] For more on Agnoia and Peripatetic notions of comprehension, see Cinaglia 2015.

τοιοῦτον ὄντα τοῦτον, ἀρχὴν δ' ἵνα λάβῃ
μηνύσεως τὰ λοιπά—τούς θ' αὑτῶν ποτε
εὕροιεν·

... so that he would go into a rage—because I led him, (although) he's not naturally that sort of person, so that the consequences would bring the beginning of new information, and eventually find their own people.

Ignorance here crucially and explicitly says that Polemon's anger subsequent to believing that Glykera was unfaithful was not natural to him, rather that it resulted from ignorance. This would go some way toward making sense of what the spectators have seen of Polemon: that he is accomplished and powerful, but that the remorse following his act of violence is a reliable manifestation of his character. It will also result in positive outcomes, assures Ignorance, and she further says, for Menander seems to feel it critical to justify (167–171):

ὥστ' εἰ τοῦτ' ἐδυσχέρανέ τις
ἀτιμίαν τ' ἐνόμισε, μεταθέσθω πάλιν.
διὰ γὰρ θεοῦ καὶ τὸ κακὸν εἰς ἀγαθὸν ῥέπει
γινόμενον. ἔρρωσθ' εὐμενεῖς τε γενόμενοι
ἡμῖν, θεαταί, καὶ τὰ λοιπὰ σῴζετε.

As a result, if anyone is disgruntled about this and thinks that it is dishonorable, they should change their mind. Because by superhuman intervention, even the bad transforms and turns into good. Goodbye and wish us well, spectators, and support what happens next.

Thus Menander anticipates that something in spurring Polemon to anger will strike a spectator as culturally undesirable and worthy of condemnation (ἀτιμίαν, 168) and includes an injunction to trust in the outcome of the unpalatable events. The note of caution here perhaps can be taken as an indication that Polemon's shearing of Glykera actually occurred on stage, a shocking visual then and now, but at least the idea that an accomplished military man violently deformed his lover is certainly reason enough for a spectator to express objections to the moral worthiness of the action. The goal of a Menander play always is to have a settled, stable domestic household. Polemon's action can easily be taken as one that permanently makes such a result impossible, and that his exile from the community (another meaning of ἀτιμία) should be the result. This again puts the core conflict of the play squarely at the tension within Polemon of his military prerogative and his culturally ratified erotic desire to have a faithful lover, which in turn should result in a stable productive marriage.

That judgment of Polemon's character is meant to be the focus of Ignorance's statement is confirmed with the very next line, when Sosias comes forward to reveal to the audience Polemon's current behavior (172–180):

ὁ σοβαρὸς ἡμῖν ἀρτίως καὶ πολεμικός,
ὁ τὰς γυναῖκας οὐκ ἐῶν ἔχειν τρίχας,
κλάει κατακλινείς. κατέλιπον ποούμενον
ἄριστον αὐτοῖς ἄρτι, καὶ συνηγμένοι
εἰς ταὐτόν εἰσιν οἱ συνήθεις, τοῦ φέρειν
αὐτὸν τὸ πρᾶγμα ῥᾶον. οὐκ ἔχων δ' ὅπως
τἀνταῦθ' ἀκούσῃ γινόμεν' ἐκπέπομφέ με
ἱμάτιον οἴσοντ' ἐξεπίτηδες, οὐδὲ ἓν
δεόμενος ἄλλ' ἢ περιπατεῖν με βούλεται.

Our man who was just so violent and warlike, who can't let women hold on to their hair, is now lying down crying. I left a meal prepared for them just now. His friends have gathered together, so he won't take it so hard. Since he didn't have any way to hear about what's going on out here, he sent me out to bring him an overcoat, but he doesn't need one. He's just sending me to keep me wandering.

Sosias' initial line is routinely cited as testimony that Polemon is in fact, underneath, a stock braggart soldier.[24] In fact it says nothing of the sort, and if anything, quite the opposite. Ignorance has already informed the audience that Polemon is not violent by nature. He had to be goaded. Here Sosias confirms that. Polemon was violent and warlike when he cut Glykera's hair, utilizing his military power and prerogative, but now his emotional distress is even greater than what the spectators witnessed on stage earlier. He lies weeping, consoled by comrades. Sensibly someone has provided a meal, but it seems he has not eaten. This is a realistic scenario of grief, evocative of the exact kind of remorse expressed by combat veterans who have momentarily directed their military violence on loved ones.[25] The scenario also indicates that Polemon has sympathetic comrades who are working to ease his suffering, the exact remedy of community promoted by health professionals today.[26] All this emphasizes, consistent with Ignorance's insistence earlier, that all will work out for Polemon, but it will take the duration of the play's performance to complete the process. At the moment, Polemon is helpless. He is disconnected from events

---

[24] Petrides 2014a:236; Gutzwiller and Çelik 588 and n24.
[25] Shay 1994:xiv–xxii, 2002:137–139.
[26] Shay 1994:187–193, 2002:168–179.

and sends Sosias out for a cloak (ἱμάτιον). It is no stretch to read symbolism into Polemon requesting additional covering from his military identity, as it is what has caused him his current pain. Sosias rightly adds that it is not what the soldier needs and he considers the order a fool's errand.

At this point another member of Polemon's household emerges and enters the stage, Doris, who is attached to Glykera and who provides another perspective on Polemon. She says (185–188):

> ... δυστυχής,
> ἥτις στρατιώτην ἔλαβεν ἄνδρα. παράνομοι
> ἅπαντες, οὐδὲν πιστόν. ὦ κεκτημένη,
> ὡς ἄδικα πάσχεις.

Poor woman who takes a soldier for partner. Lawless, the lot of them, and untrustworthy. My mistress, how you've been mistreated.

She continues (188-90):

> ... εὐφρανθήσεται
> κλάουσαν αὐτὴν πυθόμενος νῦν· τοῦτο γὰρ
> ἐβούλετ' αὐτός.

He'll be pleased to hear that she's crying now. That's what he wanted.

Here Doris, someone from Polemon's own household, voices a perspective on the situation sympathetic to Glykera.[27] Except for the exculpatory revelations by Ignorance about Glykera and her brother, characters on stage have been mostly, if not entirely, hostile to her. Doris also continues to problematize Polemon's military character. As a soldier, he is inherently lawless and unreliable. She does not, however, characterize him as a braggart or fraud. Rather, she takes a side on the conflict within Polemon's character: his identity as a soldier trumps and invalidates his identity as a law-abiding citizen and potential husband (ἄνδρα). Sosias' response, while sympathetic and supportive to Polemon in its own way, reinforces Doris' point, that Polemon is painful to Glykera and she is suffering for it.

Unfortunately two pages of the script are missing at this point, so we cannot know how the conversation continued. The script resumes at the final lines of the first act, spoken by Daos, a slave in Moschion's household, announcing the band of drunk young men who will provide the entertainment between acts. In

---

[27] Arnott gives these lines to Sosias, rather than Doris, but the criticism of Polemon seems more in line with Doris, while Sosias only wishes his master felt this way.

the next act, Daos emerges again, now with Moschion, whom the spectators see for the first time. In the course of their conversation, it is revealed just who is the true braggart of the play: Daos himself. Moschion calls out Daos as a liar and a braggart (ἀλαζών, 268).[28] As their banter continues, with Daos pleading his case that he deserves a reward for making Glykera come to Moschion's home, Moschion makes a dismissive counteroffer (279–281):

ΜΟΣΧΙΩΝ

βούλομαι δὲ προστάτην σε πραγμάτων Ἑλληνικῶν
καὶ διοικητὴν στρατοπέδων—

ΔΑΟΣ

... οἵ μ' ἀποσφάττουσιν εὐθύς, ἂν τύχῃ, κλέψαντά τι.

MOSCHION

I want to see you an overlord of Greek affairs and marshal of infantry forces.

DAOS

<text damaged> ... They'll cut my throat right away if they catch me stealing something.

This exchange is mostly cited in scholarship because of Schwartz's suggestion that the scenario here alludes to a specific historical occasion, the assassination of Alexander son of Polyperchon in 314/13.[29] For present purposes, however, more interesting is the contrast with the demonstrated character of Polemon. Polemon himself is an accomplished soldier struggling with his military abilities that impede his path toward a successful domestic life with the woman he loves. For the real braggart Daos, military power is akin to punishment, even a death sentence. Daos' refusal becomes ironic at the end of their conversation, when Moschion derisively refers to Polemon as ἐπὶ θεοῖς ἐχθρῷ πτεροφόρῳ χιλιάρχῳ "a goddamned chiliarch with a feather on his helmet" (294). Thus Moschion snubs Polemon's very real military experience as an infantry commander after threatening Daos with just such responsibilities (with Daos averse to any such

---

[28] Cf. Traill 2008:35 on Moschion himself as braggart.
[29] See Gomme and Sandbach 1973:482 for discussion of this line and also the badly damaged end of 280, for which one supplement, by Jensen, includes ξένων "mercenaries." On the "guessing game" motif here, to be compared with that of the *Rhesos*, see Fantuzzi and Konstan 2013.

opportunity) and also mocking the insignia of Polemon's military authority. While Polemon has his own struggles, bragging and pretense are not among his flaws, in contrast to Daos, who is evidently a true *alazon*, and Moschion, labeled a hothead by Ignorance, a characterization confirmed by his conversation in this scene. Indeed, Daos goes inside to promote Moschion's cause to Glykera and their mother but reemerges a failure, even confessing that he had not been in fact responsible for bringing Glykera to Moschion earlier. Moschion is an ineffective commander of Daos and Daos himself a true fraud.

Sosias now reappears with an update on Polemon. Tellingly and symbolically, Polemon has handed over implements of his military identity, his cloak (χλάμυς) and sword (σπάθη) for Sosias to surrender to Glykera. Sosias adds that this is the most miserable he has ever seen his master (κακοδαίμον᾽ οὕτω δεσπότην οὐδ᾽ ἐνύπνιον / ἰδὼν γὰρ οἶδ᾽ ... , 359–360), calling this "a bitter way to settle at home" (ὢ τῆς πικρᾶς ἐπιδημίας, 360). Polemon now fits a long-standing cultural pattern from mytho-historical narratives of successful warriors, from Agamemnon to Odysseus, who struggle to settle at home with family members.

As soon as Sosias exits on this note, Daos immediately returns to the stage and continues the narrative of Polemon, "The mercenary has arrived! Now things are really tough," he frets (ὁ ξένος ἀφῖκται. χαλεπὰ ταῦτα παντελῶς / τὰ πράγματ᾽ ἐστί, 361–362). This is the first time in the surviving portions of the script that Polemon is identified as a mercenary soldier in particular, though it is unlikely that this would have been the first such reference, unemphatic as it is here. Indeed, without context, the word Daos uses of Polemon as a mercenary, ξένος, marks him primarily as an outsider to the community. Soon Sosias reemerges and Daos retreats to comment to the audience. Sosias complains that Glykera has moved in with Moschion the "adulterer" (μοιχόν, 370), in response to which Daos comments to the audience, μάντιν ὁ στρατιώτης περιάγει / τοῦτον· ἐπιτυγχάνει τι "The soldier has himself a prophet! He's hit on it" (371–372). Soon Daos and Sosias are arguing, each standing up by proxy for their respective masters (Moschion and Polemon). Sosias challenges Daos, πότερα νομίζετ᾽ οὐκ ἔχειν ἡμᾶς .... / οὐδ᾽ ἄνδρας εἶναι; "You don't think we're real men?" (379–380), laying claim to the exact identity (ἄνδρας) Doris earlier denied Polemon. Daos responds by downgrading Polemon's military status (380–382):

ναὶ μὰ Δία, τετρωβόλους.
ὅταν δὲ τετραδράχμους τοιούτους λαμβάνῃ,
ἢ ῥᾳδίως μαχούμεθ᾽ ὑμῖν.

By Zeus, four-obol men. As long as he has four-drachma-types, we'll have an easy time fighting you.

Daos likens Polemon and Sosias to the lowest levels of mercenary pay possible, four obols for a rank-and-file soldier and four drachmas for the lowest officer, simultaneously insulting their rank and emphasizing that they are mercenaries. This military imagery continues as Sosias, who blames Glykera and laments Polemon's weakened condition, threatens Daos and Moschion in military terms: they will take the pathetic house by force (388–389). "Arm your adulterer," he snarls (ὅπλιζε τὸν μοιχόν, 390). Their peltasts, he continues, will smash everything, throwing back the "four-obol" insult at Daos (393–395), and he even calls for a pike (396). Now Daos exits and Doris returns, but the script is incomplete at this point and does not resume until the next act.

The beginning of the third act is lost in the script, but when it resumes, the siege promised by Sosias seems to be in progress. This is the first appearance of Polemon on stage since his violence and ensuing depression in the previous sequence. In one sense, as will be explicit in the scene, the siege represents Polemon exercising his military prerogative and ability. In this way, it represents a temporary surge by the problematic side of Polemon in his inner struggle, the greatest threat of his character to Menander's ideological goal (a stable, domestic neighborhood) playing out live on stage. In fact, Menander mutes the threat by staging the siege in humorously domestic terms. Although not all the details can be recovered because of the lost portion of the script, the siege party seems to consist at most of Polemon, Sosias, a *hetaira* named Habrotonon, and possibly a cook. Any other participants would have been similarly non-military. Polemon's desire is the only military threat here.

The siege scene also includes the first appearance in the extant text of another crucial character: Pataikos. Pataikos is the father to Glykera and Moschion, although none of the characters on stage, and perhaps not even the audience, at this point are aware of it. In an oblique way, then, this scene presents a confrontation between Polemon as soldier and lover and Pataikos as father-in-law. When the script resumes, well into the siege scene, it is evident that Polemon and Pataikos are already known to each other. Because of gaps in the script, it is impossible to determine whether this familiarity develops during the play or whether the two characters are said to have known each other prior to the events of the play. Either way, a certain level of mutual respect is established before their conversation in the extant portion of the script. More important for purposes of the current analysis is that Pataikos makes explicit the central conflict of Polemon, and by extension, of the play as a whole: between Polemon's prerogative as a soldier and as a lover. Although Pataikos does not yet know that he is in fact Glykera's father, and thus effectively dictating terms to his future son-in-law, he unremittingly steers Polemon toward operating not as a militarized man but as a civilian lover within the community. Sosias even interprets Pataikos' position as traitorous to Polemon's military siege ("He's betraying you and the army!" προδίδωσίν σε καὶ τὸ στρατόπεδον, 468), to which Pataikos simply retorts that Sosias should give up on the battle and sleep it off (κάθευδ'...τὰς μάχας, 469), as an unhealthy venture (οὐχ ὑγιαίνεις, 470). Pataikos then turns his attention to Polemon.

In response, Polemon offers a self-assessment, προειδὼς πάντα ταῦθ' ὁ δυστυχὴς / τηρῶν τ' ἐμαυτὸν εἰς τὸ μέλλον, "Poor me, I saw all this coming, and I was monitoring myself about what was going to happen" (472–473). Pataikos applauds Polemon's self-awareness and uses the opening to guide Polemon in a new direction (473–74). Sosias objects to Pataikos' intervention in military terms, "He'll end the war, just when domination is within reach!" (τὸν πόλεμον διαλύσεται / ἐξὸν λαβεῖν κατὰ κράτος, 478–479), punning on Polemon's name itself meaning "war." Sosias emphasizes that Pataikos is no commander (οὐκ ἔσθ' ἡγεμών, 480).[30] Losing ground with Polemon, Sosias turns to the *hetaira* Habrotonon. Characteristically of Sosias, the closest he ever comes to domestic terminology is here where he deploys military terminology with sexual overtones to rally Habrotonon to the military cause—unsuccessfully as it turns out (481–485).

Meanwhile, Pataikos continues to press Polemon to pursue his cause as a civilian lover. Like Sosias, he puns on Polemon's name meaning "war," but in order to highlight the contrast with Polemon's desire: εἰ μέν τι τοιοῦτ' ἦν, Πολέμων, οἷόν φατε / ὑμεῖς τὸ γεγονός, καὶ γαμετὴν γυναῖκά σου—"Polemon, if the situation were anything like you say, and she were your wife ... " (486–487). Polemon bristles at this and insists that he has indeed recognized her as his wife (ἐγὼ γαμετὴν νενόμικα ταύτην, 489). What Polemon fails to recognize here, of course, is that such recognition is insufficient for resolution in Menander's world. Legitimacy hinges on the bride's father granting betrothal and the subsequent ritual wedding sanctioned by the community. Polemon is sufficiently troubled by his military past not to invoke specifically martial authority or ability on his own behalf, but he has yet to yield to the requirements of the civilian community that legitimizes his domestic life within it. Pataikos exposes the deficiency in Polemon's position by asking who betrothed Glykera to him (ironically, of course, since Pataikos himself should have betrothed her, but none of the players realize this yet). Polemon replies that Glykera gave herself willingly to him (491). Pataikos in turn exposes the consequences of what he considers Polemon's untenable assertion. If Glykera has the authority to betroth herself, then she has subsequently withdrawn herself in the face of inappropriate treatment, as

---

[30] In these lines, speaker attributions and addressees are uncertain, but the most consistent way to assign lines is for Sosias to insist on military terminology; cf. Gomme and Sandbach 504–505.

her legal guardian (*kyrios*, see Gomme and Sandbach 1973:505–506 for details) could do. Polemon says he is especially pained at the idea that his treatment of Glykera has been inappropriate (τουτί με τῶν / πάντων λελύπηκας μάλιστ' εἰπών, "You hurt me most when you say that!" 493–494). Pataikos continues to push Polemon into accepting the community's (in this case probably Corinth's) sociopolitical authority for meeting Polemon's needs. He addresses Polemon's needs not as those of a former soldier but as a desperate lover (lines 494–504; cf. Lape 2004:180–183). Addressing Polemon, Pataikos says (494–499):

...ἐρᾷς,
τοῦτ' οἶδ' ἀκριβῶς, ὥσθ' ὃ μὲν νυνὶ ποεῖς
ἀπόπληκτόν ἐστιν....

...
λοιπὸν τὸ πείθειν τῷ κακῶς διακειμένῳ
ἐρῶντί τ' ἐστίν.

You're in love. I know that clearly. Consequently, what you're doing is stupid .... Persuasion is the recourse of the suffering lover.

Pataikos continues, still addressing Polemon but with reference to Moschion (501–503):

ἀδικεῖ σ' ἐκεῖνος, ἄν ποτ' ἔλθῃς εἰς λόγους.
εἰ δ' ἐκβιάσει, δίκην δ' ὀφλήσεις· οὐκ ἔχει
τιμωρίαν γὰρ τἀδίκημ', ἔγκλημα δέ.

He's wrong to the point that you can have him indicted, if you ever come to terms. If you force it, you'll lose your case. The crime allows for indictment, not for punishment.

Polemon responds in kind, in the process choosing to go forward with his identity as a young man in love, not as a wronged mercenary. In so doing, he calls on Pataikos to plead his case. Of course, once again, since Pataikos really is Glykera's legal guardian, he is in fact the man to whom Polemon needs to appeal, except that the ignorance of the characters about Pataikos' relationship to Glykera temporarily impedes this natural progression. Instead, and necessarily, Menander steers the dialogue between Pataikos and Polemon in a direction that will reveal the relationship between all the characters and thus let the chain of communally approved command over legitimate marriages run its course. Menander achieves this by having the deliriously in love Polemon decide to show Pataikos Glykera's clothing, which will be key in revealing everyone's identity (516–525).

As Polemon and Pataikos retire, Moschion takes over the stage, still caught up in the quasi-military activity earlier, referring to pikes (λόγχας, 527) and mercenaries (ξένους, 530). Much of the next several hundred lines of the script is missing entirely and the extant sections are quite fragmentary, but it is clear enough that a recognition scene enables Pataikos, Glykera, and Moschion to realize that they were father and twin children.[31] The surviving script resumes with Polemon once again, as he was earlier in the play, despondent to the point of suicide (" ... so I'll hang myself!" ἵν' ἐμαυτὸν ἀποπνίξαιμι, 976) and penitent (he assures his servant Doris that he will be completely well-behaved at 980). He believes at this point that Glykera has abandoned him, but upon hearing that she is in fact preparing to reunite with him, he is thrilled.[32]

At the prospect of facing Pataikos as Glykera's legal guardian, and potential father-in-law, however, Polemon runs inside, but Pataikos promptly betroths Glykera (1012–1014). At this point, Pataikos makes explicit that Polemon's future identity excludes his prerogative as a soldier (1016–1017): τὸ λοιπὸν ἐπιλάθου στρατιώτης ὤν, ἵνα / προπετὲς ποήσῃς μηδὲ ἓν ... "Forget about being a soldier, so you don't go out of control ... " Polemon assures Pataikos and Glykera that he will not behave badly in the future. The exchange expressly puts the reconciliation (διαλλάγηθι, Polemon asks of Glykera at 1020; cf. Gutzwiller 2012) in terms of Polemon forgoing his military prerogatives. It also shows that what is problematic about Polemon exercising his military prerogative is not that he is an arrogant fraud, a *miles gloriosus*, but that such militaristic behavior violates the civilian norms of a settled domestic husband. Indeed, this last exchange encapsulates the tension and dynamic in Polemon throughout *Perikeiromene*. At the beginning of the play he is despondent about the consequences of his violent skills costing him the support and love of the woman he considers his wife. By the conclusion of the play, he has replaced his military identity with that of a husband as sanctioned legally and ideologically by his community.

This is the political dynamic that I trace in all of Menander's plays, where he takes tensions that are potentially disruptive to the rhythms of stable domestic life in Greek communities within a broad Macedonian imperial environment and brings the characters to a point where such tensions are reconciled within their community's norms. Menander thus sets up a soldier like Polemon as inherently inconsistent with the communal norms of a Hellenic city and dramatizes his

---

[31] Furley 2015; cf. Henry 2014:114–115 on new supplements to lines 540–541.

[32] At 995, he mentions a cook, consistent with the pattern that a settled household can command an otherwise troublesome cook. Cf. Chapter 2 on cooks.

path to normalization. Polemon initially believes that he has a settled domestic life with the woman he loves, but the violent eruption of his military strength, to the point that it disfigures that same woman, leaves him in despair to the point of being suicidal. Gradually, despite the skepticism of others and a comical failure to succeed via his military prerogative in the siege scene, Polemon accepts a lawful wife, a father-in-law, and the dissolution of his military imperatives that would otherwise be inconsistent with his new civilian life. It is important to underscore again that this inconsistency is genuine, i.e. that Polemon's militarized identity really is a threat, not that he blusters or pretends that he poses an overwhelming military threat. He is not a fraud, a *miles gloriosus*; he is a former soldier without a community who forgoes the risks and prerogatives of that identity for a stable and innocent life in a stable and innocent home.

Misoumenos: A Man Wounded in Hatred ...

Using the hermeneutics and interpretive lens established for *Perikeiromene* adds clarity and cohesion to all the other plays and sequences involving soldiers in Menander. *Misoumenos*, another play that foregrounds a soldier deluded into thinking he has a stable, domestic life but who is tripped up by his military past, starring a man wounded in hatred, Thrasonides, contains many points of contact with *Perikeiromene*, as far as its incomplete script allows. On the basis of testimony in antiquity and the sheer number of different papyrus sources (still adding up to a small fraction of the complete script), *Misoumenos* was one of Menander's more popular and recognized plays. Indeed, centuries after Menander's lifetime, Arrian uses Thrasonides as an example when reporting Epictetus' teachings on the nature of freedom and slavery. This teaching aims to show that freedom and slavery hinge on making choices rather than on the identity of an oppressor. In Epictetus' version of Stoicism, acting contrary to one's desires constitutes slavery, so, for example, a Roman senator who obeys the emperor against his wishes or gives in to the wishes of a slave girl lover is more a slave than nominal slaves who live lives as they choose (e.g. *Enchiridion* 19). For Epictetus, Menander's Thrasonides serves as an example of a man with military experience who is nevertheless enslaved to his passions:

> ὅρα ἃ λέγει καὶ ποιεῖ ὁ Θρασωνίδης, ὃς τοσαῦτα στρατευσάμενος, ...
> πρῶτον μὲν ἐξελήλυθε νυκτός, ὅτε ὁ Γέτας οὐ τολμᾷ ἐξελθεῖν, ἀλλ'
> εἰ προσηναγκάζετο ὑπ' αὐτοῦ, πόλλ' ἂν ἐπικραυγάσας καὶ τὴν πικρὰν
> δουλείαν ἀπολοφυράμενος ἐξῆλθεν. εἶτα, τί λέγει;
> παιδισκάριόν με, φησίν, καταδεδούλωκ' εὐτελές,
> ὃν οὐδὲ εἷς τῶν πολεμίων οὐπώποτε.

... εἶτα ξίφος αἰτεῖ καὶ πρὸς τὸν ὑπ' εὐνοίας μὴ διδόντα χαλεπαίνειν καὶ δῶρα τῇ μισούσῃ πέμπει καὶ δεῖται καὶ κλαίει, πάλιν δὲ μικρὰ εὐημερήσας ἐπαίρεται.

See what Thrasonides says and does: He had been on military service ... first, he still went out at night. At this time Geta did not dare to venture out, but if he had been compelled by Thrasonides, he would have screamed out his bitterness and would have been lamenting his bitter slavery when he did go out. Next, what does Thrasonides say?

"A cheap little girl has made a complete and total slave of me.
No enemy ever did this to me!"

... Then he asks for a sword. With good intentions, the man doesn't provide it, and Thrasonides grows angry and sends presents to the very woman who hates him, and begs and cries, but when he has a little success, he's elated.

Arrian *Epictetus' Discourses* 4.1.19–22

Despite Epictetus (and Arrian) selectively summarizing Thrasonides' behavior in *Misoumenos*, this is valuable testimony, because the patchy nature of the fragmentary script makes it difficult, indeed mostly impossible, to trace the contours of the individual scenes with any precision, to say nothing of entire acts or the play as a whole. This passage gives some idea how the movement across the play struck an ancient audience. Moreover, the actions that Arrian/ Epictetus highlights are familiar from those of Polemon in *Perikeiromene*. Both protagonist soldiers are despondent because they are separated from the women they love. Both ask companions to bring implements or symbols of their military identity (a cloak for Polemon, a sword for Thrasonides), and in each case the companion recognizes the foolishness of the request. Moreover, the central tension in each character is the conflict between exercising their military identity and their desire for a stable domestic life with the wives they love. For Epictetus and Arrian, Thrasonides' problems result from his failure to control his emotional drives and his failure to recognize that, were he a Stoic, he could and should decide to be free in his choices, rather than dependent and enslaved to the will of others. Menander's dramatization, of course, does not correspond to this Stoic view (tending, if anything, toward second-generation Peripatetic philosophy), so it is no surprise that Arrian's account says nothing about Menander's resolution of Thrasonides' inner conflict. Epictetus wants to make the point that his own take on Stoicism is a ready antidote to Thrasonides' inner conflict, while, as we have seen, Menander has his own ideological goals and means of reaching them. Like Polemon in *Perikeiromene*, Thrasonides needs to commit to a communally approved domestic union with the woman he loves and abandon his military past, since it is incompatible with stable domestic life and the object of his desire.

The remains of *Misoumenos*' script confirm in outline the parallel dynamics between Polemon in *Perikeiromene* and Thrasonides in *Misoumenos*, along with many details. Whereas the beginning of *Perikeiromene* survives only vestigially in visual representations and via the implications of later parts of the script, a substantial portion of the opening sequence of *Misoumenos* has been recovered and reconstructed. The visual tableau of the start of the *Perikeiromene* featured a depressed soldier flanked on one side by the woman from whom he is estranged, whose good graces represent the communally approved domestic life for which he yearns, and on the other side by a companion who is frustrated with the soldier's emotional state, but more interested in restoring his confidence by shoring up his military identity and deprecating the soldier's other desires. *Misoumenos* introduces the soldier Thrasonides in the middle of a winter's night, literally just outside the house where the woman he loves is staying, apostrophizing the Night itself and the pathetic hopelessness of his current state (A1–5):

ὦ νύξ, σὺ γὰρ δὴ πλεῖστον Ἀφροδίτης μέρος
μετέχεις θεῶν, ἐν σοί τε περὶ τούτων λόγοι
πλεῖστοι λέγονται φροντίδες τ' ἐρωτικαί,
ἆρ' ἄλλον ἄνθρωπόν τιν' ἀθλιώτερον
ἑόρακας; ἆρ' ἐρῶντα δυσποτμώτερον;

You Night! You among the gods own the greatest share of Aphrodite. In you the most thoughtful and passionate speeches are spoken. Have you ever seen another man more miserable? A lover more unfortunate?

His slave Getas now joins him, and the dialogue between them starts delineating the relative identities of both characters. Thrasonides' frantic pacing prompts Getas to ironically label him a Peripatetic philosopher (περιπατεῖ φιλοσοφῶν ... περιπατῶν, 17–21), and he subsequently questions whether Thrasonides is really sleeping or awake.[33] Thrasonides responds by raising the issue of authority: why is Getas outside with him? Getas seems like a κηδεμών, a protector or guardian.

---

[33] Cf. *Adespota* fr. 1054, a strip of papyrus (PSI 847) that seems to preserve part of a dialogue featuring several questions about where a character has gone or will go (the answer repeatedly being οὐκ οἶδα "I don't know"), including the query πῶς οὖν περιπατεῖς at line 17. While attempts have been made to place this fragment among Menander's plays, no attribution has won favor. Cf. *Perikeiromene* 180 for the περιπατεῖν motif.

Now the conversation becomes more revealing about the tensions that drive the play. The pair, or at least Getas, had only recently returned from a military campaign, a successful one it seems, since Getas was responsible for transporting the material and financial rewards (33–36). Thrasonides responds by getting to the heart of his distress (ὑβρίζομαι, "I'm being abused" 37) and then analyzes the situation this way (37–40):

ὑπὸ τῆς αἰχμαλώτου· πριάμενος
αὐτήν, περιθεὶς ἐλευθερίαν, τῆς οἰκίας
δέσποιναν ἀποδείξας, θεραπαίνας χρυσία
ἱμάτια δούς, γυναῖκα νομίσας.

By that prisoner of war girl! I paid for her, promised her freedom, presented her as my housekeeper, with staff, finery, clothing, and recognized her as my wife.

Thrasonides, like Polemon in *Perikeiromene*, crucially reckons that he is already effectively married and settled with the woman he loves, so he cannot process the current antinomy between them. Next Thrasonides and Getas thrash out some details of the difficulties in his relationship with Krateia. The damage to the surviving script does not make it possible to understand all the details, but it is clear enough that Thrasonides does not yet know why Krateia hates him and Getas is misogynistically inclined to ascribe to Krateia cynical motives. Only tatters remain from the subsequent scenes, but it seems certain enough that the reason for Krateia's hostility is tied to Thrasonides' military past, for he is in possession of a sword belonging to Krateia's brother, so she believes that he is responsible for his death. Although the specifics of this belief will turn out to be untrue, two crucial dynamics are valid: (1) it is an association with Thrasonides' military past that thwarts his current domestic aspirations and (2) Thrasonides does not yet have a legal, community-sanctioned version of marriage that would validate his status as abused by a lawfully wedded wife.

Very little of the second and third acts of *Misoumenos'* script are recovered, with the few extant fragments ranging from incoherent bits to occasional bits of dialogue, but almost none permitting continuous coherent translation.[34] It is apparent, however, that gradually Krateia's background is emerging in these acts. Specifically, an old man named Demeas learns that Krateia is his daughter (206–221 = 607–623 Arnott). At this point, however, Krateia believes that Thrasonides has killed her lost brother, news of which grieves Demeas (229–258

---

[34] See Henry 2014:97–111 for valuable supplements to some of the lines here, but nothing that alters or enhances the analysis here.

= 630–659 Arnott). The key to this belief is a sword in Thrasonides' possession, which had belonged to Krateia's brother. Military implements, in this case a sword (σπάθη), but also cloaks (as for Polemon, and cf. on *Samia* below) or a shield (cf. on *Aspis* below) typically serve as physical and visual emblems of the problematic military identity of a troubled soldier in Menander (cf. Mueller 2016 and Chapter 2 above). Characters in Menander routinely extrapolate from the presence of a military prop something tragic about the past. In this case, Krateia assumes Thrasonides is her brother's killer when she sees the sword, a conclusion she draws because of his military identity (she would not draw the same conclusion upon finding the same sword in the possession of any other type of character).[35] By the middle of the third act of *Misoumenos* this tragic assumption is working against an already distraught Thrasonides. He emerges on stage to express his nervousness about the situation. He recognizes that Demeas can grant him the opportunity to consecrate his marriage to Krateia as he wishes, but he cannot conceive of his future otherwise, effectively a figure quite aware of the critical moment of his potential tragedy (259–269 = 660–670 Arnott).[36]

The fourth act of *Misoumenos* foregrounds Thrasonides for the first time since the opening sequences of the play. Menander builds up to this critical showcase, however. At the beginning of the act, Getas dramatizes events that have just taken place indoors, when Thrasonides made his appeal to Demeas and Krateia to make her his lawfully wedded wife. In contrast to Polemon in *Perikeiromene*, Thrasonides is ready, indeed eager, to pursue a legally sanctioned marriage. Like Polemon, however, he does not yet recognize that his military past is short-circuiting this opportunity. Getas presents Thrasonides' failure in terms quite abusive to Demeas and Krateia as being unfair and brutal to Thrasonides. While Getas probably does not know why Demeas and Krateia are so opposed to Thrasonides' appeal, it is also consistent of him (as it is for Polemon's companion Sosias) to be loyal to the soldier and bitter toward anyone who thwarts his desires. For all his ranting, Getas does convey the perspectives of the opposing parties in revealing ways. He summarizes Demeas' position as hoping to ransom (ἀπολυτροῦν) Krateia back from Thrasonides (298 = 699 Arnott), indicating that Demeas operates as if Thrasonides is a soldier holding Krateia captive. Thrasonides, by contrast, is seeking a wife from Demeas. Getas quotes Thrasonides pleading the case from his own perspective:

... "ἀντιβολῶ, Κράτεια, σέ,
μή μ' ἐγκαταλίπῃς· παρθένον σ' εἴληφ' ἐγώ,

---

[35] See Traill 2008:25–33, esp. n. 30, on the complex difficulties of Thrasonides' relationship with Krateia.

[36] For the following brief sequence with a cook , see Chapter 2.

ἀνὴρ ἐκλήθην πρῶτος, ἠγάπησά σε,
ἀγαπῶ, φιλῶ, Κράτεια φιλτάτη· τί σοι
λυπηρόν ἐστι τῶν παρ' ἐμοί; τεθνηκότα
πεύσει μ' ἐάν μ' ἐγκαταλίπῃς."

"I'm begging you, Krateia, don't abandon me. I took you when you were still a virgin and first was recognized as your husband. I loved you. I do love you. I cherish you, my dearest Krateia. What is so painful about being with me? You'll find out I'm dead, if you abandon me."

305–310 = 706–711 Arnott

As earlier in the play, and as testified by the reference in Arrian, Thrasonides is desperate to the point of suicide (cf the similar threat at 37–40). Also according to Arrian, Thrasonides seeks death by a sword, the same type of military tool which is blocking him from his desired goal of Krateia as his wife. In multiple ways, then, Thrasonides does not recognize how his military identity is the obstacle to his erotic desire. The same failure plagues Polemon in *Perikeiromene*, who is also despondent to the point of contemplating suicide, but futilely attempts a military siege to achieve his ends, which is no more successful than Thrasonides' ploy to manipulate Krateia's emotions (cf. an analogous ploy at lines 53–56). A short while later, Getas delineates the issue as he himself sees it, though it is unclear from the script as it is whether he is repeating what he said earlier or is only now venting this to the spectators (316–322 = 717–723 Arnott):

ἀλλ' ἐλεεῖν ὀρθῶς ἔχει
τὸν ἀντελεοῦνθ' ...
. . . .
... βοήσεται δὲ καὶ βουλεύσεται
κτανεῖν ἑαυτὸν στάς· βλέπει δὲ πῦρ ἅμα
... δράττεταί τε τῶν τριχῶν.

It's right to show pity when it's reciprocated ... He [Thrasonides] will cry and contemplate killing himself! As sure as he's standing there fired up ... and there crying into his hair!

After this outburst, Getas finally engages with the neighbor Kleinias, who has been present on stage but ignored by Getas up to this point. Very little of their conversation can be recovered from the text, but in some way the action moves toward its culmination with Thrasonides delivering an extended (fifty lines or so) monologue to the spectators. Only about half of Thrasonides' speech (a few lines near the beginning and about twenty lines toward the end) can be restored to anything meaningful, and coherence is further challenged by the complexity of the speech, as Thrasonides, like Getas earlier, seems to be repeating or freshly dramatizing multiple parts of a conversation.[37] Despite the limitations in understanding Thrasonides' performance, it is evident enough that he is still struggling to balance his desire for reconciliation with Krateia against his own sense of fairness, expressed variously in terms of his tragically bad luck, dignity, and, of course, his military identity. He recognizes that getting drunk would expose his pain (364–365 = 765–766 Arnott). He rejects that he is acting selfishly and does not understand why it is unfair to prevent Demeas from taking Krateia away (388–394 = 791–796 Arnott).[38] Obliquely, Thrasonides starts to analyze his own behavior, which at least in part stems from his military prerogatives. Ποῦ τὸ τῆς σωτηρίας ἐπίσημον; ("Where is that badge of salvation?" 396–397 = 798–799 Arnott) he asks of himself, perhaps a reference to the emblem on his military cloak of his accomplishments, much as Polemon wears in the Daphne mosaic. He contemplates resisting angry urges and acknowledges of himself "Maybe you are impetuous" (ἴσως ἰταμὸς εἶ, 399 = 800 Arnott), before pivoting again and falling back on manipulating Krateia emotionally, arguing that she was treated well and wounded Thrasonides, who gave her only good things in life (εὖ παθοῦσα ἐτιμωρήσατο / τὸν τἀγάθ' αὐτῇ δόντα, 402 = 805–806 Arnott). The very end of Thrasonides' tirade is too incomplete to comprehend in detail, but it does end the fourth act.

Unfortunately, the remains of the fifth and final act are difficult to interpret in detail, but broad parallels with *Perikeiromene* are evident. By the point that the script becomes intelligible, Getas is relaying the happy news to Thrasonides that he will be allowed to marry Krateia.[39] The details that led to this reversal are obscure, but there are indications that Thrasonides' desire for suicide played a role.[40]

Still ambiguous but more informative is a mosaic from the House of Menander at Mytilene featuring a scene labeled as from act 5 of *Misoumenos* (Figure 5).[41] None of the three characters are labeled and there are no unambiguous clues to their identity based on the remains of the script of this act. The character on the left is holding up a scarf around his neck, making the most likely interpretation that this is Getas referring to Thrasonides' potential

---

[37] See Henry 2014:111–114 for some minor supplements to this section of the script.
[38] If Handley's supplement to line 796 is correct, it is an especially appropriate line: τὰ πρόσθε γενόμεν' ἀνατρέπει "What happened in the past is tripping me up."
[39] Cf. Traill 2008:139–143 on Krateia's agency in this sequence.
[40] A possible reference to a drug in line 819 (Arnott) could be a factor.
[41] A cake mold from Ostia might represent the same scene, but even if so, it adds nothing to understanding it. For discussion, see Charitonidis et al. 1970:60 and, for an image, plate 26.3.

Figure 5: Mosaic of act 5 of *Misoumenos* from Mytilene
(drawing based on Charitonidis et al. 1970 plate 8.1).

suicide while the other two characters are reacting in horror. Again, no details are available, but near the end of the play, Getas reports to Thrasonides that his proposal is now accepted. Little remains of the script at this point beyond indications that everyone prepares for the wedding. Like Polemon in *Perikeiromene*, Thrasonides had believed that the object of his desire had abandoned him, but upon hearing that she is in fact preparing to reunite with him, he is thrilled. Part of the reconciliation must have included learning that Thrasonides had not in fact killed Krateia's brother, and thus in some fashion the specter of his past military identity was put behind him. It is a reasonable expectation, given Thrasonides' recognition of his own impetuousness, that he came to repudiate his military imperatives in some form along the way.

Sikyonios: A Stranger from a Sikyonian Land

Yet another play that was much celebrated in antiquity and fascinates (and perplexes) scholars today also features a soldier as the protagonist: Stratophanes of the *Sikyonios*.[42] Polemon of *Perikeiromene* again serves as a valuable reference point for this soldier protagonist. In contrast to *Misoumenos*, *Sikyonios* testifies more to the hostility a soldier faces from the community when attempting to settle into civilian domestic life. The maid Doris in *Perikeiromene* expresses prejudice against soldiers as unreliable and lawless. In the remains of *Misoumenos*, a prejudice against soldiers is at least implied and could have been explicit in lost parts of the script. In *Sikyonios*, the tension is explicit, testified in an isolated fragment: εὐλοιδόρητον, ὡς ἔοικε, φαίνεται / τὸ τοῦ στρατιώτου σχῆμα καὶ τὸ τοῦ ξένου, "Apparently it's easy to argue about the appearance of a soldier and mercenary" (fr. 2 = fr. 5 Arnott). While the parts of the script of *Sikyonios* that have been recovered do not make it possible to know who makes this comment or at what point in the play, there can be little doubt that it refers to Stratophanes. That this facet of a soldier's experience is more prominent than in either *Perikeiromene* or *Misoumenos* may be an accidental byproduct of what portions of each script are readable, but Stratophanes also faces more challenging hurdles to acceptance. Parallels and contrasts with *Perikeiromene* are instructive. Whereas in *Perikeiromene* the soldier Polemon becomes a rival to a man who will turn out to be the long-lost brother of the woman he loves, in *Sikyonios* the soldier Stratophanes becomes a rival to a man who will turn out to be his own long-lost brother. Actually, it is more accurate to say that Philoumene in *Sikyonios* will be revealed as a long-lost sister and Stratophanes himself will be revealed as a long-lost brother. The meaning of the fragment above could thus have carried multiple meanings, perhaps intentionally or ironically, for ξένος generally refers to an outsider, but it can also designate Stratophanes' identity as a mercenary. It is also the term used of Polemon in *Perikeiromene*, for example, thus doubly marking him as unsuitable for settled domestic life with the woman he loves, unsuitable both as an obvious soldier and as a non-citizen and thus ineligible for communally approved marriage. A crucial part of *Sikyonios* involves conflict between keeping Stratophanes at bay as a non-citizen while he is simultaneously demonstrating that he is in fact an Athenian citizen.

The controversy over and resolution of Stratophanes' identity involve, but are far from limited to, the documentation and physical tokens on which recognition of citizen identity so often hinges in Greek drama. As fragment 2 testifies, Stratophanes' appearance as a soldier played a role in this tension, and a mosaic from Kissamos on the western end of Crete shows what is almost certainly the "recognition" scene of Stratophanes, the evidence of his birth as an Athenian citizen revealed, to the evident shock of two other characters, a woman and an

---

[42] While it seems that the play was known in antiquity by both the title *Sikyonios* and *Sikyoinioi*, I follow Slater 2020 in following the singular title.

111

old man (Figure 6). Stratophanes wears the distinctive red cloak that traditionally identifies a soldier (there are multiple candidates for the identities of the
other characters).

Part of a wall painting found in Ephesus also shows a scene from the play,
but it is unclear whether it is a variation of the scene found on Crete or a
different scene.[43] It depicts two characters, one a slave and the other free, the
latter potentially Stratophanes. Since this character is not at this point wearing
the red cloak or evidently displaying any distinctive mark of being a soldier,
he may well be another character, such as Stratophanes' long-lost brother
Moschion. Nervegna would make this character the model of a Hellenistic figu-
rine from Myrina (Nervegna 2013:157, figure 17c). In favor of it being a soldier,
and thus Stratophanes, she compares the pose with that of the partial image of
a soldier from a mosaic recovered in Chania (rejected above as being Polemon
of *Perikeiromene*). For purposes of this study, without more certain identification of the scenes, only the Kissamos mosaic is especially revealing, and that
because it emphasizes the distinctive red cloak as a marker of the soldier. This

Figure 6: Mosaic of *Sikyonios* from Kissamos
(drawing based on Dunbabin 2016:67 figure 3.12).

---

[43] The best published plate of this badly faded wall painting is Dunbabin 2016:63, figure 3.5.

cloak is mentioned in an unplaced fragment from the play (fr. 3 = fr. 6 Arnott), apparently to indicate that Stratophanes previously had relatively meager property.[44] In another sense, though, the visual representation of Stratophanes has inspired thoughtful analysis of his character and the multiple components of his identity debated in the play.

Several interlocking facets of Stratophanes' identity are at play in *Sikyonios*, among them his financial status, his dress as a soldier, his mask (signal components of which are his skin and hair), his emotional expression, his political allegiance, and his association with stage tragedy.[45] Most of these are paralleled explicitly in other plays with soldiers as protagonists. The cloak is perhaps the most distinctive visual marker of a soldier, whether in surviving visual representations or from references in scripts. Stratophanes goes from being relatively poor and facing responsibility for debts to being wealthy to some degree, a dynamic at play with all of Menander's protagonist soldiers, since they have been on campaigns specifically as mercenaries. As scholars have increasingly documented, and as was noted in Chapter 2, much of Menander's theatrical world is suffused with elements from tragic theater. In *Perikeiromene* and *Misoumenos*, the soldiers flirted with suicide reminiscent of stage figures like Ajax.[46] In *Sikyonios* it is actually critical to understand the standard association of a soldier and a tragic figure. Stratophanes' dispute and rivalry with Moschion (who turns out to be his brother) plays out in part at the assembly in Eleusis. Much to Moschion's frustration, Stratophanes succeeds in persuading the assembly to accept him provisionally as a citizen while keeping Philoumene, whom both Stratophanes and Moschion desire, available for betrothal. Moschion protests the decision in part by asking of the assembled citizens, τραγῳδίᾳ / κενῇ τ' ἀγόμενος τὴν κόρην ἀφήσεται, "By means of this vapid tragedy he's going to take the girl and release her?" (262–263). Of course, a soldier veering toward tragedy is to be expected. Stratophanes earlier at the assembly had wordlessly broken down in tears and only subsequently made his appeal to be given a chance to find Philoumene's father. This emotional desperation and plea follow narrative expectations of a protagonist soldier, as does the ensuing scene where he does get to meet Philoumene's long-lost father and secures the right of marriage from him.

Other aspects of Stratophanes' identity generate attention in *Sikyonios* that do not surface as much, if at all, in other plays. As always with such fragmentary scripts and evidence, it is hazardous to speculate whether these components were in fact exceptional in *Sikyonios* or whether other plays, were they available

[44] See Chapter 4 for discussion of the wealth of the soldiers in Menander's *Kolax* and in Roman comedy.
[45] Traill 2008:16–25 sorts through the complexities of Stratophanes' relationship with Philoumene.
[46] Cf. Chapter 2 and analysis of *Aspis* below.

now in more complete forms, would feature analogous instances. Nevertheless it worth turning to these facets and determining how much might be fairly extrapolated from this particular play.

Political debate in *Sikyonios* takes more stage time and is articulated in harsher terms than anywhere else in Menander's limited recovered corpus. Given that ancient testimony explicitly says that political rancor and public vitriol were atypical of Menander, it is not unreasonable to suppose that *Sikyonios* is about as politically explicit and harsh as can be found in Menander's work.[47] This is not to say that it is revealing, however, just uncharacteristic and comparatively explicit. The longest somewhat continuous part of the script to survive contains two sequences with political overtones. The first is a bit of conversation between two men, one an "oligarch" and the other a democratic "mob" (150–168). The "oligarch" is all but certainly Smikrines, who later in the play will turn out to be Stratophanes' father. It is unclear who is his democratic opposition. For the dialogue to be logical, it must be a free citizen male, but beyond this there are no clues. It is unlikely to be Moschion, since by this point in the play he will have come out on the losing end at the assembly and not be inclined to side with democratic procedure. It could be Kichesias, who will be revealed as the father of Philoumene later in the play, and puts the respective fathers of Stratophanes and his beloved on opposing sides of the political spectrum, but this is speculative. It could even be Stratophanes himself, who would then end up in political opposition to his own father, but this is likewise speculative. Other, lesser-known characters, such as Theron the parasite, are also candidates. These uncertainties and the gaps in the conversation do not allow for a grounded analysis of Menander's political goals. Moreover, Menander is known for his ability to tailor speech to his characters, and there could well have been earlier or later sequences that developed the character and politics of one or both men, which are lost now.

Lape has analyzed *Sikyonios* with the idea that it supports staunch democratic ideology in the face of Macedonian domination. She presents a matrix of gender, physiognomy, and political vocabulary underpinning the language of the extant scenes. She points out, for example, that the democratic assembly rules rightly in favor of Stratophanes and against the effeminate and untrustworthy Moschion. Moschion is even labeled a λαύσταρος (line 266), a term of abuse leveled elsewhere at the members of the court of Philip II for their deviant behavior, implying that Moschion is simultaneously himself a deviant and a Macedonian sympathizer. Thus for Lape, Stratophanes the democrat defeats Moschion the oligarch for the hand of the virgin Philoumene in an allegory of

---

[47] Cf. the discussion of Menander's politics in Chapter 1.

the rebirth of Athenian democracy. "The drama of the democratic mercenary's return in the *Sikyonios* seems to recall the story of the men from Phyle [who led the democratic revolt against the Thirty in 403], men whom later writers credited with redemocratizing and remasculinizing the city..." (239, cf. 226-8). The opening chapter of this study updates my position, that Menander's plays are most consistent with that of a playwright who prefers a stable world predicated on Macedonian rule. While Lape repeatedly casts Moschion in the *Sikyonios* as an oligarch, it is Smikrines who is identified as such and the term λαύσταρος is attested only once in the context of Macedonians (Theopompus FGrH 115 F 224.23-39), making this sole instance an inadequate guide for whether Menander and his audience would make the association. I make no particular claims for the oligarchic or Macedonian sympathizer here, preferring to conclude only that the extant portions of *Sikyonios* are too incomplete to make legitimate claims about how Menander slanted the political tensions of his day in this play.[48]

Analysis of *Sikyonios* by Lape and others has been more fruitful elsewhere when discerning the dynamics of gender, character, and physical bodies. Lape is right to emphasize the contrast between the effeminate Moschion and masculine Stratophanes in the reported assembly scene, a contrast that plays out consequentially in this political arena in that the democrats shout down Moschion in favor of hearing out Stratophanes. She is right to spotlight that the goal of Stratophanes' desire for marriage is accomplished with a lack of agency on Philoumene's part.[49] What these contrasts in gender and body type can mean for Stratophanes has been taken up in detail by Petrides (2014a:203–207). The report of the assembly is for Petrides a particularly clear example of how Menander and spectators "read" the character of individuals via their appearance, in particular the accretion of features on their masks. Stratophanes has physical features, being young enough not to have a beard (standard in his mask and confirmed by the Kissamos mosaic, Figure 6), so the narrative instead declares that the assembly found Stratophanes masculine-looking by contrast to Moschion, whom they judge as "queer" (Petrides's translation of *lastauros*) and looking like an adulterer, that is, someone incompatible with a settled communally approved marriage, a goal that Stratophanes seeks. In terms of a soldier, since his appearance can be a source of opposition and his military identity incompatible with a communally approved goal, this is consistent with Petrides' analysis. Menander has to compensate for features of Stratophanes that would make him in effect antisocial, and so he makes him a natural-born citizen, respectful of the community's central political decision-making body

---

[48]   Cf. Cusset 2015 for a different take on the politics of the play.
[49]   Traill 2008:17–25.

(with a touch of religious reverence, given that the setting is Eleusis), and in opposition to a truly antisocial character like Moschion.[50] Unfortunately too little remains of the scenes before and after to bring out how Menander handled these other details.

The Impact of the Soldier's Absence and Aspiration

The soldiers in *Perikeiromene*, *Misoumenos*, and *Sikyonios* stand out as the protagonists of their respective plays. Whereas scholarship to date has assumed that such soldier characters are expected to be stock braggarts of the *miles gloriosus* type, the study here argues that the unspoken assumptions and expected narrative patterns are quite different. Menander's soldiers have more in common with literary and cultural forebears such as Odysseus and Ajax than literary progeny like Plautus' Pyrgopolynices or Shakespeare's Falstaff. Like Ajax in tragedy, Menander's soldiers have complex and non-traditional families, and their military experiences work at cross-purposes to settling down happily with the women they love. In their failures, Menander's soldiers contemplate the suicide that Ajax commits with devastating consequences. But Menander steers his protagonists toward reconciling with their military pasts and settling down to legally sanctioned marriages and families in their local communities. Like Odysseus, then, Menander's protagonists have the goal of having a stable home and family after completing their military service.

This goal and narrative expectation in turn propel action, create tension, and add a layer of comprehensibility to scenes and sequences in other plays that are either even more fragmentary or where soldiers and their identity are oblique in some way. The remaining sections consider instances where bringing a proper narrative expectation enhances our understanding of the dramatic action: the opening tableau of *Aspis* and the final act of *Samia*.

Aspis: The Shield and the Homefront

As with *Perikeiromene* and *Misoumenos*, Menander begins the *Aspis* with a striking tableau, and the surviving script happens to be most complete for this early sequence of the play. An entire entourage, led by an elderly man but also consisting of various staff and a prosperous train of goods, takes the stage and sets up the key emblem of this play's soldier, a collapsed shield. The prominence of the damaged shield in this scene signals that a military identity will be key

---

[50] Cf. fr. 5 = fr. 8 Arnott, κακὴ μὲν ὄψις, ἐν δὲ δείλαιαι φρένες, but unfortunately we cannot determine whose evil face belies a cowardly breast; also cf. Slater 2020 on Menander's associating the Athenian *ephebia* with Stratophanes.

to the play's central conflict. Amid the goods and mourners also comes another older man who does not belong to the entourage, while the first elderly man addresses the shield as if it were its proper bearer. He expresses dismay at an unexpected turn of events (1–3). When he first reveals his expectations, he begins with hopes of a military career (4–7):

ᾤμην γὰρ εὐδοξοῦντα καὶ σωθέντα σε
ἀπὸ στρατείας ἐν βίῳ τ' εὐσχήμονι
ἤδη τὸ λοιπὸν καταβιώσεσθαί τινι,
στρατηγὸν ἢ σύμβουλον ὠνομασμένον

I was thinking that you'd be successful and safe after the campaign, and enjoying a respectable life in the future, in the capacity of a general or military advisor.

As in *Perikeiromene* and *Misoumenos*, the soldier's colleague is supportive of the soldier's success and continued prosperity. He in fact looked forward to the soldier enjoying a senior and respected military title after serving time on the battlefield.[51] Given that the previous two plays have this subordinate character supportive of the soldier's military prerogative against the intrusion of the soldier's desire for domesticity, it is a reasonable expectation that the military hopes expressed here will be followed by an account of a domestic crisis. And indeed, the very next lines reveal one (8–10):

καὶ τὴν ἀδελφήν, ἧσπερ ἐξώρμας τότε
ἕνεκα, σεαυτοῦ νυμφίῳ καταξίῳ
συνοικιεῖν ποθεινὸν ἥκοντ' οἴκαδε,

And your sister, for whose benefit you went on the venture, settled at home with a fine husband, when you made your much-desired return home.

A settled domestic situation then does turn out to be the goal of the soldier when he returns home, not directly for himself but for his sister. This is a variation on the soldier's narrative pattern from *Perikeiromene* and *Misoumenos*, in that a soldier's military past will be an obstacle to a settled domestic household approved by the local community. The soldier, Kleostratos, like other such characters in Menander, is in key respects a successful and respected military man. He secures enough booty for his sister's dowry (six hundred gold staters,

---

[51] Cf. the discussion in Chapter 1 of fr. 191 on military titles from *Imbrians* on leaders using reasoning.

an amount mentioned at least twice, lines 35 and 82–83) plus additional riches and slaves. He seems respected and successful enough that his military prestige will carry over into his life after campaigning. Nonetheless, his campaigning leaves a legacy that interferes with settled domestic life. The booty from his military successes and his death leave his sister an heiress, soon to be desired by an unscrupulous uncle, Smikrines. The need for other members in the household to thwart Smikrines' hope of marrying the sister to take control of her inheritance drives much of the remaining plot of the play.[52]

As in *Perikeiromene* (and probably in *Misoumenos*), Menander follows a disturbing opening tableau with a divine prologue that provides some critical information for the audience but also acknowledges the harshness of the opening scenario (97–99):

ἀλλ' εἰ μὲν ἦν τούτοις τι γεγονὸς δυσχερές,
θεὸν οὖσαν οὐκ ἦν εἰκὸς ἀκολουθεῖν ἐμέ·
νῦν δ' ἀγνοοῦσι καὶ πλανῶνται· ...

Now, if something truly harsh had happened to them, it would not be appropriate for a divinity like me to follow up, but as things are, they are just ignorant and wandering.

The sentiment is similar to that in the divine prologue of *Perikeiromene*, where the speaker seeks to downplay the harshness and potential for a perceived impropriety in what has just been staged. As in the divine speech in *Perikeiromene*, the divinity delays identifying herself until she reveals not only her title but also that her identity is dynamically critical to the events that will unfold in the play. She concludes her monologue (146–148):

... λοιπὸν τοὔνομα
τοὐμὸν φράσαι· τίς εἰμι, πάντων κυρία
τούτων βραβεῦσαι καὶ διοικῆσαι; Τύχη.

It remains to say my name. Who am I? The authority for directing and guiding all this: Luck.

Indeed, Daos himself bitterly invokes Luck later in the play, when he laments passing from his master Kleostratos to the evil uncle Smikrines (line 206). Unfortunately, very little of the second half of *Aspis* survives in the script, so we cannot analyze how Menander reconciled the military past and future of Kleostratos with the domestic turmoil he finds in his wake.

---

[52] See Traill 2008:56–65 for analysis.

There is a possible ancient visual depiction of a scene from later in the play, from Nikopolis in the late third or early fourth century CE (Figure 7).[53] The central of three figures holds a round shield, and the rarity of this object both in depictions of comic scenes and in the remains of comic scripts make it probable that the scene, although unlabeled, is meant to represent Menander's *Aspis*. The man with the shield is older, and so unlikely to be the young soldier Kleostratos. The old man holds the hand of the slave, who stands to his left. In the surviving parts of the script, Daos is the only attested slave character, so he is a strong candidate. Behind the old man stands a young woman. There are two young women involved the play's plot, one the sister of Kleostratos, for whose benefit he went on military campaign and who eventually marries another young man, Chaireas. Chaireas also has a sister, who will marry Kleostratos. The woman in the mosaic could be either, but since Kleostratos' sister is a linchpin

Figure 7: Mosaic from Nikopolis, probably the *Aspis*
(based on detail from Kyrkou 2007 figure 10).

[53] Kyrkou 2007 provides discussion of the full site but links the image to satyr play (I 336–337, II fig 10 for photos); cf. Dunbabin 2016:64 and n. 72. The vestigial remains of a wall drawing on Delos and a pastiche figure currently in Milan, possibly Apulian, might be extracts from this same tableau. See MINC3 1.87 XZ4.

for the plot as we know it, she is the more likely candidate. As for the old man, since Kleostratos' father seems to be dead or otherwise not a participant in the play, the old man here should be one of Kleostratos' uncles, either the conniving Smikrines or the helpful Chairestratos. The tableau in the mosaic does not correspond to any scene that survives in the script, but since Chairestratos and Daos cooperate to thwart Smikrines and protect Kleostratos' sister, the most plausible understanding of the scene on the available evidence is that it shows, from the viewer's left to right: (1) Kleostratos' sister, (2) Chairestratos with Kleostratos' shield standing in for the soldier in his absence, who is, at this point, presumed dead, and (3) Kleostratos' slave and supporter Daos. Chairestratos and Daos are signaling their support for their plan to help Kleostratos' sister. If this is correct, the image nicely and poignantly represents the central tension of the play, showing how the loss or absence of a young man who became a soldier, represented here only by his shield, leads to consequences for a range of people in his household: his sister, his slave, and his uncle, all three distinct in terms of gender, seniority, and social status, and yet all three at risk for losses until Kleostratos returns. Put another way, the image encapsulates the ideological tensions about Menander's soldiers: that the consequences of their actions are inconsistent with, even wreak havoc on, settled domestic life.

Consequences in the *Aspis* are the focus of James's analysis of the play. Focusing on the harsh impact of a soldier's loss, she has recently analyzed *Aspis* as a whole and concludes, "Menander depicts the very specific social realities of combat-related ... PTSD, survivor guilt, and family trauma ... *Aspis* constantly recurs to loss, grief, and an ever-widening circle of survivors whose lives will be irremediably damaged by the soldier's death. The happy turn, in which the warrior returns unharmed, offered a comforting wish-fulfillment for many viewers, a fantasy of family rescue and reintegration" (James 2014:237). James perhaps paints Menander's play in darker shades than would seem familiar to Menander and ancient spectators, but the contrast she spotlights between the grim domestic situation created by the loss of Kleostratos and the happy resolution at the play's finale is valid enough. The scenario is more than just a variation on the narrative pattern at the core of other plays with soldiers. The opening sequences of the play show Menander carefully calibrating his scenario in response to ideological pressures and toward his own ideological goals. Menander wants his soldier to be successful, but the career goal of being a general or military advisor runs afoul of both his ideological goal of a stable domestic community and of those in the audience whose political and military interests might not line up with a soldier like Kleostratos having military glory. The mission to provide for his sister is then a shrewd one on Menander's part. It fulfills the narrative task of positioning Kleostratos' military past in opposition to the resolution of domestic conflict and does so in a way that makes his motive ideologically acceptable for Menander's own goals and those with quite different agendas. Chapter 2 includes analysis of Isaeus 2, where a defendant, a former mercenary, is enmeshed in a complicated inheritance case involving his sister. The specific family tree is different, but the fundamental tension for the speaker in court is the same as in *Aspis*. Kleostratos has left Athens on military service for financial gain. That he does so in service of a respectable marriage for his sister provides ideological cover for his mercenary service. Nonetheless, both Isaeus' court speaker and Menander are necessarily oblique about the mercenary aspect of the campaign abroad for financial gain. Isaeus' speaker keeps references to his mercenary activity to a minimum and as much as possible in line with jurors' democratic leanings. Menander subordinates the military goal to the consequences on the domestic front. In terms of the broader empire building in Menander's lifetime, the site of Kleostratos' campaign, by the Xanthus river in Lycia, was at best a minor front, which serves Menander's purpose well, for the campaign itself does not have major political and military baggage as a site of conflict. Scholars have analyzed the specifics of the unusually graphic account of the military situation in which Kleostratos is lost. Lamagna and other scholars struggle to make precise sense of how to evaluate the military failure of the campaign,[54] but I suggest such evaluation would just be distracting for Menander. The description in fact meets all his dramatic needs: (1) it provides a scenario where Kleostratos is lost but can and will return later in the play; (2) it does not directly impugn Kleostratos' ability as a soldier; and (3) Menander can still convey that mercenary service, even when successful in terms of financial reward, is inconsistent with the desirable goal of stable households.

There is again tragic coloring, provided by the first elderly speaker, who reveals himself to be Daos, Kleostratos' pedagogue (11–18).[55] Daos will even explicitly call for staging a tragedy to resolve the play's central domestic conflict (δεῖ τραγῳδῆσαι πάθος / ἀλλοῖον ὑμᾶς, 329–330). From grief to ideological tension to tragedy, these are the foci by which to understand how the expected narrative of a soldier character in Menander shapes and colors a drama even by its absence or distortion. The expectation of a stock *miles gloriosus* plays no role here.

---

[54] Lamagna 2014:61–71.
[55] See Groton 2020:243–244 for a brief analysis of Daos' distinct speech patterns and characterization in this play.

Samia: When Not to Be a Soldier

The last act of Menander's *Samia* again shows how Menander dramatizes and then redresses the communal ideological tensions of the soldier character, this time by reversing the standard narrative pattern. Where protagonist soldiers have been conflicted young men in love who settle down to marry, in *Samia* a young man in love who is about to marry threatens to use a soldier narrative to disrupt others' judgments about his own character.

The protagonist is the young man Moschion, another sexually mischievous young man who has gotten the girl next door pregnant. New Comedy being what it is, there has been a series of misunderstandings (which include his being mistaken for an adulterer, not unexpected, given the youth's name), but by the last act of the play, Moschion is cleared to marry the girl. By the final act of the play, the young man has a very strong, stable domestic obligation to two families. Indeed, at the beginning of the scene, Moschion emphasizes that his love for the girl controls him and he therefore cannot abandon this responsibility (630–632):

νῦν δ' οὐ ποήσω διὰ σέ, Πλαγγὼν φιλτάτη,
ἀνδρεῖον οὐθέν· οὐ γὰρ ἔξεστ', οὐδ' ἐᾷ
ὁ τῆς ἐμῆς νῦν κύριος γνώμης, Ἔρως.

As it is, for your sake, dearest Plangon, I won't do anything really manly.
It's just impossible. The master of my mind, Love, forbids it.

Because of the various misunderstandings during the course of the first four acts of the play, however, Moschion feels that he needs to teach his adoptive father a lesson to prevent being mistreated in the future. To do so, he plans to scare (φοβῆσαι, 635) his adoptive father, Demeas, by threatening to become a mercenary soldier. In performance, he might employ a mask consistent with what Pollux describes for soldiers, but the script as we have it provides no help on this point. The script is explicit, however, about two props that he uses. The script is also fairly direct about what threat each prop represents.

To dramatize his threat, Moschion orders his slave Parmenon to bring him the necessary props: a military cloak and sword (χλαμύδα καὶ σπάθην τινὰ / ἔνεγκέ μοι, 659–60). Moschion assures the audience at this point that this is just a performance to teach his foster father a lesson (664–668):

... πρόσεισι νῦν ὁ πατήρ· δεήσεται
οὗτος καταμένειν, δηλαδή. δεήσεται
ἄλλως μέχρι τινός· δεῖ γάρ. εἶθ', ὅταν δοκῇ,

πεισθήσομ’ αὐτῷ. πιθανὸν εἶναι δεῖ μόνον
ὅ, μὰ τὸν Διόνυσον, οὐ δύναμαι ποεῖν ἐγώ.

This is when my father will show up. He'll ask me to stay, of course.
He'll ask in some other way for a while, because he'll have no choice.
Then, when I'm ready, I'll let him convince me. It's got to be convincing,
though, by Dionysus, since I can't really go through with it.

In the meantime, however, Parmenon ignores the order and the notion of
Moschion as a soldier and instead harps on the point that the young man is
supposed to be preparing for his wedding.[56] In fact, Moschion has to slap the
poor slave hard enough to split his lip open to get him to go get the requested
props (670–681):[57]

ΠΑΡΜΕΝΩΝ

ὑστερίζειν μοι δοκεῖς σὺ παντελῶς τῶν ἐνθάδε
πραγμάτων, εἰδώς τ’ ἀκριβῶς οὐθὲν οὐδ’ ἀκηκοὼς
διὰ κενῆς σαυτὸν ταράττεις εἰς ἀθυμίαν τ’ ἄγεις.

ΜΟΣΧΙΩΝ

οὐ φέρεις;

ΠΑΡΜΕΝΩΝ

ποοῦσι γάρ σοι τοὺς γάμους· κεράννυται,
θυμιᾶτ’, ἐνῆρκτ’, ἀνῆπται θύμαθ’ Ἡφαίστου φλογί.

ΜΟΣΧΙΩΝ

οὗτος, οὐ φέρεις;

ΠΑΡΜΕΝΩΝ

σὲ γάρ, σὲ περιμένουσ’ οὗτοι πάλαι.
μετιέναι τὴν παῖδα μέλλεις; εὐτυχεῖς· οὐδὲν κακὸν
ἐστί σοι. θάρρει· τί βούλει;

---

[56] Cf. *Adespota* 1007 in Chapter 4 and *Georgos* fr. 4, where someone urges a young man not to sit by
while wedding preparations are going on, but other than a reference to battles (μάχαις) in fr. 7,
there is no hint of a soldier character or military references in the extant portions of the script
of this play.

[57] See Cox 2013 and Konstan 2013 on the violence here.

ΜΟΣΧΙΩΝ

νουθετήσεις μ᾿, εἰπέ μοι,
ἱερόσυλε;

ΠΑΡΜΕΝΩΝ

παῖ, τί ποιεῖς, Μοσχίων;

ΜΟΣΧΙΩΝ

οὐκ εἰσδραμὼν
θᾶττον ἐξοίσεις ἅ φημι;

ΠΑΡΜΕΝΩΝ

διακέκομμαι τὸ στόμα.

ΜΟΣΧΙΩΝ

ἔτι λαλεῖς οὗτος;

ΠΑΡΜΕΝΩΝ

βαδίζω. νὴ Δί᾿, ἐξεύρηκά γε
τόδε κακόν.

ΜΟΣΧΙΩΝ

μέλλεις;

ΠΑΡΜΕΝΩΝ

ἄγουσι τοὺς γάμους ὄντως.

PARMENON

I think you're behind on everything that's going on in there. You understand exactly nothing. You've heard nothing. There's no reason to beat yourself up or lose heart.

MOSCHION

Do you have them?

PARMENON

They're putting on your wedding! The wine is being mixed, incense is smoking, Hephaistos' fire is cooking the meat ...

MOSCHION

Hey you, do you have them?

PARMENON

It's YOU they've been waiting on forever! What are you waiting for? Get the girl! This is your lucky day! Nothing to worry about! Cheer up! (*Pausing while Moschion scowls.*) What do you want?

MOSCHION

You're going to preach to me, are you??

[*He slaps Parmenon.*]

PARMENON

Boy, what are you doing, Moschion?

MOSCHION

Get in there quick and get what I asked for!

PARMENON

My lip is split!

MOSCHION

Why are you still talking?

PARMENON

I'm going, but Zeus, I've found some pain.

MOSCHION

Are you still here?

PARMENON

They really are putting on your wedding!

When Parmenon does return with the props, Moschion makes use of the cloak first. The role of the cloak is to indicate that Moschion will, by becoming a mercenary, not go through with his wedding. There is never any discussion of where Moschion might go, his potential life as a soldier, etc. The cloak simply means that Moschion's military career vacates his role as a husband.

So, first his adoptive father Demeas comes out. He recognizes the symbolism of the cloak. He does not address military life but reminds Moschion of his duties as a good son (695–712). In this he is nearly successful, since Moschion's whole performance is about restoring respect to their relationship, but then Nikeratos, the girl's father and thus Moschion's future father-in-law, storms in and puts Moschion back on the defensive. Nikeratos, too, recognizes the symbolism of the cloak (χλαμύς. ἀπαίρειν οὑτοσί που διανοεῖται, "A cloak! This guy has it in mind to take off," 717), but his response is to bind Moschion to the community as a confessed criminal, i.e. as an admitted adulterer.[58]

In response to this, with the threat of the cloak having failed, Moschion deploys the other prop, the sword. The idea here is that the sword is a threat not to obey the laws of the community by force of violence. Since this is comedy, however, no military weapon can withstand the anger of a grumpy old man. Nikeratos simply orders Moschion to hurry up and put down the sword (οὐ καταβαλεῖς τὴν σπάθην θᾶττον; 719–720) and Moschion gives up (ἀφείσθω, 721) and has to resort to trying to save face by asserting that he has been persuaded not to leave and become a soldier. This attempt to assert any superiority, however, merely aggravates Nikeratos even more, and Demeas in fact has to step in to restrain Nikeratos, which he does by reasserting the primacy of the wedding that is to happen. To defuse the situation and Nikeratos' temper, Demeas orders the bride brought out immediately (ἔξω κόμιζε δεῦρο τὴν νύμφην, 724). Over the course of the scene, then, the threat of the soldier is a complete failure and completely subservient to the domestic and legal rules governing civilian life.

Once again, knowing the expected narrative pattern of the soldier in Menander's comedy brings coherence to a scene. Moschion's threat to become a soldier raises the specter of soldier characters who need to be reconciled to domestic stability. The old men, and Menander's spectators, recognize this. Moschion as a soldier is defined and recognized solely in a negative way: he is threatening to take on an identity that is fundamentally incompatible with his going forward as a communally approved husband. Demeas responds accordingly, invoking Moschion's responsibilities as a dutiful son, an identity that he knows that Moschion inhabits. Nikeratos, by contrast, threatens to recategorize

---

58 Once again, a young man named Moschion is effectively in conflict with a stable marriage, even being accused of being an adulterer; cf. Moschion in *Sikyonios*.

Moschion not as a soldier but as a different type of antisocial character, an adulterer. Moschion and Demeas react against this threat. Again, none of this involves the *miles gloriosus* narrative.

Short Bits

A recurring motif of this study, as is inevitable in virtually any analysis of Menander, is the fragmentary state of the scripts and visual evidence for his plays. Every play and scene involving soldiers is incomplete to some degree. For the sake of thoroughness, this final section surveys the remaining scraps in Menander's corpus that involve soldiers, with an eye toward what enhanced understanding is to be gleaned from them by keeping the appropriate cultural, ideological, and narrative expectations in mind.

There are tiny scraps of as many as three other plays that could have had soldiers as protagonists or at least plot points. The tattered papyrus strips that constitute Ant. 55 (P. Antinoopolis 55 = *Fabula Incerta* 7 Arnott) include a speaking character possibly named Thrasyleon (line 55), whose name is a title known from a few brief fragments (181–185 PCG; Tiii]).[59] References to an adulterer (line 59) and Moschion a little later (line 66), raise the intriguing possibility that once again a soldier comes into rivalry and conflict with a young man named Moschion associated with adultery. A type of legal dispute (πρόκλησις) is involved, and Arnott points to Demosthenes 39.1–5 for a real-life case of this class of dispute, though how much the play's plot involved this type of procedure is necessarily speculative.

Another variation of the protagonist soldier seems to have played out in Menander's *Carthaginian* (*Karchedonios*).[60] Of the few scraps of the play that survive, a snatch of dialogue indicates that the Carthaginian character claims maternal descent from a Carthaginian general and declares his intention to marry an Athenian girl once he is properly registered in Attica (30–40). This would set up the familiar tension between the protagonist's military and foreign identity and his desire for legitimized marriage. Scattered remains from another papyrus scrap mention marriage and some military equipment within a few lines, so there could have been dialogue or monologue about the Carthaginian soldier's situation, but beyond this there is virtually no information.[61]

---

[59] Julian *Beard Hater* 249c, the source of Tiii, indicates that this soldier is beardless, hence we can expect that he was a young man and a candidate to be a protagonist in love.

[60] For Alexis' play of the same name, see the analysis of Plautus' *Poenulus* in Chapter 4.

[61] There is a chance that P.Oxy 3966 = *Fabula Incerta* 9 Arnott, some scrappy lines referring to marriage preparations, also comes from this play, but even if so, it adds little to nothing about how the character's military identity was treated.

A few papyrus scraps of a script (*Fabula Incerta* 6 Arnott) from an unidentified play of Menander may point to a plot, or background to a plot, that involves
a soldier. The fragmentary beginning of the script (preserved in P. Antinopolis
15) includes a young man venting his frustration about his situation and, with
a companion slave, opening a container with various objects in it. Among the
objects is a half of a cloak (line 24), of a type that does routinely designate a
soldier (χλαμύς). Another papyrus scrap linked to the same play (B1 P. Berlin
13982 = P. Schubart 23) mentions a sword (ξίφος, line 9) and maybe a reference
to it being rusted (19–22). If these are recognition tokens, they could indicate
that someone who was a soldier will be recognized as a parent, but even this is
speculative and nothing else in the meager remains hints at what role a soldier
character might play.

There remains, of course, another crucial component to Menander's
corpus, a component with plays and testimony critical for the tradition of
the *miles gloriosus*: the renditions in Latin by Plautus and Terence. Two plays
from this tradition which also have some traces recovered from Menander's
scripts, *Synaristosai* and *Kolax*, will be analyzed in the next (and final) chapter
of this study. Indeed, the *Kolax* will emerge as a critical play for the reputation
of Menander's soldiers and in the Latin tradition, especially where the soldier
thrives in Terence's version of the *Eunuch*. At least as importantly, however, the
chapter will tell how the Roman renditions of Greek New Comedy in the generations following Menander made standard the comic soldier who would come
truly to be the stock expectation for centuries and millennia, a stock expectation that was then, almost inevitably once Menander's own scripts were lost
completely for a millennium, read back onto Menander himself.

So on the road to Rome ...

4

From Menander's Soldiers to the
Miles Gloriosus on the Roman Stage

L ARRY GELBART, COAUTHOR OF the book for the 1962 musical *A Funny Thing Happened on the Way to the Forum*, reflecting nearly thirty years later on the authors' and composer's debt to Plautus, writes, "I believe it is safe to say that there is not a joke form, comic character, or farcical situation that exists today that does not find its origin in Plautus's work. Forum contains at least one taste of his original flavor. When Miles Gloriosus, the impossibly pompous, braggart warrior, gets a huge laugh (and he always does) by stating 'I am a parade!' the audience is responding to a line that is over two thousand years old."[1] Scholars are prone, by contrast, to analyze Plautus' comedy as a hybrid of inheritances from Greek New Comedy traditions suffused with elements more immediately accessible to Plautus' Italian audiences. Indeed Eduard Fraenkel's seminal tome on such elements remains a sine qua non of Plautine scholarship nearly a century after its initial publication (1922, 1962, 2007; cf. Christenson 2020). With regard to the tradition of the *miles gloriosus*, however, Gelbart is closer to the truth than scholars have recognized. Previous chapters have laid out the case that soldier characters in Menander and Greek Comedy were not fundamentally braggarts. This chapter shows the consequences of reorienting soldiers in the Greek comic tradition in this way for understanding how soldiers on the Roman stage stand in meaningful contrast to their predecessors.

As much as Menander's soldiers have been misunderstood, Plautus has been underappreciated for his role in crystallizing the soldier character that has had a long, productive life in subsequent theatrical tradition. Generally the relationship between soldier characters in Plautus' plays and those in Menander's plays is in parts both refreshingly direct and frustratingly indeterminate. The directness derives from the fact that undeniably Plautus knew Menander's plays, read

---

[1]   Gelbart 1991:3–4; cf. Gordon 2014 for a focus on Stephen Sondheim's songs in this show, including Miles Gloriosus' entry song, which Gelbart is quoting. On the 1966 film adaptation, see Gonçalves 2020:462–465.

his scripts, and used them in the process of creating his own plays, including those with soldier characters. The indeterminacy derives from uncertainty about Plautus' methods with respect to Greek theater in general, poor documentation of Plautus' theatrical environment, and distance, both chronological and cultural, between the two playwrights.[2] Nearly a century elapsed between the end of Menander's career and the theatrical activity in Italy documented by the surviving scripts and testimony from the late third to mid-second century BCE.[3] Some strands of continuity between the "New Comedy" of Menander's generation and comic theater in Italy two generations later are explicit, however. The scripts of Plautus and Terence testify to the practice of translating, in a broad sense, plays from the Greek tradition for audiences in Roman and other Italian traditions. How soldier characters fit into this tradition finds expression in a few statements in the scripts. In one play, Plautus has the character of a soldier's slave introduce the play this way:

> comoediai quam nos acturi sumus
> et argumentum et nomen vobis eloquar.
> Alazon Graece huic nomen est comoediae,
> id nos Latine gloriosum dicimus.

> Of the comedy that we are going to perform, both the plot and title I will tell you: the comedy's title in Greek is "*Alazon*." In Latin we say this as "*gloriosus*."

> *Miles Gloriosus* 84–87

The *miles gloriosus* of this play, Pyrgopolynices, has come to epitomize the Greek *alazon* and Latin *gloriosus*. Other references in the scripts of Plautus define and contribute to modern scholarly understanding of soldier characters on the early Roman stage. In *Captivi*, Plautus lists the *miles gloriosus* among characters that will not be included (58), since it is to be an atypical comedy, thus testifying by inversion to a braggart soldier as an established and expected character

---

[2] For a survey of what is known of Plautus' theatrical environment, see Moore 2020.

[3] For a survey of Plautus vis-à-vis the Greek theatrical tradition, see Nervegna 2020. Goldberg 2005:87–114 and Feeney 2016:94–98, 102–107, 139–143 each, in contrasting ways, address the contours and gaps in the development of Roman drama during this period. Feeney teases out a broad spectrum of Roman engagement with Hellenism, one focus of which was drama. This dynamic has much in common with that of Anderson, cited below with respect to the *Miles Gloriosus*. More cautiously, Goldberg finds much of the same evidence helpful for illuminating first-century BCE perspectives on the past rather than as illumination of third-century practice and perspective. As appealing as Feeney's model is, I side with Goldberg's caution on this issue, as I do not see that later Roman sources embed detailed and reliable information about Plautus' original practices.

(cf. a similarly oblique comment in Terence's *Eunuch*, on which see the discussion below). In *Truculentus*, again by inversion, Plautus testifies to the expectations for the *miles gloriosus*. Plautus brings on a soldier character, here named Stratophanes, who attempts to distinguish himself from the *miles gloriosus* stereotype. In response to the implicit expectation that he is a *miles gloriosus*, the actor and character declares (482–484):

> Ne exspectetis, spectatores, meas pugnas dum praedicem:
> manibus duella praedicare soleo, haud in sermonibus.
> scio ego multos memoravisse milites mendacium ...

> Don't wait for me to declare my battles, spectators! I am in the habit of making declarations with my hands, and not with speeches. I understand that many soldiers have recalled total lies ...

Thus Plautus plays Stratophanes as soldier against the tradition and expectation that a *miles gloriosus* will expound on military accomplishments by having him explicitly separate himself from that tradition. As Stratophanes also indicates, key to the character is that the soldier brags of accomplishments which the spectators recognize as false, unbelievable, and even hypocritical. Stratophanes himself, despite his initial claims, fulfills the expectations of the stereotypical *miles gloriosus*. Following his initial declaration that he is no hypocrite, and then claiming that he does not rely on speeches, Stratophanes delivers a speech on hypocrisy (485–499). He then reveals the purpose of his visit to Athens, to check on his girlfriend whom he left pregnant (*ad amicam ... / ... quam gravidam hic reliqui meo compressu*, 497–498). His girlfriend, Phronesium, is a prostitute. She is in fact borrowing a baby to convince Stratophanes that he is a father, a role he is too eager to embrace. When informed by one of Phronesium's fellow prostitutes that he has an "absolutely delightful boy" (*puerum nimium lepidum*, 505), Stratophanes immediately asks after the baby's resemblance to himself (*Ehem, ecquid mei similest?* 505). Upon hearing that the newborn requested a sword and shield, Stratophanes feels assured that the child is his (*Meus est, scio iam de argumentis*, 507), and yet he only ratchets up the bravado. He expects the baby to have grown up, joined the army, and won spoils of war (*iam magnust? iamne iit ad legionem? ecquae spolia rettulit?* 508). At the suggestion that this might be an unreasonable expectation of a baby born only four days earlier, Stratophanes is impatient and asserts that a son of his would be ready for battle in the womb (510–511):

> inter tot dies quidem hercle iam aliquid actum oportuit.
> quid illi ex utero exitiest prius quam poterat ire in proelium?

Over that many days he should have accomplished something already.
What's the point of his leaving the womb before he can go into battle?

Despite the initial metatheatrical protest, Stratophanes is now squarely in the realm of a classic *miles gloriosus*. Yet, as much as this absurd boasting is emblematic of the character type, it is also an example beyond any that survives from the remains of Greek scripts (Chapters 2 and 3).[4]

While it is convenient and efficient to assume that Plautus was transplanting a popular stock character from the Greek stage to Roman *fabula palliata*, the testimony and scripts on both the Greek and Roman side are not consistent with such a simple operation. Although hundreds of titles of fourth- and third-century BCE Greek comedies are attested, Plautus' lines are the only testimony for the title *Alazon*, and attempts to identify a Greek predecessor for *Miles Gloriosus* have remained unhelpfully speculative.[5] Furthermore, Plautus' lines quoted above do not necessarily say that he is using a Greek model titled *Alazon*, as he could be giving the Greek and Latin equivalents for his play's title. Plautus did sometimes use Greek titles, as for *Acharistio*, *Agroecus*, *Colax*, *Dyscolus*, *Phago*, and possibly *Schematicus*. Play titles can be deceiving, however, as *Epidicus* and *Stichus* among the surviving plays have Greek-looking titles but these turn out to be the names of characters, so a Greek title for *Miles Gloriosus* is possible but not certain, making its relationship to Greek predecessors even more nebulous. This nebulousness also casts shadows over *Truculentus*, which scholars on multiple grounds have argued is Plautus' own creation, not indebted to any particular Greek ancestor, which likewise leaves Stratophanes without a discrete Greek antecedent.[6]

---

[4] Papaioannou 2010 pairs Stratophanes with Thrasonides in *Misoumenos* (cf. Chapter 3) to highlight the rarity of the *gloriosus* type in Menander, though she seems to read Stratophanes as less reliant on stock expectations than I do here.

[5] See Mastromarco 2009:17–19 for a recent review of this topic. Fontaine 2010 and 2014a:526–527 resurrect the idea that the opening scene of *Miles Gloriosus* owes a debt to Menander's *Kolax*. Such an assertion cannot be disproven, given the limited evidence, but the parallels Fontaine cites are slight, and he does not even address the added complication of Plautus' own known direct adaptation of Menander's *Kolax* (frr. 54–57 Monda).

[6] Notably, E. Lefèvre and the "Freiburg school" have emphasized the centrality of the native dramatic traditions of impromptu performances in Plautus. See Lefèvre 1991:175–200 for *Truculentus* in particular. My analysis of soldiers in Plautus' plays is not predicated on the position of the Freiburg school. Indeed I do not see any reason to believe that Plautus adhered to a single process vis-à-vis Greek scripts in composing his own scripts. Perhaps studies of this sort can add something to the conversation. My focus is to highlight a pattern that seems to involve whether a specifically Menandrian model was in play or not. On a different tack, I am sympathetic to and supportive of Marshall's model of Plautus' scripts as flexible documents that spurred performances with the expectation of live improvisation. I do not expect that my analysis of the passages here would differ meaningfully because someone does or does not subscribe

The examples of *Captivi* and *Truculentus* indicate that the character of the *miles gloriosus* was established enough for Plautus to play both with and against the expectations of the stereotype. Plautus' prominent deployment of the character type in some plays and his metatheatrical manipulation of the type in other plays also raise the intriguing possibility that Plautus himself was instrumental in the popularity of the *miles gloriosus*, so that Plautus is toying with his own theatrical legacy that transformed the Greek *alazon* into the *gloriosus*. Two other plays of Plautus also fit this pattern of featuring a standard braggart soldier but lacking evidence for an established Greek model, *Curculio* and *Epidicus*.[7] It is worth analyzing the characteristics of these four Plautine braggart soldiers (Therapontigonus in *Curculio*, the unnamed soldier in *Epidicus*, Pyrgopolynices in *Miles Gloriosus*, and Stratophanes in *Truculentus*) before moving on to Plautus' plays that have known precedents in Menander's corpus. Certain characteristics and dynamics unite these four examples of soldier characters on the Roman stage but also offer contrasts with soldier characters known from Menander and other Greek predecessors.[8]

Accordingly this analysis traces five characteristics and notes contrasts in these characteristics with the Greek precedents analyzed in Chapters 2 and 3: (1) The *miles gloriosus* brags about military achievements that other characters and the audience recognize as untrue, while the *miles* himself is oblivious to others recognizing his false bravado. (2) The *miles* is wealthy with sufficient monetary resources to lay financial claim to a female prostitute slave, one inevitably desired by a free young man without comparable financial resources. (3) The *miles* is thus a rival claimant to the play's protagonist, who will in the end secure the girl that both characters pursue, while the *miles* will fulfill neither his desire nor his claim. (4) The *miles* stands in further contrast to the protagonist in that the *miles* is marked as a non-Roman soldier. The *miles gloriosus*, insofar as he is non-Roman, is defined to a Roman audience as inferior militarily. (5) Plautus reinforces this cultural assumption and expectation by staging the inferiority of

---

to Marshall's model. By contrast, however, I do think, pace Marshall 2006:ix, that Terence's scripts are predicated on the expectation of a more stable performance and with substantial self-consciousness about the relevance of Greek scripts. This is not to say that Terence is not creative or limited by this dynamic, but that, as the prologues to the scripts make explicit, these issues were not tacit nor was there broad agreement.

[7] For the debates about how much or little Plautus relied on Greek predecessors in composing these two plays, see Lefèvre 1991:89–93 on *Curculio* and Arnott 2001 on *Epidicus*.

[8] The slim remains of Plautus' *Cornicula* (frr. 62–69 Monda) imply the presence of a soldier, but nothing about a Greek precedent and nothing certain about the soldier's role and character in the play. Bias from Menander's *Kolax* will be a focus of analysis in connection with Terence's *Eunuch* later in this chapter.

the *gloriosus*. In every play, a subordinate character dominates the non-Roman *miles gloriosus*.

The first characteristic, the soldier's braggadocio coupled with his lack of self-awareness, goes to the heart of defining the stock character on the Roman stage and is conversely scarce in soldier characters in earlier Greek comedy (Chapter 2), especially in Menander (Chapter 3). Pyrgopolynices in *Miles Gloriosus* remains the preeminent example of the character in Plautus. In the opening scene of the play, Pyrgopolynices discourses about his military achievements while the parasite Artotrogus both bolsters the soldier's egotism and banters with the audience to mock the braggart's absurd claims (1–78). The motif dominates all the later scenes where Pyrgopolynices appears, especially when he is set up for the supposed affair with a Roman matron (947–1129, 1200–1393). In the last scene of the play, he receives his comeuppance (1394–1437). In the scope and extent of the *miles gloriosus'* presence, this play exceeds all other plays known from the Greek or Roman tradition, but the crucial dynamic of the obtuse braggart plays out in other comedies. Thus Therapontigonus in *Curculio* blusters that his anger can lay waste to towns (534) and even kings obey him (555–556), the soldier in *Epidicus* expects gratitude from all mortals (443), earning explicitly the epithet *gloriosus* (301), and Stratophanes in *Truculentus*, as noted above, boasts about not falling into the stereotype even as he fulfills its expectations.[9] As discussed in Chapter 2, this bragging motif is attested in Greek comedy at most as one strand in the presentation of soldiers.

The role of the *gloriosus* in the action of a play consistently hinges on his financial wealth, in that he has sufficient monetary resources to lay financial claim to a female prostitute slave, one inevitably desired by a free young man without comparable financial resources. Accordingly, Pyrgopolynices in *Miles Gloriosus* can afford to send off one such prostitute, Philocamasium, with a load of gifts, including the freedom of the slave Palaestrio, just in order to pursue an illicit relationship with a matron (1200–1215). In the process, the *gloriosus* sets the girl free to be with the play's young male protagonist and relinquishes his claim on her. Therapontigonus in *Curculio* commits thirty *minae* to purchase another such prostitute, Planesium, and subsequently, when he turns out to be Planesium's brother, can agree to a "dowry" of feeding the parasite Curculio in perpetuity (662–667). The soldier in *Epidicus* is wealthy with gold (*multo aureo potens*, 153) sufficient enough that he agrees to buy a prostitute at double the normal price (301, 449–451, 463–471, where the transaction is for sixty *minae*, twice the thirty *minae*, e.g. in *Curculio*). In *Truculentus*, Stratophanes'

---

[9] Similar to these scenes is *Pseudolus* 917–918, where Harpax is proxy for a soldier. Cf. Richlin 2017:233–255 and 2018:450n47.

wealth is sufficiently expected as a braggart soldier that his girlfriend prostitute lays plans to steal his property (18–21) and later Stratophanes desperately provides lavish gifts in order to stay in her favor (529–533). In the remains of Greek comedy, by contrast, the financial resources of a soldier character may be relevant, mainly by inference or consequence of his mercenary service, but the flamboyant wealth of these soldiers in Plautus has no certain parallel on the Greek stage (see below for comments on the wealth of Bias in Menander's *Kolax*, which focuses on Bias' social mobility, not the extent of his wealth, and his analogue Thraso in Terence's *Eunuch*).

Perhaps the most crucial contrast between soldiers in Menander and those in Plautus is defined by their relationship to a play's protagonist. Overwhelmingly in Plautus' plays and in Greek New Comedy so far as it is attested, there is a young elite male who hopes to, and eventually does, secure a long-term relationship, most often marriage, with a woman he desires.[10] In Plautus this romantic protagonist is never a soldier.[11] The *miles* is instead a rival claimant to the play's protagonist, the young man who will in the end secure the girl that both characters pursue, while the *miles* will fulfill neither his desire nor his claim. The *miles gloriosus* in Plautus and Terence is thus never the protagonist, but instead a blocking character, a rival and threat to the protagonist of the play, who is still a young man in love (Duckworth 1952:264–265; Rosivach 1998). Thus in *Epidicus* the *gloriosus* is a rival and threat to the young man Stratippocles, in *Curculio* Therapontigonus is a rival and threat to Phaedromus, in *Truculentus* Stratophanes is a rival and threat to Diniarchus, and in *Miles Gloriosus* Pyrgopolynices is a rival and threat to Pleusicles. Additionally, in *Pseudolus* the soldier Polymachaeroplagides, represented on stage only by his proxy Harpax, is a rival to the young protagonist Calidorus. By contrast, in Menander, whenever sufficient evidence or testimony makes it possible to determine a soldier's role in a plot, he is himself a protagonist, one of several variations of the young man in love, one who will ultimately be successful in securing marriage with the woman he desires.[12]

Further reinforcing the contrast between the *miles gloriosus* and the Roman audience is that the *miles* is a non-Roman soldier. In *Truculentus*, Stratophanes

---

[10] Plautus provides the key exceptions of *Captivi* and *Amphitryo*, the former explicitly characterized as unorthodox by Plautus and the latter often characterized as of a somewhat different genre than palliata; see Christenson 2000:45–55. Cf. James 2020 on Plautus' comedies being surprisingly unsupportive of marriage as resolution.

[11] Stratippocles in *Epidicus* is something of an unsuccessful soldier and his father apparently an accomplished one, but the *miles gloriosus* in the play is a separate character and a rival.

[12] See James 2020 and Gold 2020 on how Plautus problematizes marriage as a successful resolution in his comedies.

is Babylonian (84, 202, 391–392, 472). In *Miles Gloriosus*, Pyrgopolynices has recruited mercenaries for King Seleucus (75–76). In *Curculio*, Therapontigonus meets the title character in Caria and has dealings in Epidaurus (338–341), as well as with "kings" (555). *Epidicus*, set at Athens, has its *miles gloriosus* come from Euboea (153), with another (fictional) one from Rhodes (300–301). The father Periphanes and protagonist Stratippocles are unique examples of citizen-soldiers of the locale where a play is set, but they are distinct from the outsider *miles gloriosus*. Periphanes assures the Euboean *gloriosus* that he has far more to boast about than the soldier does (451–452), and he has already told the audience that he used to boast about his achievements as a young man.[13]

Whereas in Menander the citizen identity of a soldier can be problematic, something to be negotiated or revealed as properly belonging to the local community he seeks to join, the *miles gloriosus* in Plautus is and remains a foreign outsider.[14] Along these lines, even assuming wrongly that the braggart soldier was a stock character held over from Greek comedy, scholars have long sensed that Plautus was deploying the type toward distinctly Roman ends. Grimal (1968), for example, argues that the Greek original behind the *Miles Gloriosus* would have satirized Demetrius the Besieger as an insolent buffoon, a topical source of humor that Plautus would have reworked considerably for his Italian audiences.[15] Leach (1979) promoted Plautus' creative trajectory further, arguing that the ridicule of the foreign soldier Pyrgopolynices and the slave Palaestrio's military metaphors fit the exuberance that came with the wave of military successes the Romans enjoyed around the time of the play's performance (about 205 BCE).

Also analyzing the lead slave Palaestrio and the soldier Pyrgopolynices in *Miles Gloriosus*, and following Leach's lead, Anderson summarizes how Plautus deploys his soldier characters for a Roman audience vis-à-vis their Greek character:

> The soldier is a Greek mercenary, fighting for money, not for any principle, certainly not in defence of his home and country against a

---

[13] If 431–434 are really by Plautus, on which point see Duckworth 1940 *ad* 431–434, Lowe 2001:67 and Arnott 2001:87, who finds this sequence especially Menandrian, but, as Chapter 3 shows, his examples are not characteristic of Menander at all. Additionally, in *Pseudolus* the soldier Polymachaeroplagides, represented on stage only by his proxy Harpax, who threatens to deprive the young protagonist Calidorus of his beloved, is referred to consistently as Macedonian (51, 346, 617).

[14] For the *miles gloriosus* as outsider in general, see Brown 2004:2–4 and more broadly McKechnie 1989:79–101.

[15] Cf. *Cornicula* fr. 63 Monda, possibly also referring to a mercenary serving with Demetrius Poliorcetes.

national enemy. That sets him drastically at odds with Roman soldiers, who were conscripted in times of emergency. There were Greek mercenaries in Hannibal's armies, and Roman soldiers had encountered such mercenaries in numerous battles during the third century, losing some engagements but always winning the war in the end. The plot of the comedy takes this male braggart and symbolically unmans him: it exposes him as a liar and coward, as an unromantic and unattractive fool who is brought to the verge of castration, condign punishment for his silly male egotism and his gullible leap into entrapment as an adulterer. The mercenary soldier emerges as the very opposite of the Roman soldier: he represents, in fact, the contemptible features of Greek corruption. Now it becomes obvious why Plautus attributes to the clever slave, who engineers the humiliation of the soldier, metaphorical terms connected with Roman military practice. Palaestrio, by his intrepid wit, exhibits basic qualities with which the Roman audience identifies, and when the military imagery is added by the poet, Palaestrio becomes a victorious exponent of the Roman ideological conflict with the tired but still boastful and glaringly corrupt Greek civilization.[16]

Anderson's point jibes well with the current study. Menander staged soldiers that addressed a key cultural anxiety of his day, turning on the ways soldiers could be disruptive to the goals of Macedonian imperialism. Menander met this anxiety with plays showing that retiring mercenaries need to forgo their military imperatives and settle into domestic lives, abiding by the norms of their Greek communities. Plautus and his Italian audiences have their own anxieties about mercenary soldiers, but the needs of their communities are quite different. For them, mercenaries are part of the threat to Roman soldiers and to Roman prosperity in general.[17] Plautus mocks and defuses this anxiety by making the soldier a foreign mercenary who is in fact no threat at all, only a stupid braggart.

Put another way, the diffusion of anxiety about deploying military power in a domestic setting differs according to cultural context. Menander focused on a particular anxiety about destructive military might, about the use of military prerogatives off the battlefield by a former mercenary who has no allegiance to the norms of his community, resolving the tension by having the veteran's

---

[16] Anderson 1993:145–146; pace Segal 1968:124, who thinks the Greek characterization of the soldier is not critical for his humor value.

[17] See Rawlings 2011:50–51 on mercenaries being associated in the early Republic with the armies of Roman's enemies. See Burton 2020 on military and imperial motifs in general in Plautus.

erotic desires channeled to live according to the laws and expectations of a lawful husband, forgoing his prerogatives as a soldier. By contrast, Plautus assigns the positive associations of military power, those of Roman soldiers, to the protagonists of his plays, the young man in love or a subordinate in his service, and deflates the military power of Rome's enemies in the figure of the *miles gloriosus*, a foreign mercenary who is all talk and no walk.

In this context, Roman military language is an element recognized as a motif distinct to Plautus compared to the Greek scripts he utilized, most famously documented and categorized in Fraenkel's seminal analysis of elements that resonate as distinctly Plautine enhancements or additions to the plays of Greek predecessors.[18] Fraenkel analyzes how Plautus imbues primarily his slave protagonist characters with Roman military motifs, while Plautus suffuses dialogue involving soldiers more with Greek motifs drawn from stage tragedy. While this method separates Plautus from earlier Greek practitioners, it is impossible on the available evidence, unfortunately, to assess how much these Plautine elements distinguished him from his Italian contemporaries and predecessors. Indeed in general there is little that can be asserted with confidence to orient the development of this character in Plautus or Terence within broader trends in Roman drama, beyond basic speculation.[19] It is sensible, for example, to think that Atellan farce staged soldier characters, but no evidence or testimony survives to confirm it.[20] Additionally, Terence implies that Naevius' adaptation of Menander's *Kolax* included the soldier character (on which, see the discussion of Terence's *Eunuch* later in this chapter), but beyond such shadowy hints, we must rely on the extant scripts of Terence and Plautus to understand soldiers in the early phases of Roman theater.

Plautus' Roman military language not only differentiates the cultural orientation of characters and props but also reinforces a hierarchy of Roman cultural values vis-à-vis those of other cultures. With regard to the *miles gloriosus* character, Plautus not only consistently ensures that the soldier is an obvious fraud, but he doubles his failure as a militarized man by staging at least one sequence establishing that the *miles gloriosus* is inferior to another character whom a Roman audience would rank beneath that of a Roman citizen soldier. Plautus' prominent tricky slaves are an easy example, as they make use of military imagery and

---

[18] Fraenkel 2007:159–166 and Hanson 1964.

[19] For the broader context of orienting Plautus and Terence in the chronological development of Roman drama, see De Melo 2014, Fontaine 2014, and Petrides 2014b.

[20] L. Pomponius Bononiensis wrote several "Maccus" plays, one of which is *Maccus Miles*, but this is a century or so later than Plautus. See Manuwald 2011:267–270; Plautus' *Amphitryo* features the title character as a victorious general returning home, thus distinct from the mercenaries under discussion here. On the soldier jokes here, see Richlin 2018:447–448.

dominate their social betters.[21] Within this framework Anderson (1993:144–146; cf. Richlin 2018:447–454) analyzes the example of the slave Palaestrio achieving dominance over Pyrgopolynices in the form of Roman superiority over an eastern Greek-style soldier in *Miles Gloriosus,* and this paradigm plays out similarly in the other plays with a *miles gloriosus.* Plautus achieves this double level of dominance with characters of lower social rank. In *Curculio* it is the parasite in service to the young protagonist who swindles the soldier first at gambling and later by proxy, in disguise as a phony freedman to Therapontigonus, in order to swindle the soldier on behalf of the banker Lyco. In *Epidicus* Periphanes, the father of the play's young hero, is an Athenian citizen who had served as a mercenary in his younger days (449–451); he assures the Euboean soldier that he has far more to boast about than the *gloriosus* does (451–452). Periphanes thus establishes his own military credentials as superior to that of the *gloriosus,* but he is Athenian (read, Greek) and thus inferior and "other" compared to a Roman soldier. Moreover, he will be tricked by his own social inferior, his slave *Epidicus* (Brown 2004:4). In *Truculentus,* the soldier Stratophanes engages in a showdown fight with another social inferior, the cook Cyanus. Here Stratophanes' military sword barely wards off the kitchen knife that Cyanus wields (600–630, esp. 615 *si tu in legioni bellator clues, at ego in culina clueo,* "If you are famous as a warrior in the army, I am famous in the kitchen!")[22] Stratophanes' inferiority as a soldier continues, as his failed attempts to hold his status, to say nothing of actually having leverage, rely entirely on his financial resources. He repeatedly invokes his gifts to assert victory and respect, first with the cook (618) and subsequently with the young man Strabax and the prostitute Phronesium, all to no avail (900, 911, 945–967).

All these dynamics of Plautus' soldiers in *Curculio, Epidicus, Miles Gloriosus,* and *Truculentus* should then be compared with the soldier characters who appear in Plautus' plays that have a demonstrated pedigree from Menander, since we can now contrast these soldier characters with those in other plays of Plautus and tease out commonalities with soldier characters known directly from the remains of Menander's own scripts. Thus with regard to soldiers, it is necessary to reconfigure the impact of Menander on this Roman tradition. Menander's shadow over Roman comedy in general is a subject far larger than the one I am undertaking here, but with respect to the *miles gloriosus,* Menander

---

[21]   See Feltovich 2020 and Witzke 2020:335–336 on Pyrgopolynices' (failed) masculinity along similar lines. On the "Greekness" of the play's setting, see Papaioannou 2020:290–291.

[22]   See Biers 1985 for a clay mold that may well depict a cook struggling with a soldier and thus potentially hint at a Greek New Comic predecessor for the scene in *Truculentus.*

has a direct inheritance nowhere but in Terence's *Eunuch*.[23] None of Plautus' plays with a *miles gloriosus* proper have known antecedents in Menander. While Plautus' silence about Greek predecessors should receive due caution and not be taken as proof that he did not utilize a Menander play for any of these paradigmatic braggart soldiers, this pattern is unlikely a mere coincidence. Still, so far as possible, scholars should be careful to distinguish Menander from Greek New Comedy as a whole and from the substantive differences implemented by Roman playwrights. Conflating Roman practice with that of Menander can be necessary and valid on some topics, but the temptation can result in distortion. For example, Petrides writes, "Of all the ways to write and play the *miles gloriosus* Menander's typical choice, a reflective, sentimental mode, which redeems the soldier and usually, through timely *anagnorisis*, rehabilitates him into the society of citizen men, may have been the least representative of the norm. On the contrary, the *palliata* provides an image of the *miles* much more attuned with the semantics of *alazoneia* ... " (2014a:213). Petrides makes explicit what most scholars say only in summary fashion or obliquely, that Roman *palliata* preserve the iconic *miles gloriosus*, and Menander's soldiers are to be analyzed as deviations.[24] Petrides goes on to analyze the dynamics between the *miles gloriosus* and the parasite characters in terms of their physiognomics, especially their masks. Much of what Petrides says about these scenes is illuminating and does not depend on Greek masks, Peripatetic philosophy, or that Roman theater used masks, although he does subscribe to all these ideas. For the most part, his analysis stands as a perceptive and enlightening explication of communication between playwrights, performers, and their spectators. My argument means that his analysis of the *Miles Gloriosus* reveals more of Plautus' dramaturgy than Menander's.[25]

While the evidence does not support Plautus relying on Menander for the *miles gloriosus* tradition, Plautus did of course know and absorb Menander's plays. Three surviving scripts of Plautus undoubtedly have Menander plays as antecedents. One of these, *Stichus*, derived from one of Menander's *Adelphoe* plays, has no soldier character. The other two, *Cistellaria* (drawing on Menander's *Synaristosai*) and *Bacchides* (Menander's *Dis Exapaton*), carry over motifs of soldier characters that we have observed in Menander's plays, but do not have *miles*

---

[23] Ireland 2010:392–396 and Fontaine 2014b are both good starting points with bibliography.

[24] Papaioannou 2010 makes a similar observation but in the context of how Roman Comedy in a sense responds to "postclassical" Greek comedy.

[25] Petrides is thin on the Roman *miles gloriosus* outside of Plautus' *Miles Gloriosus*, sometimes to the point of distortion, such as when he mistakenly identifies the character Diabolus in *Asinaria* as a soldier (2014a:219).

gloriosus characters. These are scenes and motifs in Plautus that reflect the type of soldier Menander did deploy, which is not the *miles gloriosus*.

When Plautus does render Menander into his own plays, vestiges or motifs of non-*gloriosus* soldiers appear. In *Cistellaria*, for example, the young lover Alcesimarchus makes a series of requests to his slave for military equipment. Eventually the whole sequence is deemed a bit of temporary insanity (284–297). This is not bragging, but linking military imagery to the play's hapless protagonist. The motif is also reminiscent of Moschion in Menander's *Samia*, when the young man impetuously demands a sword and cloak to dramatize his lesson to his adoptive father (cf. discussion in Chapter 3). It is hazardous to reason that Plautus here is directly adapting a scene from Menander's original, but it is notable that a known Plautine rendering of a Menander play has this parallel. Moreover, although Alcesimarchus' request for military paraphernalia is dismissed as mad, later in the play the desperate youth melodramatically emerges and threatens suicide by sword (940–950). This is also somewhat reminiscent of *Samia*, but more of Menander's soldiers like Polemon in *Perikeiromene* and Thrasonides in *Misoumenos* threatening suicide, and of course of many variations of the melodrama of pathetic young men in love.[26]

For the relationship of Plautus to a Menander original, Plautus' *Bacchides* has generated more scholarly attention than any other pairing, because of the papyrus finds that make direct comparison possible of a few corresponding pages of each of this play with Menander's *Dis Exapaton*.[27] As it happens, however, none of the surviving bits of Menander's play contain or refer to a soldier, so no direct comparison of this character is possible. Nonetheless, the role of the soldier Cleomachus in Plautus' play has suggestive analogues to the known soldiers in Menander.

The first scene in *Bacchides* referring to the soldier is a dialogue between the young protagonist in love, Pistoclerus, and the object of his desire, the (Athenian) Bacchis. This Bacchis wants Pistoclerus present when the soldier arrives, in order to protect and eventually liberate her sister, the other "Bacchis" (45–108). Where other young men in Plautus take on military characteristics, albeit foolishly like Alcesimarchus, here the young man Pistoclerus imagines himself in contrast to the soldier at an imagined banquet (69–73). None of this

---

[26] Cf. discussion of Alexis fr. 236 in Chapter 2. Two of Plautus' plays derived from Philemon have analogous motifs. Charinus in *Mercator* 830–884 uses the metaphor of sailing and Lesbonicus' slave Stasimus envisions life as a mercenary's slave at *Trinummus* 595–599 and 718–726. Cf. Fraenkel 2007:161 and Richlin 2018:449–450 for military motifs in Plautus plays derived from Philemon.

[27] See Fontaine 2014a:519–526 for analysis and bibliography.

reveals anything of the soldier's character, however, braggart or otherwise, just that he is an obstacle to the couple's desires, as is standard in Plautus.

The next scene to involve the soldier does not include his actual appearance. At 573–610, an unnamed parasite arrives in service of the soldier Cleomachus. The parasite refers to the soldier as *hominis nequam atque improbi / militis qui amicam secum avexit ex Samo*, "a disgusting no-good soldier who took his girl-friend from Samos" (573–574). Pistoclerus, despite contrasting himself with the soldier earlier in the play, now threatens violence against the parasite as proxy for the soldier (594–605).[28] As routinely in Plautus, a subordinate offers superiority over a non-Roman soldier, the rival to the play's young male protagonist. A parasite also routinely undercuts his soldier's standing, but notably, nothing so far actually constitutes braggadocio, direct or implied, from the soldier in question. The soldier is referred to negatively, even by his own proxy, but because he is an obstacle, not derided as a *gloriosus*.

Indeed when Cleomachus himself finally appears (842–905), it is not false bravado which characterizes him but anger and danger.[29] This is Cleomachus' only appearance in this rather extended play, and he is not even the dominant character on stage. More importantly for the plot, Chrysalus, the slave of another young man in love, Mnesilochus, uses the appearance of Cleomachus to swindle money from Mnesilochus' father, Nicobulus, by convincing the old man that Cleomachus is in fact the husband of the Bacchis that Mnesilochus loves. As Anderson says, soldiers are about emasculating rivals to Roman protagonists, so this is what Plautus accomplishes here. The slave Chrysalus dupes the young man's father and outwits the soldier, getting the father to pay money and getting Cleomachus to agree to surrender his hold on Bacchis' sister and accept abuse. Cleomachus just wants his money and has no apparent reaction to Chrysalus' abuse, in contrast to a *miles gloriosus*, who would never stand for such insults. Inversely, a *miles gloriosus* finds and reproduces praise where insults are slipped in.

As expected, nothing here suggests that Plautus inherited a *miles gloriosus* from Menander's play. Indeed, despite routine assertions, on the available evidence it is not necessary that there was a soldier character in the *Dis Exapaton*.[30] The reasoning is that Cleomachus is too critical for the plot structure of *Bacchides* not to have been in Menander's original, but too little can be determined about the antecedents of the complex and diffuse plot for this to be taken for granted. The same argument could be made about Thraso in Terence's

---

[28] See Petrides 2014a:216–220 for analysis of this phenomenon. *Pseudolus* similarly has the soldier represented, in this case exclusively, by proxy.

[29] Pace Lefèvre 2011:172–174, who maintains the standard line that all soldiers are stock braggarts.

[30] Lefèvre 2011:172 "muß auch bei Menander" is typical.

Eunuch, for example, but he is known to be interpolated from a different play. In terms of Menandrian dramatic practice, if Cleomachus does have a predecessor in the *Dis Exapaton*, Plautus would seem to be preserving a character that is driven by anger, a trait well attested among Menander characters (Groton 1987, Reiss 2012:319–331). In Plautus, however, again the dominance of a lower-status figure over the *gloriosus* is more important, as becomes even clearer following the exit of Cleomachus from the stage. The slave Chrysalus now takes the place as a dominant soldier, as he delivers a long rant on himself as a heroic warrior in the Trojan War (925–978, analyzed by Fraenkel 2007:163–166 as a premiere example of Plautus' creative departure from Greek practice). He subsumes the pinnacle of the Greek warrior tradition even as the foreign soldier leaves humiliated.

Plautus' most complex deployment of a soldier character and military motifs comes in yet another play, the *Poenulus*. The relationship of the play to its Greek antecedents is also unusually complex, for the principal model seems to have been Alexis' *Karchedonios*, but scholars have noted several passages where Plautus echoes Menander.[31] Additionally, no one would deny that Plautus calibrated this play to a Roman cultural context in intriguing ways. In *Poenulus* Plautus deploys a *miles gloriosus* but also refracts the various associations of a soldier character. The *miles* himself is Antamoenides, who in his first appearance on stage engages in boastful banter that marks him as a classic *miles gloriosus* (471–503). Shortly afterward, however, the young protagonist Agorastacles recruits a slave Collybiscus, to pretend to be Antamoenides (578–721), thus adding an actor pretending to be a *miles gloriosus* in a play which already features one.[32] Metatheatrically Collybiscus memorizes his lines better than actors at 581 and carries "stage" money at 596. This mock *miles gloriosus* prompts comments that make explicit the dynamics that Anderson describes, notably at 603, where helpful bystanders (some *advocati*) describe the desire of the soldier as finding a place "where you will love, drink, and go completely Greek" (*ubi ames, potes, pergraecere*, 603). Later, they add corroborating details that the soldier is a foreigner (*peregrinum*, 656), specifically a Spartan mercenary (*latro in Sparta fuit*, 663). The young man's allies are willing to have this soldier "plundered" (*diripiundum*, 646) even by a pimp (though the morality of the action, as far as it could benefit the pimp, does occasion some discussion, 633–642).[33]

---

[31] Arnott 2004:68–70 finds both Alexis and Menander imaginative but Menander's expression at a higher level.

[32] Arnott 2004:67 focuses on Collybiscus pretending to be a *miles gloriosus* in a play with a real one.

[33] Manuwald 2004:222 finds Antamoenides an unorthodox *miles gloriosus*, since he is not boastful nor a customary client of pimps.

By the time Antamoenides himself returns to the stage, the situation has changed considerably, in that the Carthaginian Hanno has been revealed as the father of the object of the soldier's interest, Adelphasium. It seems that in this concluding sequence Plautus draws on a more Menandrian characterization, as he does in *Bacchides*, as Antamoenides becomes angry when he sees the Carthaginian friendly with Adelphasium. The complexity of this scene and the play in general include having Antamoenides vent some stereotypical racism toward the Carthaginian Hanno, who is in some ways allowed an intriguing collection of positive character traits.[34] This anger recalls the *Perikeiromene*. Plautus has the scene pivot quickly, so that everyone on stage soon gangs up on the pimp.[35]

In sum, none of the examples of a true *miles gloriosus* (defined as a soldier who brags, and/or is goaded to brag, about demonstrably false military exploits) that Plautus presents have known antecedents in Menander, and indeed Greek precedents for any of his *milites gloriosi* are all but impossible to identify. Based on the analysis of Greek remains of soldiers in comedy outside Menander, the evidence from Plautus is most consistent with him taking one minor strand of staging a soldier and making it canonical.

Where the Braggarts Are: Flatterers and Parasites

Menander's contribution to the history of the *miles gloriosus* turns out to reside in the refraction of a single soldier character, Bias, in his comedy *Kolax* ("Flatterer"). This refraction is all the more disparate now because traces of the play are available only in a jumble of fragmentary chunks of evidence. These lines of evidence will inevitably limit and shape the investigation into this play and its soldier character, and a survey of this material will facilitate explaining how the subsequent analysis will proceed. Papyrus scraps preserve some lines, most incomplete, from Menander's play. The most extensive papyrus (P.Oxy 449 + 2655) itself does not cover a continuous portion of the play but rather parts of five excerpts from the script, the purpose of the excerpts being uncertain (Arnott 2.156-63; Pernerstorfer 15-21). In most cases, speakers and addressees of the lines preserved on the papyri are uncertain, yet it does not seem that Bias is present in any of the preserved scenes. But there are a number of statements by characters that can plausibly be taken as referring to the soldier. A handful

---

[34] See Franko 1996 for analysis of Antamoenides' abuse of Hanno, with a survey of the scholarly discussion of this dynamic.

[35] Plautus' manipulation of the scene is complex and not completely understood, as the last lines of the script have been supplemented or replaced to degrees not completely clear at this point. See Barsby 2004:107-108 on additions and interpolations in this section of the play.

of quotations from *Kolax* appear in other writers, the most important for our purposes being those cited in Plutarch in his essays on flatterers. Plutarch's interest is primarily in the flatterer who goads the soldier, but his quotations and comments indirectly preserve samples of Bias' statements and behavior.[36]

Menander's *Kolax* also drew an uncharacteristic amount of attention from Roman playwrights, as Terence tells us in the prologue to his *Eunuch*: *Colacem esse Naevi, et Plauti veterem fabulam: / parasiti personam inde ablatam et militis*, "There is a *Colax* by Naevius, and another by Plautus, one of his early plays, the characters of the parasite and soldier taken from there" (25–26, translation following Barsby 1999:86). Among the meager fragments of these two Latin renditions of Menander's *Kolax*, nothing is illuminating about the soldier character (Monda 66–67 for Plautus; Ribbeck 11–12 for Naevius). It is Terence's own *Eunuch*, however filtered and repurposed by Terence for his own purposes, that provides the most sustained rendition of Menander's Bias, which Terence explains briefly this way (30–34):

Colax Menandrist: in east parasitus colax
et miles gloriosus: eas se non negat
personas transtulisse in Eunuchum suam
ex Graeca. sed eas fabulas factas prius
Latinas scisse sese id vero pernegat.

There is a *Flatterer* of Menander: in it is a parasite flatterer, and a braggart soldier. These characters, he admits, he transferred into his own *Eunuch* from the Greek. But that he knew of these earlier Latin versions that had been made he absolutely does deny.

As far as the soldier character is concerned, Terence claims to work directly from Menander's soldier in the *Kolax*, without reference to what Plautus and Naevius had done with the character. This does not mean, however, that Terence transferred Menander's Bias with no filter, for Terence, in identifying his new soldier as a *miles gloriosus*, is acknowledging that the character comes with its own traditions and expectations. Terence makes this dynamic explicit in the following lines, where he catalogs characters, motifs, and ideas, including the *miles gloriosus*, that comic playwrights should have license to deploy (35–40; contrast the list at *Heauton Timorumenos* 37–39, which does not include the *miles*

---

[36] There is a similar snatch of dialogue in Athenaeus. Pernerstorfer 2009:137–146 argues that Plutarch *Moralia* 61c should be added to the fragments of *Kolax*, and this would provide a snatch of dialogue involving Bias, but elsewhere Plutarch makes explicit that this saying is to be attributed to the sage Bias of Priene (*Moralia* 147b).

gloriosus). Accordingly, we can say that Terence read and utilized the soldier character of Bias in Menander's *Kolax*, but he was conscious that the character he was deploying in his own play, *Eunuch*, was to be an iteration of the *miles gloriosus* tradition, by this point established at least as far back as Plautus. It will be valuable, therefore, to measure Terence's own single example of a *miles gloriosus* against the characteristics identified for Plautus' versions of the type. That Terence's version will meet these criteria, however, is not sufficient evidence that Menander's version also did, so we will have to consider what elements can be verified for Menander, since Terence is working when the criteria embedded in Plautus' plays are an established expectation for soldier characters in a way that they were not in Menander's time. In this context, too, it is intriguing that Plautus, Naevius, and Terence all took the soldier from Menander's *Kolax*, especially if we view the attention paid to this particular play against the backdrop of the soldier character not being an established stock character, but a stage phenomenon that acquired consistency and popularity. The meager remains of all but Terence's play make conclusions about the appeal of *Kolax* speculative, but still I would like to suggest the possibility that an instantiation of a soldier character in *Kolax* which was amenable to being retooled as a *miles gloriosus* made the play appealing to playwrights of Roman comedy. When the braggart soldier was an established, expected, and popular part of Roman comedy, playwrights would be motivated to make use of Greek plays that had characters that could reasonably be transferred to the Roman stage in this mold, especially from the plays of Greek New Comedy's leading playwright. Speculative as this suggestion is, if this particular soldier was outside the norm for Menander, but in a way that was conducive to being repurposed on the Roman stage, it would fit the fact that Menander's *Kolax* inspired three separate playwrights while none of his other plays foregrounding soldiers have known Latin versions. The reception of Menander's *Kolax* and Terence's *Eunuch*, discussed further below, will have more to offer on this possibility.

Perhaps not coincidentally, the other character that Terence interpolates from Menander's *Kolax*, the flatterer himself, whom Terence identifies with the double epithet *parasitus colax* ("flatterer parasite," 30), also had a dynamic progression. Alexis' *Parasitos*, according to ancient testimony, was crucial in the theatrical history of the character who flattered and manipulated someone who, typically but not necessarily oblivious to the parasite's manipulation, would provide sustenance.[37] Here Petrides's rich analysis of performance dynamics between parasite and soldier in Plautus' *Miles Gloriosus* gives an idea

---

[37] Arnott 1996:542–545. For a survey of the broader debate about the terms *parasitos* and *kolax*, see Pernerstorfer 2009:151–166, Arnott 2010:322–324, and Ruffell 2014.

how complex yet compelling the exchanges were (2014a:216–220). It also gives a sense of a type of scene that Terence knew was successful and popular, which provides some motivation for him to interpolate these two characters as a pair and make the interaction between them a feature of all three scenes that feature the soldier in the play. The pairing of the soldier and flatterer also allows for attention to be paid to differences in reactions to the characters, in the sense that a reader, audience member, or spectator can choose to focus on one of the interlocuters more than the other. At least on available evidence, it is the dynamic of the flatterer that dominates the play's reception, but it is an ancient reader of Terence's *Eunuch* who finds something remarkable in the staging of the soldier character, consistent with the notion that Terence took a Menandrian example of a soldier who, in retrospect, had characteristics associated with the *miles gloriosus*, but Terence advanced the depiction in a significant way.

The analysis here of the soldier from Menander's *Kolax*, then, will run differently from that in the previous chapter, where investigation proceeded as much as possible in line with spectators' experience of the plays in performance. Too little is known, and even this with too little certainty, to proceed the same way through Menander's *Kolax*. In this case, the reflections of later authors who had fuller experience of the play will provide more helpful perspectives, which can then illuminate the fuller but filtered and repurposed workings of Terence in his *Eunuch*. Throughout, though, the central claim abides: that for Menander the braggart soldier was neither an expected nor central type and that, while the particular case of Bias in *Kolax* has traits in common with the braggart, it was on the Roman stage that the *miles gloriosus* took hold and Terence's recasting of the character capitalizes on the more fully developed tradition.

The first step is to contextualize and analyze two later sources that had fuller access to Menander's *Kolax*, Plutarch and Donatus, even if these sources themselves now provide only fragments from their own understandings of the play. Centuries after Menander's, Plautus', and Terence's careers, New Comedy continued to be common on theater stages around the Mediterranean world but also became a staple of literary education, with Menander the leader on the Greek side (Fantham 1984 and Nervegna 2013) and Terence in Latin.[38] The reception of Menander's Bias and Terence's corresponding Thraso in these two later ancient commentators provides valuable perspective on this tradition. These commentators, differing in time, language, and geography, probe the ways to learn moral lessons from the impact of Menander's and Terence's soldiers, each from a different perspective on the centrality of the soldier being a braggart. In the Greek tradition, Plutarch in the second century CE provides valuable

---

[38] See Augoustakis and Trail 2013: 363-428 for various stages of Terence's reception.

testimony about Menander's *Kolax*, but always in the context of the play's title character, the flatterer, where the soldier is but one potential victim.[39] Somewhat later in the Latin tradition, the scholar Donatus reflects on Terence's distinct take on the soldier character. Given the dominance of the *miles gloriosus* in the Latin tradition, Donatus feels the need to explain the nuances that Terence brings to the character which he expects readers would not discern without being alerted to them.

In the case of Menander and Plutarch, the soldier Bias in *Kolax* is a subordinate and replaceable figure compared to his companion, the flatterer Strouthias.[40] As such, divergent from Menander's practice in other plays, the soldier's companion is not his loyal slave but a manipulative parasite. Plutarch trumpets the moral lessons to be gleaned from this dynamic in Menander, but he makes explicit that the victims of flattery extend well beyond the soldier. Plutarch cites the soldier and the parasite only in the context of learning how flatterers operate in order to guard against them. He elaborates:

ἔνιοι μὲν οὖν κολακεύοντες αὐτοὺς ὥσπερ γαργαλίζουσι καὶ φυσῶσιν, ἔνιοι δὲ κακοήθως οἷόν τι δέλεαρ μικρὸν εὐλογίας ὑποβάλλοντες ἐκκαλοῦνται τὴν περιαυτολογίαν, οἱ δὲ προσπυνθάνονται καὶ διερωτῶσιν, ὡς παρὰ τῷ Μενάνδρῳ τὸν στρατιώτην, ἵνα γελάσωσιν·

A: "πῶς τὸ τραῦμα τοῦτ' ἔχεις;"
B: "μεσαγκύλῳ·"
A: "πῶς, πρὸς θεῶν;"
B: "ἐπὶ κλίμακα πρὸς τεῖχος ἀναβαίνων."
ἐγὼ μὲν δεικνύω ἐσπουδακώς, οἱ δὲ πάλιν ἐπεμυκτήρισαν.

Some flatterers effectively titillate people and puff them up, while others elicit self-praise by maliciously scattering a crumb of commendation like bait, and still others cross-examine and ask leading questions, as with the soldier in Menander, in order to raise a laugh:

Speaker A: "How did you get this wound?"
Speaker B: "From a javelin."

---

[39] Contrast Epictetus' use of the soldier Thrasonides in Menander's *Misoumenos*, nearly contemporary with Plutarch. While both are concerned with the moral implications of Menander's characters. the two men differ in many ways, not least that Plutarch was a Platonist and Epictetus was a leading Stoic, on which see Chapter 3.

[40] On Plutarch's use of comedy, including stereotypes of comic soldiers, for moralizing ends, see Xenophontos 2012, esp. 626–628 on Menander's soldiers, although this study focuses on the *Parallel Lives*. For citations of Menander in Plutarch generally, see Casanova 2005.

A: "By the gods, how?"
B: "I was climbing up a ladder to a wall … "
I demonstrate—seriously!—but they booed again!

> *Moralia* 547c = Arnott fr. 7 = Pernerstorfer fr. 8; not in
> Sandbach (translation modified from Arnott)

Plutarch does not identify the Menander play, but Arnott (fr. 7) and Pernerstorfer (fr. 8) reason that Plutarch is citing *Kolax*, since he cites it elsewhere (see below) and the scenario matches nothing else known in Menander's corpus. Whether from *Kolax* or not, the entire quotation is spoken by the flatterer. He is recounting a brief snatch of dialogue with a soldier, but the nauseating performance is all by the flatterer himself. He inquires about a wound, which the soldier says he received from a javelin while on a ladder approaching a wall, presumably in a siege. There is nothing evidently outrageous about this; it is the flatterer's exuberant demonstration that follows which draws a negative reaction (though it is not possible to figure out for whom the flatterer is performing). For Plutarch's purposes, the point is what the flatterer makes happen, not that a soldier is a braggart.

The same context and limitations apply to another citation in Plutarch, this one just following the passage above. As an example of how irritating self-praise can be, Plutarch observes that it aggravates even the flatterers who provoke it:

καὶ κόλακι καὶ παρασίτῳ καὶ δεομένῳ δύσοιστον ἐν χρείᾳ καὶ δυσεγκαρτέρητον ἑαυτὸν ἐγκωμιάζων πλούσιός τις ἢ σατράπης ἢ βασιλεύς· καὶ ‘συμβολὰς ταύτας ἀποτίνειν μεγίστας’ λέγουσιν, ὡς ὁ παρὰ Μενάνδρῳ,

σφάττει με, λεπτὸς γίνομ’ εὐωχούμενος,
τὰ σκώμμαθ’ οἷα τὰ σοφὰ καὶ στρατηγικά,
οἷος δ’ ἀλαζών ἐστιν ἀλιτήριος.

ταῦτα γὰρ οὐ πρὸς στρατιώτας μόνον οὐδὲ νεοπλούτους εὐπάρυφα καὶ σοβαρὰ διηγήματα περαίνοντας,

Even for a flatterer and parasite in desperate need, it is hard to endure and tolerate a wealthy man or satrap or king puffing himself up. They even describe it as paying a huge fee, like the man in Menander:

He slaughters me. I'm lightweight on the highlife!
Such clever and strategic humor.
What a pretentious bastard he is!

This is what it's like in the presence of not just soldiers and the nouveaux riches when they embark on their extravagant excesses of praise ...

Moralia 547e = fr. 8 Arnott = fr. 9 Pernerstorfer;

not in Sandbach

Again, the citation is from Menander, yet not explicitly from *Kolax*. Plutarch is not quoting a bragging soldier but the flatterer's supposed frustration—ironic in this case, as the dynamic is of his own making—and Plutarch is explicit that the soldier is here just one possible candidate for the source of the self-praise that irks the flatterer.

In another essay on flattery, Plutarch does cite *Kolax* explicitly, but he still remains focused on the mechanics of flattery, using the parasite Strouthias toying with the soldier Bias as an example.[41] This time Plutarch uses lines from *Kolax* as examples of a flatterer's technique, so as to identify and guard against their wiles:

καθάπερ ὁ Στρουθίας ἐμπεριπατῶν τῷ Βίαντι καὶ κατορχούμενος τῆς ἀναισθησίας αὐτοῦ τοῖς ἐπαίνοις

Ἀλεξάνδρου πλέον τοῦ βασιλέως πέπωκας

καὶ

γελῶ τὸ πρὸς τὸν Κύπριον ἐννοούμενος

As when Strouthias is wandering around with Bias and dancing all over his lack of awareness with his "praise":

You drank more than King Alexander!

and

I laugh when I think of that one about the Cypriot.

Moralia 57a = fr. 3 Arnott and Pernerstorfer[42]

Again, what Plutarch cites is the flatterer speaking and making the outrageous statements, not Bias the soldier. The point is what the flatterer facilitates, not what Bias the soldier says. Plutarch's caution about how a flatterer operates

---

[41] See Pernerstorfer 2009:31–40 on the problem of the two names attested for the flatterer.

[42] A metrical line embedded shortly after this passage (Sandbach fr. 6 = Arnott fr. 10 = Pernerstorfer fr. 11), about the way a flatterer hunts his prey, may also be from *Kolax*.

is consistent with what the Latin scholar Donatus observes and also with a surviving quotation from the *Kolax* (see lines 86–94, quoted below).

The two lines cited by Plutarch open up a small window to view the mechanics of Terence translating Menander for his own audiences and purpose. Terence interpolated Menander's Strouthias and Bias as Gnatho and Thraso respectively into his rendering of Menander's *Eunuch*. The joke about Alexander disappears completely, while the joke about a Cypriot is transferred to mocking Rhodians, a contentious topic at Rome in Terence's day (Starks 2013:136–138). Terence preserves the dynamic of the flattering parasite teasing out humor at the soldier's expense as he does so (419–422):

THRASO

… quid illud, Gnatho?
quo pacto Rhodium tetigerim in convivio,
numquam tibi dixi?

GNATHO

numquam; sed narra, obsecro.
plus miliens audivi.

THRASO

Gnatho, did I tell you about the hit I scored on the Rhodian at a party?

[*GNATHO gestures "no."*]

I never told you?

GNATHO

Never! So please tell me!

(*To the audience*) I've heard this a thousand times.

Thraso repeats the joke and Gnatho feigns uncontrollable laughter. Thus in this small example, Terence preserves the interpersonal dynamics but changes the specific topic, a technique attested elsewhere, although Terence also, as later in the *Eunuch* itself, makes much more dramatic changes.[43]

It is an intriguing snatch of dialogue from later in this scene that prompted acute analysis from the scholar Donatus in the fourth century CE. In Terence's

---

[43] For a survey of the many issues embedded in Terence's adaptation, see Barsby 1993.

play, Thraso is in love with the prostitute Thais, as is a young male protagonist, Phaedria. Gnatho, ever prodding Thraso, encourages the hapless soldier
to find ways to make Thais jealous. Thraso for once counters Gnatho: *siquidem
me amaret, tum istuc prodesset, Gnatho,* "If somehow she were in love with me,
Gnatho, then that could work" (446). In the fourth century CE, when Terence
was established as a key author in Roman education, the scholar Donatus used
this line to extrapolate principles about Terence and comic theater (*ad* 446):

> hic uersiculus personam militis et Gnathonis continens pro oeconomia
> inducitur, qua uerisimile fit facile militem ferre posse anteponi sibi
> Phaedriam, qui se semper intellexerit non amari. nam si hoc tollas,
> aut excludendus est Phaedria aut ex dolore militis in hac fabula fit
> exitus tragicus. Et hoc miles ut sapiens locutus est. ergo meminisse
> conuenit ridiculas personas non omnino stultas et excordes induci
> a poetis comicis, nam nulla delectatio est, ubi omnino qui deluditur
> nihil sapit. Stultitia autem est in his quattuor modis: aut non uenire in
> mentem quod oportet aut si uenerit non tenere aut bonum consilium
> non admittere aut malum admittere. uide ergo, ut hoc, quod commode
> miles uiderat, non tenuerit totumque amiserit. hoc autem idcirco
> interposuit poeta, ut ostenderet, quid ueneni haberet assentatio, per
> quam non modo errantes decipiuntur ac praecipites eunt, uerum etiam
> sapientes interdum sanique euertuntur.

This line efficiently demonstrates the characters of the soldier and
Gnatho. It becomes realistic that the soldier can easily endure Phaedria
being preferred to himself, since he has always realized that she is
not in love with him. Because, if you delete this line, either Phaedria
has to be blocked out or the conclusion of the play becomes tragic as
a consequence of the soldier's grief. Here the soldier has spoken as a
perceptive man. So it is beneficial to keep in mind that ridiculous characters are not dramatized as stupid and blockheaded all the time by
comic poets. For there is no pleasure when the person being played is
a complete moron. Foolishness, in turn, operates in one of four ways:
(1) someone does not realize what is necessary; (2) they realize it but
do not act on it; (3) they fail to come up with a good idea; or (4) they
pursue a bad idea. You can therefore see here that what the soldier
had properly seen he does not grasp and fails completely. The poet has
inserted this to show the toxic effect of assent, through which not only
do those who stray get caught up and run straight on anyway, but even
those who remain perceptive and turn out to be sane.

While Donatus starts with Terence's technique, he develops his initial observation into a series of principles about how alert, sensible people still lapse into error.[44] That a flatterer like Gnatho leads otherwise smart and important people into ruin dominates ancient aphorisms about flattery. This analysis of flattery is similar to that of Plutarch and also explicitly a concern of Menander's play, the meager papyrus remains of which include this contribution along the same lines (the speaker and addressee are uncertain):

... εἷς ἐστιν, εἷς
δι' οὗ τὰ πάντ' ἀπόλωλε, τρόφιμε, πράγματα
ἄρδην. λέγω σ[......]ν· ὅσας ἀναστάτους
πόλεις ἑόρακα, τοῦτ' ἀπολώλεκεν μόνον
ταύτας ὃ νῦν διὰ τοῦτον ἐξεύρηκ' ἐγώ.
ὅσοι τύραννοι πώποθ', ὅστις ἡγεμὼν
μέγας, σατράπης, φρούραρχος, οἰκιστὴς τόπου,
στρατηγός—οὐ [...] ἀλλὰ τοὺς τελέως λέγω
ἀπολωλότας—νῦν τοῦτ' ἀνῄρηκεν μόνον,
οἱ κόλακες· οὗτοι δ' εἰσὶν αὐτοῖς ἄθλιοι.

There's a single man who wrought all this thorough destruction, master, I tell you .... All the cities I've seen wrecked, this one thing destroyed them. Because of him, I've discovered this one thing. Every dictator ever, any great commander, satrap, stationed officer, founding father, general—I'm talking specifically about those who got destroyed—this one thing ruined them: flatterers. They are the source of the misery.

Kolax 86–94 Sandbach = C190–199 Arnott =
Pernerstorfer 91–100[45]

The Greek and Latin traditions about the impact of flatterers have both commonalities and differences.[46] Donatus is at pains to show that a *miles gloriosus* is not exclusively a moron, but both traditions are primarily concerned with the

---

[44] On Donatus' technique, see Jakobi 1996:149–152; cf. Demetriou 2014:217–219, on Donatus' characterization of Thraso's misuse of language in character as stupid, and Goldberg 1986:107–108.

[45] I follow Pernerstorfer's ἑόρακα, rather than ἑόρακας, in line 94.

[46] For a collection of variations on this theme, see Athenaeus 248d–262a, which collects a number of lines from comedies related to flattery: Cf. Diphilus fr. 23 (Athenaeus 6.254e) for a shorter version; Anaxilas fr. 32 at 254d; Anaxandrides fr. 43 at 255a; Alexis fr. 262 at 255b; Antiphanes fr. 200 (*Soldier*) at 257e; Antiphanes fr. 142 at 258d; Alexis fr. 233 at 258f; Eubulus fr. 25 at 260c–d; Anaxandrides fr. 50, Aristophanes fr. 172, and Sannyrio fr. 11 all at 261f; Philemon fr. 7, Philippides fr. 8, and Diphilus fr. 48 at 262a. Of Menander's *Kolax*, Athenaeus says only κεχαρακτήρικε δὲ ὡς ἔνι μάλιστα ἐπιμελῶς τὸν κόλακα Μένανδρος ἐν τῷ ὁμωνύμῳ δράματι, "Menander crafted the most indelible portrait of a flatterer in his play of that name" (6.257e); cf. Eupolis *Kolakes* fr. 172

victims of flattery. In this sense, the Greek comic generalizations square with Plutarch's moral analysis of flattery. Donatus' note veers into the same territory, focusing on the detrimental effect of flattery on even thoughtful people. Two things are worth emphasizing so far: for Menander, the soldier character is deeply embedded in dynamics about the flattery of accomplished and important people. The testimonia and reception of *Kolax* are consistent with this, and Terence to a degree carried it over into his *Eunuch*. The analogous didacticism in both the Latin and Greek traditions foretell the legacy the *miles gloriosus* character will have on Western theater.[47] Plautus provides paradigms of the exuberant idiocy of the character.[48] Terence and Menander, with the single paradigm of Bias/Thraso, embed the character in a dialogic matrix with moral lessons that will prove essential in using the character purposefully in later comedy.

That said, it is worth tracing further where Terence seems to depart from Menander's characterization of Bias and where he also makes use of the *miles gloriosus* as established by Plautus' day. The papyrus scraps recovered of the script of *Kolax* indicate, for example, the considerable wealth of the soldier Bias. Someone, quite likely Bias, has a notable reputation (δόξῃ μέγαν, 16 = B15 Arnott). In another sequence, although the lines are partial, Bias is explicitly mentioned, and the remains indicate a contrast between the drudgery of his previous military life and his current affluence (27–41 = B26–40 Arnott). As elsewhere, other characters do not assume the soldier has a good character, and the tale of Bias' good fortune elicits this diatribe from some character (46–53 = B45–53 Arnott):

ὀμνύω ...
. . . .
ἐβόων ἂν αὐτῷ παρακολουθῶν ἐν ἀγορᾷ·
"ἄνθρωπε, πέρυσι πτωχὸς ἦσθα καὶ νεκρός,
νυνὶ δὲ πλουτεῖς. λέγε, τίν' εἰργάζου τέχνην;
τοῦτο γ' ἀπόκριναι· πόθεν ἔχεις ταῦτ'; οὐκ ἄπει
... τί διδάσκεις κακά;
τί λυσιτελεῖν ἡμῖν ἀποφαίνεις τἀδικεῖν;"

---

for a precedent in Old Comedy. Plautus *Colax* fr. 63 Monda focuses on how flatterers deceive kings.

[47] See Guastella 2020, esp. 437 on the commedia dell'arte, and Franko 2020.

[48] See Feltovich 2020 on Pyrgopolynices as an archetype. On stock characters and stereotypes more generally, see O'Bryhim 2020.

I swear I'd follow him and shout out downtown, "Sir, a year ago you were nothing more than a beggar, the walking dead, but now you're rich! Explain: what job did you work so hard at? Answer that! Where did you get it from? ... Why must you be a lesson in evil? Why be an obvious lesson that crime pays?"

Another character, evidently a pimp, expresses his own anxiety about the money involved (128–132 = E 233–237 Arnott = 134–138 Pernerstorfer):

... ἢ μί᾽ ἐλάμβανεν
ὅσον οὐχὶ δέκα, τρεῖς μνᾶς ἑκάστης ἡμέρας
παρὰ τοῦ ξένου. δέδοικα δ᾽ οὕτω λαμβάνειν·
ἐκ τῆς ὁδοῦ γὰρ ἁρπάσονθ᾽, ὅταν τύχῃ,
αὐτήν. δικάσομαι, πράγμαθ᾽ ἕξω, μάρτυρας

The girl by herself brings almost as much as ten, three minas per day from the mercenary. I'm afraid of bringing in so much, because they'll kidnap her when there's a chance. I'll end up in court, a whole mess, witnesses ...

While Terence implies that his Thraso has considerable wealth, this becomes only a vehicle for his exploitation (see below), not an explicit cause of anxiety, as it appears to be in Menander's *Kolax*. Plutarch, however, may well be recalling the association of the soldier and his new wealth when he cites soldiers and the nouveaux riches together in the context of flattery (*Moralia* 547e, quoted above).

To step back to a broader perspective, the surviving scraps of the script of Menander's *Kolax* provide only limited testimony for how Menander handled the narrative trajectory of the soldier Bias. The consistent elements found in other Menander plays showcasing soldier characters make filling some gaps plausible, but the distinctiveness of the parasite-soldier pairing also makes reconstruction hazardous. Having the complete script of Terence's *Eunuch* is therefore extremely valuable and illuminating, yet anything but straightforward for understanding Menander. An analysis of Terence's play, in view of previous analyses of soldier narratives in Menander and Plautus, suggests in broad terms where Terence likely retained something of Menander's characterization, where he continued the tradition of Plautus, and where he put his own distinctive stamp on the resolution.

In Terence's *Eunuch*, the soldier Thraso has three scenes: (1) his dialogue with the parasite Gnatho, (2) an aborted domestic "siege" of Thais' brothel to kidnap the girl Pamphila, and (3) the resolution of the play where Thais and her lover Phaedria agree to allow Thraso to remain in Thais' company for exploitation. The first scene consists primarily of the flattery by Gnatho, as analyzed above. This flattery continues into the other two scenes at constantly shifting levels.

As Barsby observes of the siege scene, "in performance it must have been the visual highlight of the play" (1999:229).[49] Thraso leads a ragtag military offensive to lay siege to Thais' brothel with the goal of kidnapping Thais' "sister" Pamphila. Shortly thereafter, however, confronting the girl's brother, Chremes, and faced with the revelation that Pamphila is a freeborn Athenian citizen, Thraso withdraws. No comparable scene is well preserved among the remains of Menander's scripts, but it does seem that such a farcical siege took place in *Perikeiromene*, where the action was driven by the protagonist soldier Polemon trying to use his military prerogative to take possession of the woman he loves (see Chapter 3). Implicitly there is something of this desperation in Terence's scene, given Thraso's awareness of the unrequited passion he feels for Thais, but Terence contextualizes Thraso as an ultimately inept foreign invader, entirely congruent with the domination achieved by Roman-style protagonists in Plautus. As Thais says bluntly to Chremes, *sane quod tibi nunc vir videatur esse hic, nebulo magnus est / ne metuas*, "Truth is, while he might look like a man to you here, he is as mighty as mist. Don't be afraid." (785). Thraso is no real military threat.

The scene brings into conflict the desires and motivations of no fewer than four characters: Thais looks out for the interests of herself and her sister Pamphila. Gnatho wants to manipulate Thraso for his own benefit but, as Plutarch testifies explicitly in his citing of Gnatho's model Strouthias, becomes impatient in his dealings with Thraso. Thraso himself wants Thais and is actually more perspicacious (when not clouded by Gnatho's flattery) than Gnatho realizes. Finally, Chremes is Pamphila's brother and rightly proclaims her citizenship status, but he is insecure and ineffective when left to his own devices. Over the course of the fifty-line scene, two of these motivations win out: Pamphila's identity as an Athenian citizen trumps Thraso's desire and coincides with Thais' desire. Thraso's ineffectiveness as a soldier defuses the siege and leaves Chremes dominant in protecting his sister and Gnatho still needing a way to promote his own interests.

The subtlety Terence brings to the scene in part turns on the dynamic identified by Donatus, that Thraso is not a moron. Before even setting up the

---

[49] The entire scene is in emotional trochaic septenarii, but soldiers are generally nonmusical. Moore 2004:149 of *Poenulus*, observes, "Antamoenides, the other blocking character [than the pimp], is also disassociated with music." Cf. Moore 2012:258 that blocking characters generally do not sing. Prof. Moore kindly directed me to Collart 1970, which demonstrates that soldiers sing least of all characters.

siege, Thraso declares, *Mane / omnia prius experiri quam armis sapientem decet*, "Wait! Trying everything before weapons is the mark of the wise." (789–790). Indeed, in his limited way, Thraso is wise but misled by flattery, although his flatterer Gnatho is oblivious to this, as he rejoins sarcastically (and unhelpfully), *di vostram fidem!, / quantist sapere! numquam accedo quin abs te abeam doctior* "May the gods give me strength. What wisdom. I've never come near you without leaving wiser" (790–791).

Once Chremes and Thais have taken the sociopolitical high ground of defending Pamphila as a citizen, they exit the stage, leaving Thraso uncertain of what to do and vulnerable to Gnatho's manipulation. Gnatho immediately takes the opportunity to convince Thraso that the women will still succumb to Thraso's desire, and so Thraso assents to disbanding the makeshift army (811–815). Thus Thraso's military action faces defeat before a combination of civic righteousness and the weakest of Roman citizens, a prostitute and a hapless youth. Like other *milites gloriosi*, Thraso departs the stage defeated by Roman superiority.

For the last of Thraso's three scenes, the finale of the play, Thraso returns, desperate to surrender to Thais for whatever concessions that he can manage. Gnatho, as ever, works to manipulate Thraso to his own advantage by any opportunity he can pursue. As happens repeatedly in the play, Thraso plunges ahead, while Gnatho in frustration tries to find a way to turn the situation to his advantage (Thraso enters determined to surrender to Thais, 1025–1026; Gnatho expresses his sarcastic frustration with Thraso's decision at 1027–1028). The reality of Pamphila's Athenian citizenship, however, allows for an ideologically approved resolution of the plot without a role for Thraso and Gnatho, as they soon recognize (1043). Again in desperation, Thraso implores Gnatho to negotiate some foothold, a dependency that Gnatho is finally happy to exploit (1054–1061).

Gnatho's, and Terence's, unorthodox solution has attracted and prompted much discussion and speculation.[50] Since the understanding seems to be that Thais and her young lover will allow Thraso some access to Thais so long as he is financially advantageous, an arrangement that in the context of Roman comedy, and largely in the cultural context of the Western tradition, remains unorthodox, what Terence meant to convey to his audience remains as intriguing as it does indeterminate. For purposes of the present study, however, there is a definite constant: the subordinate exploitation of the soldier Thraso. The shock

---

[50] See Victor 2012, who focuses on Gnatho's oratorical prowess in bringing about the resolution and Brown 2013, who uses *Eunuch* to illuminate Terence's distinct manipulation of the tradition of Greek New Comedy.

and challenge of the arrangement derives from the young male protagonist agreeing to it, that he will share possession of the object of his desire, who is a prostitute to begin with, with a foreign mercenary, even if only for purposes of extorting financial benefit. Even though, as Donatus says, Thraso is not entirely a moron, there is no particular sympathy or expression that he suffers disproportionately to his status and identity. Simply, as the young male protagonist lover states bluntly, "he deserves it" (*dignus est*, 1088; cf. Barsby 1999:280–288).

Thus again the tradition on the Roman stage hinges on the Roman audience feeling comfortably superior to the *miles gloriosus*, this empty foreign braggart. The complexity of Terence's Thraso, as identified by Donatus, spawned references and explication repeatedly over the centuries, while Plautus' Pyrgopolynices provided a paradigm of the exuberant blusterer ultimately brought low for his arrogance.[51] For all its subtleties and potential, this tradition remains distinct from the Greek tradition, at least as far as Menander is concerned. It is the legacy of Plautus and Terence, imbued with influences from later Greek and early Italian playwrights that are today impossible to measure, that makes the braggart soldier a long-running, successful character on stage, as Larry Gelbart's reflection at the start of chapter recognizes. Menander's tradition was one where the soldier was an earnest and troubled protagonist, whose troubles in one instance involved a manipulative flatterer, and his susceptibility to this flattery brought him at least partially in line with what would become the Roman tradition. It remains to offer final reflections, then, on what this recovered legacy of Menander's characterization of soldiers offers distinct from the Roman inheritance.

---

[51] See Derrin 2017 on early print references to Terence's Thraso, and generally Turner and Torello-Hill 2015, along with Feltovich 2020 (on Pyrgopolynices).

Epilogue

It happens all the time
Seek and ye shall find
Love in the age of war

Men without Hats, "Love in the Age of War,"
lyrics by Ivan Doroschuk

THE INTRODUCTION TO THIS STUDY briefly suggested that the dynamics and narrative trajectories of soldier characters in Menander's plays represent an untapped resource for using soldiers' experiences in Greek antiquity that could be informative and beneficial for veterans and their communities today. The body of this study began by situating Menander in the cultural and political context of his day to suggest what motives and aims he had in constructing his soldier narratives as he did. The last chapter ended with the somewhat different, yet interdependent, Greek and Roman traditions that each represent extrapolated moral codes from the dynamics of soldier characters in comic theater in the later centuries of the Roman empire.

To move along summarily and all too rapidly, after New Comedy enjoyed widespread viewing around the Roman empire, live theater was gradually demonized and theaters closed as Christians occupied seats of imperial power and reconfigured the cultural activities of the empire's communities. Menander, Plautus, and Terence became authors in books with unequal vitality in the late antique and medieval worlds. Menander's scripts ceased to be copied and preserved, so he remained an author of reputation more than direct citation and, when theater revived in Europe centuries later, Menander was recovered only as a shadow looming behind Plautus and Terence. It was the scripts of Plautus and Terence, therefore, which featured the characters who became the reference points for the braggart soldiers on stages in the theaters of Europe and beyond. Given Menander's indirect legacy, it was not illogical to impose on him antecedents of Pyrgopolynices and Thraso, thought to resemble them in all but superficial ways. It was not illogical, as portions of Menander's scripts became available once again, when faced with soldiers that bore deep traits that do not align with the familiar specimens of the *miles gloriosus*, to credit Menander with creative variation and departure from the norm. Not illogical, but, as it has turned out now that significant portions of his plays are available directly, wrong.

The more important result, however, is not negative, but positive. Reorienting the context for Menander's soldier characters and realigning the theatrical precedents he did draw on reveals a fascinating and rewarding theatrical tradition. Menander, as he did so often, absorbed the tragic tradition, in this case warriors who struggled and failed to return to domestic life successfully. Aligning this tradition with the marginalized mercenaries of his day, Menander addressed the tension surrounding militarized men without the concomitant bonds to their communities traditional in polis armies. He dramatized these men making choices to prioritize new opportunities for a sanctioned family life. These men, previously estranged by their own skill, now become accepted members of families and communities. In Plautus and Terence these men are figures to be mocked and dominated to soothe the anxieties of their audiences. For Menander's audiences, these men become neighbors, husbands, and citizens. Perhaps, just perhaps, during an era of much military frustration and upheaval across the Roman world and when, as archaeology suggests, images of Menander in private homes were as widespread as they ever were, this acceptance was a factor in the daughter of Poplius Claudius Thrasyboulos (see Introduction) finding it appropriate to join on her father's tombstone both his military career and his performance of the "wise" Menander.

To close this study, I offer snapshots of scenes from Menander that could spur productive conversations about struggles that some veterans, their loved ones, and their communities recognize. That Menander dramatizes these dynamics in a certain way does not mean that I expect individuals or groups to sanction or subscribe to Menander's resolution of these same conflicts. Indeed, I expect a healthy conversation would involve departing from some of paths Menander takes in favor of other avenues that Menander never pursues. But if starting with Menander's dramatization of issues assists anyone in finding new paths to a settled life that previously seemed beyond comprehension, this study of Menander will have achieved one of its most desired goals.

Toward this end, the following are notes on scenes in Menander's scripts that dramatize tensions beyond just the specific ones of his time and place. The Appendix merges these into a continuous performance script (on which see the introductory note there).

1. The opening tableaus of *Perikeiromene* or *Misoumenos*: The opening scenes of both plays, preserved rather differently in terms of their scripts and visual representations, offer depictions of analogous tensions. In both plays, a soldier

has fallen in love with a woman whom he reckons as a wife, although the marriage is not legally recognized where they reside. In both plays, the woman leaves him because of violence that she associates with his military past. In both plays, the soldier is desperate and confused about how to be reconciled to the woman. In both plays, the soldier has a loyal companion who supports him as a soldier and is suspicious of the woman. In very similar ways, then, both scenes set up a conflict about the soldier, in that he has a yearning for a stable, domestic, loving home life, which is eluding him, while he has support from a comrade aligned with his military prerogatives.

2. The opening tableau of *Aspis*: This is a vivid dramatization of the gap a departed soldier can leave in his household. In this case, a soldier is wrongly presumed dead, but no one in his home knows that. His friend grieves for the lost soldier and the prosperous life that he had anticipated once the soldier returned. The loss of the soldier also leaves his sister vulnerable to the unsavory behavior of others in the household. The damaged shield on stage thus stands for the missing soldier and a symbol of his (temporary) failure to serve and protect his family.

3. The public hearing in *Sikyonios*: This is the most difficult scene to perform for a modern audience, because many of the details are specific to the setting of the play and because the debate itself is reported indirectly, if dramatically. Nonetheless, more than any other surviving scene from Menander, this episode dramatizes the resentment sometimes felt by a soldier who is perceived and even demonized as an outsider. In this case, the soldier is proven to be a legitimate member of the community and the assembly supports his request to settle in a home with the woman he loves.

4. The confrontation in *Perikeiromene*: While the resolution of this play is somewhat fragmentary in the script, it remains the best and most explicit dramatization of resolving conflicts like those in the opening of this play and of the *Misoumenos*. Here the soldier and his future father-in-law confront directly the conflict between the soldier's military prerogatives and the commitments necessary for settled domestic life. I emphasize here that I do not expect anyone today involved in an analogous situation would find the resolution to this struggle to be as simple and quick as Menander portrays it. But I submit that there is something valuable in watching Menander dramatize in compressed form that there is a path to a healthy family life for all the individuals involved.

Finally, I have argued that Menander's political and ideological drive for these dramatizations lies rooted in his desire for stable Macedonian imperial control over his own home polis and people. Some, many even, will not find such motivation appealing, comforting, or even palatable. As theater has long demonstrated on stage, the goals and drives of human beings are rarely, if ever, simple and congruent with the easy desires of spectators and audiences. Nonetheless, Menander developed a uniquely creative style of theater that Greeks and others for centuries marveled at and appreciated. In recovering one rich vein in his creative mine, militarized citizens of the twenty-first century, who struggle with acceptance and integration into their communities as citizens, neighbors, and family members, can look to a tradition that was and is aware of them, a tradition hopeful of well-earned domestic peace, maybe even culminating in love in an age of war.

Appendix

A Performance Script Based on Fragmentary Menander Plays Featuring Soldier Characters

THIS APPENDIX OFFERS A performance script. The ideal performance would spur a conversation about the issues raised in this study, about the effects of combat experience on individuals as they subsequently adjust to civilian life, about how their relationships with their partners change, about how comrades and family respond to this adjustment, all in aspiration of the kind of dialogue that follows the performances by groups like Theater of War (theaterofwar.com) and the Warrior Chorus project (http://www.warriorchorus.org/).

This script differs from the ones in those projects in some significant ways. Those productions face the challenge of condensing longer works like the *Iliad*, *Odyssey*, or individual plays of Greek tragedy down into a compact yet coherent performance. The script here, by contrast, stitches together several scenes from different incomplete scripts to form a continuous, coherent performance. The sources are domestic comedies rather than epic or tragic dramas, and, while some of the issues raised are the same, the domestic scenes focus on different issues and their tone is often distinct. The hope is that these differences make the potential of this script beneficial exactly for these distinct differences. Moreover, any performers of this script can and should modify and enhance it for the individuals and communities who participate.

As anyone who has participated in live theater knows, for both performers and audience, delivering and absorbing a performance is a substantially different process from reflective analysis of a script and the related realia of a play. The fragmentary state of most of Menander's scripts, not to mention the relatively short life of Menander in modern performance on the stage, makes conveying his plays a daunting challenge even for specialized audiences, to say nothing of spectators new to them.

This particular script has been composed not primarily to showcase Menander, though I hope it does that, but to deliver economically the narrative patterns and dynamics that I hope this study has unpacked in his plays. This script knits together scenes from three different fragmentary plays in continuous form, taking advantage of repeated motifs in Menander's plays that make substituting one scene for another less disruptive than it might be for other plays and playwrights in other genres. I have endeavored to make everything here an honest and direct translation of what Menander wrote in his scripts, although inevitably, as with any author distant in time and culture, some embedded glossing is necessary (Parker 1992) as well as some elliptical condensing, since live performance does not permit external glossing and obscurity only impedes an audience engaging with what is already a challenging experience.

The script comprises four scenes: (1) the opening of *Aspis*, (2) the end of act 1 of *Perikeiromene*, (3) the opening sequence of *Misoumenos*, and (4) three snippets from the last half of *Perikeiromene*. The goal has been to present something of a continuous story across the scenes. Accordingly, characters have been streamlined and stabilized across the scenes, as described below.

Characters

PMC. Former Private Military Contractor: Menander's soldiers are all former militarized men who went on campaign for pay. While in modern terms they are called "mercenaries," this appellation calls to mind adventurers of a type that is not appropriate for Menander's characters in this vein. The proper modern analogy is the private military contractor, an individual who is paid for their role in a military campaign but is not a conscripted soldier or officer. PMCs face many of the same challenges and dangers as other military personnel, including struggles when they return to civilian life, but they are comparatively "invisible" culturally. It is one hope that linking their identity and experiences to the challenges dramatized in this venue gives them a voice. While this character has a different name in each of the three plays excerpted here, for ease of comprehension in performance he has only this label, PMC, in the script.

BUDDY. Consistently in Menander, the PMC character has a supportive male comrade. As with the PMC himself, this character has a different name in each of the three plays excerpted here, but for ease of comprehension in performance, he has only this name, Buddy, in the script.

DAVIS. In Scene 1, the soldier's comrade is an older man and mentor to PMC, somewhat different from BUDDY. In Greek his name is Daos, so I have given him the more accessible, but similar, name of Davis.

CREEPER. The evil uncle in the first scene is named Smikrines in Greek, and there is little subtlety to his rotten intentions, so I have named him accordingly.

GIRL. As with the PMC and BUDDY, this character has a different name in each of the three plays excerpted here, but for ease of comprehension in performance, she is labeled "Girl" in the script. Affectionate references, however, reflect the individual names (e.g. Glykera in *Perikeiromene* has a name that literally means "sweet," so PMC refers to her as "sweetheart" or "sweetie," where in the Greek he uses her name).

GIRLFRIEND. More than one different type of female companion and ally to the PMC's beloved is condensed here.

DADDY. Father of GIRL: The discovery of a character's true parents is a routine event in Menander's brand of comedy. In this script, the GIRL's father is Pataikos in Greek, but it easier for comprehension in real time just to refer to him by his relationship to the other characters, even when that relationship is not yet known.

SUPERVISING GODDESS. A recurring feature of Menander's comedy is a divine figure who conveys critical information to the play's audience. Parts of two such occurrences are excerpted in this script. The actor performing this role can also easily deliver the settings and transitions.

Scene 1: The Shield and the Homefront (*Aspis* 1–113)

A group of assistants enter the stage, setting up a number of items evidently captured on military campaign. While the treasure should be a source of prosperity, the mood is somber. The last item to be brought is a large shield which has been damaged, indeed buckled to the point that it would be unusable on the battlefield. An older man named DAVIS, visibly distraught, carefully sets up the shield up. He speaks to it heartbroken, as if the shield itself were its owner, who is now missing in action. CREEPER looms and reacts as DAVIS speaks.

DAVIS

What a day this is, my boy, nothing like I thought it would be, and I'd thought about it plenty: what I was expecting when we pursued this venture. I really thought you'd be back safe and honored from the campaign, and you'd be set for the rest of your life in style, with a title like general or consultant. And your sister, since she's the reason you went in the first place, so that you could provide for her until you came home, and she'd be married to a man you'd approve of. And then there's me. For my good service, I expected some rest from my long aches and pains in my old age. But as it is, you were snatched away, dead. I can't make sense of it. I was your mentor, young man, but I've come back, taking this shield, which didn't save you. You maintained it just fine often enough, though. You were a real man with a big soul, like no one else.

CREEPER steps up to talk to DAVIS. As will become clear, he has bad intentions, but he always tries (unsuccessfully) to come off as being caring and sympathetic.

CREEPER

What an unexpected twist of fate, Davis.

DAVIS

Awful.

CREEPER

What happened? How did he die?

DAVIS

For a soldier, the job is to find some way to survive. The road to destruction is wide open.

CREEPER

But explain it to me, Davis.

DAVIS

There's a river in Lycia, across the sea to the east, called the Xanthus. We saw plenty of action there, and had plenty of luck, too. The enemy had retreated and abandoned the field. But as things tend to be, it would have been helpful NOT to luck out. After a fall, you watch your step! Our attitude led us into the future with no discipline. A lot of us had left the barracks, looted the villages, wasting the crops, selling off prisoners of war. Everybody was making lots of money.

CREEPER

Great!

DAVIS

My charge collected some six hundred in gold, a real haul, and this whole crowd of prisoners you see around you here. He told me to sail over to Rhodes to a man he knows there to deliver them, and then to come back to him.

CREEPER

So what happened then?

DAVIS

I was going to head out at dawn, but on that very day—and the lookouts missed this—the enemy took position on a hill and waited. From some deserters they'd learned that our forces were all spread out. Later in the day the army was back in their tents from that rich land that was now stripped bare. What happened next was inevitable: most the men were partying ...

CREEPER

That's just terrible.

DAVIS

Yes, I think it was a surprise attack. I'd been gone for a day and it happened in the middle of the night, while I was patrolling the campground, guarding the prisoners and the money. I heard a ruckus, screams, running, shouting, the men calling out each other's names. That's how I heard what happened. But there was still some luck. There was a solid ridge up there, where we all crowded. They flowed in: the cavalry, guards, infantry, all wounded.

CREEPER

It was lucky for you that you'd been sent away earlier.

DAVIS

At dawn we threw up some defenses and waited. Those who'd been scattered in the raids I was talking about were now finding their way back to us. Three days later we started to move again. We'd gotten information that the Lycians were heading to their villages in the highlands to take their captives.

CREEPER

And you saw our man fallen among the dead?

DAVIS

It was impossible to identify him for sure. They'd been lying out there for three days and their faces were bloated.

CREEPER

Then how do you know?

DAVIS

He was lying there with his shield, all bashed up, which I think is why the enemy didn't just take it. Our helpful commander forbid individual cremations, seeing how much time it would take for each one, so he grouped all the remains together and burned them. He buried them as rapidly as possible and immediately broke camp. We slipped off down to Rhodes first, and then there we waited for some days, and sailed back here. Now you've heard the whole story.

CREEPER

You say you brought six hundred in gold?

DAVIS

Yes.

CREEPER

And some silver?

DAVIS

Forty pounds of it or less. Ready to inherit?

CREEPER

What? You think that's why I asked? God no.
And the rest was seized?

DAVIS

For the most part, except for what I grabbed at first. Some coats and cloaks are inside. You see the crowd here.

(*Indicating those who brought the shield and other items.*)

CREEPER

I don't care about that. He ought to be alive.

DAVIS

OUGHT to be ...

Let's go inside to report this miserable story to those who deserve the news least.

CREEPER

And then I'd like to talk to you, when you've got time.

(*to the audience*)

I think I'll go inside, too, to contemplate the gentlest way of getting a grip on them.

SUPERVISING GODDESS as LADY LUCK

(*to the audience*)

If something really bad had happened to these people, it wouldn't be proper for a goddess like me to follow up, but as it is, they just don't know the truth. They're wandering, lost. Pay attention and you'll get the real story: When the enemy's surprise attack happened, the PMC had a fellow soldier in his tent, and when the alarm kept sounding, the troops marched out, arming themselves with whatever they had nearby. That's how our man's comrade came marching out with the shield here [indicating the shield set up on stage]. He was killed immediately. The shield lay there on top of the young man's bloated corpse and our old friend here

[*indicates DAVIS*]

made his honest mistake. Our man marched out in someone else's equipment and ended up captured. He's alive and he'll end up safe back here before long. That's what you need to know about that for now ...

[*The play continues by focusing on the CREEPER's plot to marry the PMC's sister, so that he can inherit the property that the PMC brought back from his campaign. Eventually, the lost soldier returns alive, but very little of the script of that part of the play survives.*

So instead, we transition to another play, where another SUPERVISING GODDESS is again explaining some backstory to events on stage. In this play, the PMC has heard from his comrade BUDDY that his GIRL has been unfaithful, because BUDDY saw the GIRL and a young man in the neighborhood hugging and kissing. Upset at hearing this, PMC took the GIRL and forcibly cut off her hair, hence the title of the play, Perikeiromene, the Girl with Her Haircut. The GIRL as a result has moved in with a woman next door, who is the young man's mother by adoption. A SUPERVISING GODDESS now comes on stage to explain that not all is as it appears ...]

Scene 2: Her Hair Cut [*Perikeiromene* 121–190]

SUPERVISING GODDESS as IGNORANCE

The GIRL's DADDY had twin children, a boy and a GIRL, but their mother died in childbirth and he gave up the babies. An old woman found and raised them. A local wealthy woman who lives right here wanted a child, so she adopted the boy, but the old woman raised the GIRL herself. After some years, the war and trouble in town continued and the old wealthy woman was reduced to poverty. The little GIRL is all grown up now—she's the one you just saw—and this impulsive young PMC from Corinth fell in love with her. So the old woman gave the GIRL over to him as if she were her own daughter. Soon the old woman, yielding to the fact that she was heading toward the final turn in the road of her life, no longer hid what had happened, but told the GIRL, now a young woman, how she had come to have her. At the same time, she gave the girl what she had when she was found as a baby, and explained that the girl has a twin brother. The lady was thinking ahead about how human life works, and in case the girl might need assistance one day. She also saw that the brother was the GIRL's one true relative and thus set up protection against some unintended consequence that could happen because of ME, for I am the embodiment of IGNORANCE. She also saw that the boy was wealthy and partied, while the girl was young and attractive, and the PMC to whom she had entrusted the girl was, well, unreliable.

So the old woman died and the soldier bought this house here, not far away at all, so the GIRL lives in the same neighborhood as her brother, but she doesn't want to damage her brother's future when it appears so bright and he can enjoy his good luck, so she hasn't disclosed her identity. Quite accidentally she was spotted by him, though, and he's rather forward, if you know what I mean, so he's been intentionally hanging around her house. And it was late in the day, the GIRL was sending off an assistant on an errand, so when he saw her outside the entrance, he ran straight up and kissed her and hugged her. She recognized him as her brother, so she didn't run away, but that BUDDY guy saw the incident. He relayed the whole incident, how the boy said he'd like to see her again when she had time. The GIRL was standing there crying, because it was impossible for her to have the freedom to do that.

This was the spark that flamed up into what happened next, so that PMC went into a rage—well I actually pushed him to it, he's not really that kind of man—but it marks the beginning of revealing the rest, and so everyone will find what's rightfully theirs. So, if this upsets anyone and they think that it's dishonorable, change your mind. With god's help, the bad turns into the good it was destined to be. Spectators, goodbye, wish us well, and support the rest of the play.

BUDDY

(*to audience*)

Our violent warrior of just a little while ago, the one who can't let women keep their hair, is lying on the couch crying. I just found a breakfast that was made for him—his comrades are gathered around him for the same reason—so he can endure this time more easily. I guess because he can't get any news about what's happening, he sent me out to get him his dress uniform, which he doesn't need. He just wants me on a fool's errand.

GIRLFRIEND

(*enters, talking back into the house*)

Of course, dear, I'll go see ...

BUDDY

(*to audience*)

That's the girl's girlfriend. She's developing nicely, easy on the eyes. The ladies are living in style, looks like to me. I'll head over.

GIRLFRIEND

(*going to house next door, where the GIRL has retreated*)

I'll knock on the door. Don't see anyone outside. Poor thing, who's got a soldier for a man. No respect for rules, none of them. Can't trust 'em. Oh girlfriend, you poor thing.

(*keeps knocking*)

> Hey you!

(*to audience*)

> Oh, he'll be happy that she's crying when he finds out. It's just what he wanted. HEY! Listen to me!

Scene 3: A Man Wounded in Hatred (*Misoumenos* 1–100)

[*In the* Hair Cut, *the scene where the PMC comes out to talk to his BUDDY is missing, but this is a scene from another play, with a similar situation, in that the PMC's GIRL hates him, but in this case he does not know why. Here are the PMC and BUDDY together talking about the situation.*]

PMC

> O Night!

> Since you own the greatest share, among the gods, of Aphrodite, of sex, and it's in your shadows that the greatest erotic thoughts are spoken, then my question to you is: have you ever seen another human being more wretched? A lover more cursed by the stars? I'm standing at my own door now, in the alley, pacing up and down, both ways, until now, when you, Night, are nearly half complete. I could be asleep holding my beloved, since she's near me—just in there inside. I could, and I want to, like any totally crazy lover would, but I won't. But standing, shivering in the cold of the open winter sky is preferable, and talking to you ...

BUDDY

(*to audience*)

> Oh god, a night not fit for a dog, as they say, but my guy acts like it's midsummer and is pacing like a professor. He's not getting anywhere, either, except wasting time down the road of his life.

[*PMC keeps wandering as if sleepwalking. BUDDY tries to get his attention.*]

> Poor guy, why don't you just go to sleep? Your pacing rattles me. Or are you already asleep? Stop: if you're awake and can see me ...

PMC

(*finally noticing BUDDY*)

BUDDY, did YOU come out here? What do you want? Are you following orders? Not mine! Is this on your own initiative?

BUDDY

No, sleeping men give no orders.

PMC

Buddy, you're more like my personal guardian out here.

BUDDY

Just go inside now and count your blessings, sir.

PMC

Blessings? Some miracles! Buddy, I'm cursed! You just haven't had time to figure it out yet. You just got home yesterday but it's been forever for me.

BUDDY

When I left the camp and ventured out, you seemed in plenty good spirits. It was my assignment to bring back all the assets we acquired, so I was the last one back. But what's upsetting you?

PMC

It's pathetic. I'm being abused.

BUDDY

By who?

PMC

By that girl prisoner that I bought. I promised to set her free. I put her in charge of my house, provided her with a staff, money, clothes. I recognized her as my wife!

BUDDY

What? Your WIFE is abusing you?

PMC

I'm so embarrassed, but she's a real tiger.

BUDDY

Explain this to me.

PMC

She HATES me!

BUDDY

I think you have your magnet backwards. You're thinking crazy.

PMC

It's inhumane.

BUDDY

SHE is not the boss here! YOU figure out what YOU are going to do about this!

PMC

I actually have a plan. I'm standing here waiting for a thunderstorm tonight. Thunder, lightning, the whole works. Then I'll be lying in bed, holding her.

BUDDY

Say what?

PMC

I'll shout out, "Hey little girl, I have to go out to see Mr. So-and-So"—I'll make up something. Any woman hearing that will immediately say, "It's raining, you poor thing ... "

BUDDY

Oh yeah, that's going to happen.

PMC

(*fantasizing*)

"Please look at me, dearest. When you ignore me, it drives me to distraction, frenzy, pain, madness."

BUDDY

> You sad-ass. What?

PMC

(*still fantasizing*)

> "But if I hear just a few loving words, I'll sacrifice to every god there is."

BUDDY

> What's this strange trouble about, anyway? Can't say you're especially repulsive. Military pay doesn't work in your favor, but you're easy on the eyes. So find some other desirable girl your own age.

PMC

> Go to hell! We have to solve this. We must get to the cause of it!

BUDDY

> Women are polluted witches, sir, that's the root of it.

PMC

> Stop it!

BUDDY

> Sir, from what you're saying, she's just using you!

Scene 4: Her Hair Cut [*Perikeiromene* 467–525]

[*Now we return to the* Hair Cut. *Remember that the GIRL has never met her father. Next in this play, her DADDY shows up, but no one on stage realizes yet that they are father and daughter. Also in the meantime, the PMC, in desperation, has attempted a sort of military siege on the house to get his GIRL back, but his "army" consists of his BUDDY, a chef, and a prostitute, so it has not been successful. At this point in the play, the girl's DADDY is trying to calm down the PMC. DADDY will later be revealed as the PMC's father-in-law, but neither of them knows that yet.*]

DADDY

(*to PMC*)

> Leave here and sleep it off, my man. Let the fighting go. It's not healthy for you. I can talk to you now that you're not so drunk.

PMC

Less drunk? ... I barely had a drink! Damn. I knew all this was going to happen. I was charting my own course for the future.

DADDY

That's better. Let me convince you of something.

PMC

What are you going to tell me to do?

DADDY

Now you're asking the right questions, so I can tell you the rest.

BUDDY

(*to audience*)

Sound the alarm!

DADDY

(*to PMC*)

Send him inside and his whole "contingent," too.

BUDDY

(*to PMC*)

You're blowing the war! He'll end the campaign when victory is still in your grasp!

PMC

(*to BUDDY*)

Is the old guy here sabotaging me?

BUDDY

(*to PMC*)

HE'S not your commander!

DADDY

(*to BUDDY*)

Oh for god's sake, go away!

BUDDY

Fine, I'm gone.

(*To the prostitute*)

OK, missy, I bet you can still besiege an erect tower and march up some luscious squeezable territory ... hey, wait, where are you going, lady cocksucker? Embarrassed? What's it matter to you?

(*Exit chef and prostitute*)

DADDY

(*to PMC*)

If this has happened at all like you said it happened, soldier man, and she's really your wife—

PMC

How can you say that?

DADDY

It matters.

PMC

I treated her like my wife!

DADDY

Don't shout. Who betrothed her?

PMC

What do you mean? She did herself.

DADDY

That's fine. So maybe she liked you well enough and now she doesn't anymore. She left you because you weren't treating her right.

PMC

What? Not treating her right? That really hurts when you say that.

DADDY

You're in love. I truly understand that. So what you're doing now is brainless. Where are you hoping to get her? Where will you take her? She's in charge of her own life. There's only one remedy for someone suffering from love: persuasion.

PMC

But that guy seduced my girl and that was wrong!

DADDY

He was wrong, so present your case against him, if you can come around to a conversation. But if you use force, you'll lose your case. What he did wrong warrants a lawsuit, not physical punishment.

PMC

Not even now?

DADDY

Not even now.

PMC

I don't know what to say to her as a woman. I'll just choke. My sweetheart left me! She left me, my sweetheart. But if you think it can happen—you were close and you talked to her before often enough—go and get her to talk. Be my ambassador, please please.

DADDY

That actually sounds like a good idea to me. You're on to something there.

PMC

And you're really good with words ...

DADDY

Reasonably.

PMC

So PLEASE, you have to! My salvation depends on it. If I was ever wrong at all with her, if I don't keep trying my absolute loving best, if you could just see her when she's all made up—

DADDY

No need, really.

PMC

Oh god, you should just see her, you'd have pity on me.

DADDY

Oy.

PMC

Come over here. Her clothes. She looks stunning in one of these. You probably haven't seen her—

DADDY

I have.

PMC

And she's so tall, worth looking at just for that. But what am I doing? I'm droning on about her height. Oh god. My brain is a thunderstorm, teeming off the rails.

DADDY

No, it's OK.

PMC

You HAVE to see them! Come on over!

DADDY

Go on. I'll come in.

(*They exit inside.*)

Scene 5: *Perikeiromene* 708–724

[*The following scene is missing, but next we see the GIRL confront DADDY about the idea that somehow she was unfaithful, although (again) neither of them know yet that they are father and daughter.*]

GIRL

> ... so you think I left the house to shack up with that other man? I visited his mother! You think that I was trying to make him marry me? Because she would marry her rich son to me? Or to be his mistress? Wouldn't I try to hide that we were having an affair? He put me up in his father's house! You think he kept me there as his mistress? You think I'd be so stupid as to visit his mother, move in with his father, and have an affair with their son? What kind of slut do you take me for? How can you believe that of me?

DADDY

> In the name of god, I want everything you say to be true. I believe you!

GIRL

> Just go back anyway. Let HIM abuse some OTHER girl next time.

DADDY

> He didn't mean to ...

Scene 6: *Perikeiromene* 976–1025

[*In missing scene, DADDY and GIRL learn that they are father and daughter and the "other man" is her brother. But there is still the matter of whether PMC and GIRL will be reconciled or not. PMC, still desperate and now thinking that with these new discoveries he will never win favor again with his beloved, is in conversation with GIRLFRIEND.*]

PMC

> I'm going to strangle myself!

GIRLFRIEND

> Poor thing, no!

PMC

> What else can I do? How can I live without her? I'm cursed.

GIRLFRIEND

She'll come back to you ...

PMC

God, yeah right.

GIRLFRIEND

IF you'll conduct yourself in a less improper way ...

PMC

I'll keep trying, that's for sure.

GIRLFRIEND

Good.

PMC

That's incredibly good. Go on.

(*GIRLFRIEND exits*)

And I'll leave you to your reward tomorrow. But listen to something that I have to say.—She's already gone.—oimoi!—O my darling, you have complete power over me. You kissed your brother, not an adulterer. I did you wrong acting like a jealous, vengeful fury, drunk and insane. I just wanted to strangle myself. Only thing I got right.

(*GIRLFRIEND returns*)

Oh you're back, what is it?

GIRLFRIEND

Good news. She's coming back to you!

PMC

She's not just taunting me?

GIRLFRIEND

No, she definitely wants to come to you. She's putting on a dress that her father gave her. You have to get ready to celebrate quick!

PMC

God you're absolutely right! There's a chef in the house, so he can grill a pig!

GIRLFRIEND

What about everything else we need?

PMC

We'll deal with all that later. Just have him slaughter the pig—no, wait, I better do it myself. I'd better get a wreath from the altar so I perform the ritual right for the gods.

GIRLFRIEND

That'll be a better look for you anyway.

PMC

And get my sweetheart!

GIRLFRIEND

She's coming out with her father anyway.

PMC

Him, too? What should I do?

(*PMC runs off in a panic.*)

GIRLFRIEND

Oh dear, he ran away. I'll go in to try to help, too.

(*FATHER to GIRL, as they enter*)

I really like that you say you will reconcile with him. When you get lucky, you should make a fair settlement, that's how Greeks behave. Somebody needs to run, get that PMC quick!

(*PMC returns to stage.*)

I'm coming out! I was making a sacrifice. I was so happy when I heard my sweetheart found her family!

DADDY

That's good of you. Now listen to this: I am also giving you my blessing and permission to marry her formally.

PMC

I do.

FATHER

And I'll give you some money to settle down together.

PMC

You are kind and generous.

DADDY

From now on, son, no more playing the soldier, so you don't do anything rash again.

PMC

O great gods, just a little while ago I was about to die and then I act rashly again? I don't blame my sweetheart now. My beloved, just so we are reconciled.

GIRL

As it turned out, your lawless behavior ended up being the beginning of a good end to the story.

PMC

Yes!

GIRL

That's why in the end you are forgiven.

PMC

That is great to hear. Sir, please join me in celebrating.

Bibliography

Anderson, W. S. 1993. *Barbarian Play: Plautus' Roman Comedy*. Toronto.

Anhalt, E. K. 2018. *Enraged: Why Violent Times Need Ancient Greek Myths*. New Haven.

Apostolakis, K. 2014. "In the Twilight of Political Satire: Timocles and the Orators." In *Κωμικός Στέφανος: νέες τάσεις στην έρευνα της αρχαίας ελληνικής κωμωδίας*, ed. M. Tamiolaki, 103–124. Rethymnon.

Arnott, W. G. 1981. "Moral Values in Menander." *Philologus* 125:215–227.

———. 1996. *Alexis: The Fragments; A Commentary*. Cambridge Classical Texts and Commentaries 31. Cambridge.

———. 1997. "Further Notes on Menander's *Sikyonioi* (vv. 110–322)." *Zeitschrift für Papyrologie und Epigraphik* 117:21–43.

———. 2001. "Plautus' *Epidicus* and Greek Comedy." In Auhagen 2001:71–90.

———. 2004. "Alexis, New Comedy and Plautus' *Poenulus*." In Bair 2004:61–91.

———. 2010. "Middle Comedy." In Dobrov 2010:279–331.

Augoustakis, A., and A. Traill, eds. 2013. *A Companion to Terence*. Malden.

Auhagen, U., ed. 2001. *Studien zu Plautus'* Epidicus. Script Oralia 125. Tübingen.

Avramović, S. 2015. "Legal Standing and Civic Identity of Athenian Mercenaries: A Case Study." *Anali Pravnog fakulteta u Beogradu* (= *Annals of the Faculty of Law in Belgrade*) 63.3. https://anali.rs/legal-standing-and-civic-identity-of-athenian-mercenaries-a-case-study/.

Bair, T., ed. 2004. *Studien zu Plautus'* Poenulus. Script Oralia 127. Tübingen.

Baragwanath, E. 2019. "Heroes and Homemakers in Xenophon." In *The Epic Journey in Greek and Roman Literature*, Yale Classical Studies 49, ed. T. Biggs and J. Blum, 108–129. Cambridge.

Barigazzi, A. 1965. *La formazione spirituale di Menandro*. Turin.

Barsby, J. 1986. *Terence. Eunuch*. Warminster.

———. 1993. "Problems of Adaptation in the *Eunuchus* of Terence." In *Intertextualität in der griechisch-römischen Komödie*, ed. N. W. Slater and B. Zimmermann, 160–179. Stuttgart.

———. 1999. *Terence. Eunuchus*. Cambridge.

———. 2004. "Actors and Act-Divisions in *Poenulus* and Its Greek Original." In Bair 2004:93–111.

Bassett, S. E. 2008. "The Late Antique Image of Menander." *Greek, Roman, and Byzantine Studies* 48:201–225.

Bayliss, A. J. 2011. *After Demosthenes: The Politics of Hellenistic Athens*. London.

Beek, A. 2020. "Mercenaries and Moral Concerns." In *Greek and Roman Military Manuals: Genre, Theory, Influence*, ed. C. Whately and J. Chlup, 121–135. New York.

Belardinelli, A. M. 1994. *Menandro. Sicioni*. Bari.

Berthaume, G. 1982. *Les rôles du mágeiros*. Leiden.

Bettali, M. 2013. *Mercenari: Il mestiere delle armi nel mondo Greco antico*. Saggi.

Biers, W. R. 1985. "Culinary Chaos: A Scene from New Comedy." *Antike Kunst* 28:40–44.

Billings, J. 2014. *Genealogy of the Tragic: Greek Tragedy and German Philosophy*. Princeton.

Blanchard, A. 2014. "Reconstructing Menander." In Fontaine and Scafuro 2014:239–257.

Blume, H. D. 2001. "Komische Soldaten: Entwicklung und Wandlung einer typischen Bühnenfigur in der Antike." In *Rezeption des antiken Dramas auf der Bühne und in der Literatur*, ed. B. Zimmermann, 1751–1795. Stuttgart.

Börm, H. and N. Luraghi, eds. 2018. *The Polis in the Hellenistic World*. Stuttgart.

Bosworth, A. B. 1980. *A Historical Commentary on Arrian's History of Alexander I*. Oxford.

Boulay, T. 2014. *Arès dans la cité: Les poleis et la guerre dans l'Asie Mineure hellénistique*. Studi ellenistici 28. Pisa.

Bowie, E. L. 1988. "Who Is Diceaopolis?" *Journal of Hellenic Studies* 108:183–185.

Brown, P. 2013. "Terence and Greek New Comedy," in Augoustakis and Traill 2013:15–32.

Brown, P. G. McC. 2004. "Soldiers in New Comedy: Insiders and Outsiders." *Leeds International Classical Studies* 3.08:1–16.

Bulloch, A., E. S. Gruen, A. A. Long, and A. Stewart, eds. 1993. *Images and Ideologies: Self-Definition in the Hellenistic World*. Berkeley.

Burton, P. J. 2020. "Warfare and Imperialism in and around Plautus." In Franko and Dutsch 2020:301–316.

Cambitoglou, A., C. Aellen, and J. Charnay. 1986. *Le Peintre de Darius et son Milieu*. Hellas et Roma 4. Geneva.

Cameron, A. 1970. *Agathias*. Oxford.

Carey, C. 2015. "Menander on the Poetics of Comedy." In Green and Edwards 2015:13–25.

Carter, D. M., ed. 2011. *Why Athens?: A Reappraisal of Tragic Politics*. Oxford.

Cary, M. 1951. *A History of the Greek World from 323 to 146 BC*. 2nd ed. London.

Casanova, A. 2005. "Plutarco e Menandro." In *Plutarco e l'età ellenistica*, ed. A. Casanova, 105–118. Florence.

Casson, L. 1976. "The Athenian Upper Class and New Comedy." *Transactions of the American Philological Association* 106:29–59.

Caston, V., and S.-M. Weineck, eds. 2016. *Our Ancient Wars: Rethinking War through the Classics*. Ann Arbor.

Charitonidis, S., L. Kahil, and R. Ginouvès. 1970. *Les mosaïques de la maison du Ménandre à Mytilène*. Antike Kunst Beiheft 6. Bern.

Christenson, D., ed. 2000. *Plautus. Amphitruo.* Cambridge.

———. 2020. "*Novo modo nouom aliquid inventum*: Plautine Priorities." In Franko and Dutsch 2020:77–91.

Cinaglia, V. 2015. *Aristotle and Menander on the Ethics of Understanding.* Leiden.

Cole, E. 2019. "Post-Traumatic Stress Disorder and the Performance Reception of Sophocles' *Ajax*." In *Looking at Ajax*, ed. D. Stuttard, 151–160. London.

Collart, J. 1970. "Le soldat qui ne chante pas (quelques remarques sur le rôle du miles chez Plaute)." In *Mélanges Marcel Durry* (= *Revue des études latines* 47 bis), 199–208. Paris.

Constantinides, E. 1969. "Timocles' *Ikarioi Satyroi*: A Reconsideration." *Transactions of the American Philological Association* 100:49–61.

Cox, C. 2013. "Coping with Punishment: The Social Networking of Slaves in Menander." In *Slaves and Slavery in Ancient Greek Comic Drama*, ed. B. Akrigg and R. Tordoff, 159–172. Cambridge.

Crowley, J. 2014. "Beyond the Universal Soldier: Combat Trauma in Classical Antiquity." in Meineck and Konstan 2014:105–30.

Csapo, E. 1999. "Performance and Iconographic Tradition in the Illustrations of Menander." *Syllecta Classica* 10:154–188.

———. 2010. *Actors and Icons of the Ancient Theater.* Chichester.

Csapo, E., H. R. Rupprecht Goette, J. R. Green, and P. Wilson, eds. 2014. *Greek Theatre in the Fourth Century B.C.* Berlin.

Csapo, E., and P. Wilson. 2015. "Drama outside Athens in the Fifth and Fourth Centuries BC." In Lamari 2015:316–395.

Cusset, C. 2003. *Ménandre ou la comédie tragique.* Paris.

———. 2015. "Ménandre: une comédie sans carnaval ni politique?" In *Carnaval et comédie: Actes du colloque international organisé par l'équipe PLH-CRATA, 9–10 décembre 2009, Université de Toulouse Le Mirail*, ed. M. Bastin-Hammou and C. Orfanos, 161–177. Besançon.

de Marcellus, H. 1996. "IG XIV 1184 and the Ephebic Service of Menander." *Zeitschrift für Papyrologie und Epigraphik* 110:69–76.

De Melo, W. D. C. 2014. "Plautus' Dramatic Predecessors and Contemporaries in Rome." In Fontaine and Scafuro 2014:447–461.

Demetriou, C. 2014. "Performing Terence's Characters: A Study of Donatus' Interpretation." In *Terence and Interpretation*, Pierides Studies in Greek and Latin Literature 4, ed. S. Papaioannou, 223–239. Newcastle upon Tyne.

Derrin, D. 2017. "Crackinge Thraso: The Braggart Soldier Image in Sixteenth-Century Sermons and Religious Polemic." *English Studies* 98.7:704–716.

Ditadi, G., ed. 2005. *Teofrasto: Della Pietà*. Este.

Dobrov, G., ed. 2010. *Brill's Companion to the Study of Greek Comedy*. Leiden.

Doerries, B. 2015. *The Theater of War: What Ancient Greek Tragedies Can Teach Us Today*. New York.

Dohm, H. 1964. *Mageiros: Die Rolle des Kochs in der griechisch-römischen Komödie*. Munich.

Duckworth, G. E. 1940. *Plauti Epidicus*. Princeton.

———. 1952. *The Nature of Roman Comedy: A Study in Popular Entertainment*. Princeton.

Dunbabin, K. M. D. 2016. *Theater and Spectacle in the Art of the Roman Empire*. Ithaca, NY.

Duncan, A. 2015. "Political Re-Performances of Tragedy in the Fifth and Fourth Centuries BC." In Lamari 2015:297–315.

Dunn, F. 2020. "Affective Suspense in Euripides' *Electra*." In Marshall and Marshall 2020:73–86.

English, S. 2012. *Mercenaries in the Classical World to the Death of Alexander the Great*. Barnsley.

Fantham, E. 1984. "Roman Experience of Menander in the Late Republic and Early Empire." *Transactions of the American Philological Association* 114:299–309.

Fantuzzi, M., and D. Konstan. 2013. "From Achilles' Horses to a Cheese-Seller Shop: On the History of the Guessing Game in Greek Drama." In *Greek Comedy and the Discourse of Genres*, ed. E. Bakola, L. Prauscello, and M. Telò, 256–274. Cambridge.

Feeney, D. C. 2016. *Beyond Greek: The Beginnings of Latin Literature*. Cambridge, MA.

Feltovich, A. 2020. "Archetypal Character Studies: Masculinity and Power." In Franko and Dutsch 2020:179–191.

Ferrari, F. 1996. "La Maschera negata: Riflessioni sui personaggi di Menandro." *Studi classici e orientali* 46:219–251.

Fittschen, K. 1991. "Zur Rekonstruktion griechischer Dichter Statuen, 1. Teil: Die Statue des Menander." *Athenische Mitteilungen* 106:243–279.

Fontaine, M. 2010. "*Colax Menandrist...*" Review of *Menanders Kolax: Ein Beitrag zu Rekonstruktion und Interpretation der Komödie*, by M. J. Pernerstorfer. *Classical Review* 60:379–380.

———. 2014a. "Between Two Paradigms: Plautus." In Fontaine and Scafuro 2014:516–537.

———. 2014b. "The Reception of Greek Comedy in Rome." In Revermann 2014:404–423.

Fontaine, M., and A. C. Scafuro, eds. 2014. *The Oxford Handbook of Greek and Roman Comedy*. Oxford.

Fortenbaugh, W. W. 1981. "Theophrast über den komischen Charakter." *Rheinische Museum für Philologie* 124:246–260.

Fox, R. L., ed. 2004. *The Long March: Xenophon and the Ten Thousand*. New Haven.

Fraenkel, E. 2007. *Plautine Elements in Plautus*. Trans. F. Muecke and T. Drevikovsky. Oxford.

Franko, G. F. 1996. "The Characterization of Hanno in Plautus' *Poenulus*." *American Journal of Philology* 117:425–452.

———. 2020. "Plautus in Early Modern England." In Franko and Dutsch 2020:445–459.

Franko, G. F. and D. Dutsch, eds. 2020. *A Companion to Plautus*. Malden.

Funke, M. 2016. "The Menandrian World of Alciphron's Letters." In *Athenian Comedy in the Roman Empire*, ed. C. W. Marshall and T. Hawkins, 223–238. London.

Furley, W. 2015. "The Text and Staging of the Recognition Scene in Menander's *Perikeiromene*." In Green and Edwards 2015:31–43.

Gaiser, K. 1967. "Menander und der Peripatos." *Antike und Abendland* 13:8–40.

Gelbart, L. 1991. Introduction to *A Funny Thing Happened on the Way to The Forum*, by B. Shevelove, L. Gelbart, and S. Sondheim, 1–10. New York.

Germany, R. 2013. "*Andria*." In Augoustakis and Traill 2013:225–242.

Giglioni, G. B. 1984. *Menandro o La politica della convivenza: La storia attraverso i testi letterari*. Biblioteca di Athenaeum 3. Como.

Gold, B. K. 2020. "The Wife in Charge, the Husband Humiliated: Stock Characters in Evolution." In Franko and Dutsch 2020:165–178.

Goldberg, S. 1986. *Understanding Terence*. Cambridge.

———. 2005. *Constructing Literature in the Roman Republic*. Cambridge.

Gomme, A.W. and F.H. Sandbach. 1973. *Menander: A Commentary*. Oxford.

Gonçalves, R. T. 2020. "Reception Today: Movies and Theater." In Franko and Dutsch 2020:461–471.

Gordon, R. 2014. "'Old Situations, New Complications': Tradition and Experiment in *A Funny Thing Happened on the Way to the Forum*." In *The Oxford Handbook of Sondheim Studies*, ed. R. Gordon, 63–80. Oxford.

Gould, T. 2009. "Comedy." In *The Oxford Handbook of Philosophy and Literature*, ed. R. Eldridge, 95–116. Oxford.

Green, P. 1990. *Alexander to Actium: The Historical Evolution of the Hellenistic Age*. Berkeley.

Green, R. and M. Edwards, eds. 2015. *Images and Texts: Papers in Honour of Professor Eric Handley CBE FBA*. Bulletin of the Institute of Classical Studies: Supplement 129. London.

Griffith, G. T. 1935. *The Mercenaries of the Hellenistic World*. Chicago.

Grimal, P. 1968. "Le *Miles Gloriosus* et la vieillesse de Philemon." *Revue des études latines* 46:129–144.

Grossmann, G. 1968. "Das Lachen des Aias." *Museum Helveticum* 25:65–85.

Groton, A. H. 1987. "Anger in Menander's *Samia*." *American Journal of Philology* 108:437–443.

———. 2020. "To Name or Not to Name? New Comedy's Answer to a Very Old Question." *Classical Journal* 116:241–248.

Guastella, G. 2020. "From Ferrara to Venice: Plautus in Vernacular and Early Italian Comedy (1486–1530)." In Franko and Dutsch 2020:429–443.

Gutzwiller, K. 2012. "All in the Family: Forgiveness and Reconciliation in New Comedy." In *Ancient Forgiveness: Classical, Judaic, Christian*, ed. C. Griswold and D. Konstan, 48–75. Cambridge.

Gutzwiller, K. and Ö. Çelik. 2012. "New Menander Mosaics from Antioch." *American Journal of Archaeology* 116:573–623.

Habicht, C. 1993. "The Comic Poet Archedikos." *Hesperia* 62:253–256.

———. 1997. *Athens from Alexander to Antony*. Trans. D. Schneider. Cambridge, MA.

Hale, J. 2013. "Not Patriots, Not Farmers, Not Amateurs: Greek Soldiers of Fortune and the Origin of Hoplite Warfare." In *Men of Bronze: Hoplite Warfare in Ancient Greece*, ed. D. Kagan and G. F. Viggiano, 176–193. Princeton.

Handley, E. W. 1965. *The Dyskolos of Menander*. London.

Hanink, J. 2014a. *Lycurgan Athens and the Making of Classical Tragedy*. Cambridge.

———. 2014b. "Literary Evidence for New Tragic Production: The View from the Fourth Century." In Csapo, Rupprecht Goette, Green, and Wilson 2014:189–206.

Hansen, M. H. 1986. *Demography and Democracy: The Number of Athenian Citizens in the Fourth Century B.C.* Herning.

Hanson, J. A. 1964. "The Glorious Military." In *Roman Drama: Studies in Latin Literature and Its Influence*, ed. T. A. Dorsey and D. R. Dudley, 61–66. London.

Hanson, V. D. 1989. *The Western Way of War: Infantry Battle in Classical Greece.* New York.

Harding, P. E. 2015. *Athens Transformed, 404-262 BC.* London.

Hartwig, A. 2014. "The Evolution of Comedy in the Fourth Century." In Csapo, Rupprecht Goette, Green, and Wilson 2014:207–230.

Heap, A. M. 2019. *Behind the Mask: Character and Society in Menander.* London.

Henderson, J. J. 1990. "The *Dêmos* and the Comic Competition." In Winkler and Zeitlin 1990:271–313.

———. 2014. "Comedy in the Fourth Century II: Politics and Domesticity." In Fontaine and Scafuro 2014:181–198.

Henrichs, A. 1993. "The Case of Menander: A Crisis of Identity?" In *Images and Ideologies: Self-Definition in the Hellenistic World*, ed. A. Bulloch, E. S. Gruen, A. A. Long, and A. Stewart, 180–187. Berkeley.

Henry, W. B. 2014. "5198: Menander, *Misoumenos* 123-54 Sandbach/523-34 Arnott + 5198: Menander, *Misoumenos* 352-65 Sandbach/753-66 Arnott + 5200: Menander, *Perikeiromene* 540-41 Sandbach/523-34." *Oxyrhynchus Papyri* 79:97–115.

Hunter, R. 1985. *The New Comedy of Greece and Rome.* Cambridge.

———. 2003. *Theocritus and the Archaeology of Greek Poetry.* Cambridge.

Hurst, A. 1990. "Ménandre et la tragédie." In *Relire Ménandre*, Recherches et rencontres 2, ed. E. W. Handley and A. Hurst, 93–122. Geneva.

———. 1992. "Ménandre incompris?" *Actes du XXIVème congrès international de l'APLAES, Tours*, 45–60.

———. 2010-2011. "Ménandre et le méchant légaliste." *Hyperboreus* 16–17 (= *Festschrift Alexandre Gavrilov*):281–289.

———. 2015. *Dans les marges de Ménandre.* Recherches et rencontres 33. Geneva.

Iapichino, L. 1999. "I diecimila di Senofonte: Tecniche di combattimento, equipaggiamento militare e approvvigionamento degli strumenti di guerra." *Rivista storica dell' antichità* 29:91–105.

Ireland, S. 2010. "New Comedy." In Dobrov 2010:333–396.

Iversen, P. A. 2010a. "P. Oxy. X 1235, Lachares 'The Tyrant,' and Menander's *Imbrioi.*" http://dx.doi.org/10.2139/ssrn.1605346.

———. 2010b. "Was Menander a Democrat?" Paper presented at Annual Meeting of the American Philological Association, Anaheim, CA, January 7, 2010.

———. 2011. "Menander's Thaïs: '*Hac primum iuvenum lascivos lusit amores.*'" *Classical Quarterly*, n.s., 61:186–191.

Jacob, C. 2013. *The Web of Athenaeus*. Trans. A. Papaconstantinou. Hellenic Studies 61. Washington, DC.

Jakobi, R. 1996. *Die Kunst der Exegese im Terenzkommentar des Donat*. Berlin.

James, S. L. 2014. "The Battered Shield: Survivor Guilt and Family Trauma in Menander's *Aspis.*" in Meineck and Konstan 2014:237–260.

———. 2020. "Plautus and the Marriage Plot." In Franko and Dutsch 2020:109–121.

Jendza, C. 2020. *Paracomedy: Appropriations of Comedy in Greek Tragedy*. Oxford.

Johnson, O. 2018. *Ruins: Classical Theater and Broken Memory*. Ann Arbor.

Jones, A. H. M. 1957. *Athenian Democracy*. Oxford.

Kaldellis, A. 1999. "The Historical and Religious Views of Agathias: A Reinterpretation." *Byzantion* 69:206–252.

Katsouris, A. G. 1975. *Tragic Patterns in Menander*. Athens.

Konstan, D. 1995. *Greek Comedy and Ideology*. Oxford.

———. 2010. "Ridiculing a Popular War: Old Comedy and Militarism in Classical Athens." In *War, Democracy and Culture in Classical Athens*, ed. D. Pritchard, 184–200. Cambridge.

———. 2013. "Menander's Slaves: The Banality of Violence." In *Slaves and Slavery in Ancient Greek Comic Drama*, ed. B. Akrigg and R. Tordoff, 144–158. Cambridge.

———. 2014. "Crossing Conceptual Worlds: Greek Comedy and Philosophy." In Fontaine and Scafuro 2014:278–294.

Konstan, D. and M. Dillon. 1981. "The Ideology of Aristophanes' *Wealth.*" *American Journal of Philology* 102:371–394.

Konstantakos, I. M. 2008. *"Rara coronato plausere theatra Menandro?* Menander's Success in His Lifetime." *Quaderni urbinati di cultura classica* 88:79–106.

———. 2011. "Ephippos' *Geryones:* A Comedy between Myth and Folktale." *Acta Antiqua Academiae Scientiarum Hungaricae* 51:223–246.

———. 2015a. "Machon's Alexandrian Comedy and Earlier Comic Tradition." *Aevum* 89:13–36.

———. 2015b. "On the Early History of the Braggart Soldier. Part One: Archilochus and Epicharmus." *Logeion* 5:41–84.

———. 2016. "On the Early History of the Braggart Soldier. Part Two: Aristophanes' Lamachus and the Politicization of the Comic Type." *Logeion* 6:112–163.

Kyriakou, P. 2018. *Theocritus and His Native Muse: A Syracusan among Many.* Trends in Classics Supplement 71. Berlin.

Kyrkou, T. 2007. "Η έπαυλη του Μάνιου Αντωνίνου στη Νικόπολη: Παρατηρήσεις σε ένα σύνολο ιδιωτικής κατοικίας στη Νικόπολη." In *ΝΙΚΟΠΟΛΙΣ Β΄: Πρακτικά του Δευτέρου Διεθνούς Συμποσίου για τη Νικόπολη (11-15 Σεπτεμβρίου 2002),* ed. N. D. Karabelas & M. Stork, 1.333-345. Preveza.

Lamagna, M. 2014. "Military Culture and Menander." In Sommerstein 2014:58–71.

Lamari, A., ed. 2015. *Reperformances of Drama in the Fifth and Fourth Centuries BC: Authors and Contexts.* Trends in Classics 7.2. Berlin.

———. 2017. *Reperforming Greek Tragedy: Theater, Politics, and Cultural Mobility in the Fifth and Fourth Centuries BC.* Berlin.

Lape, S. 2004. *Reproducing Athens: Menander's Comedy, Democratic Culture, and the Hellenistic City.* Princeton.

Lauriola, R. 2009. "The Greeks and the Utopia: An Overview through Ancient Greek Literature." *Revista Espaço Acadêmico* 97:109–124.

Leach, E. W. 1979. "The Soldier and Society: Plautus' *Miles Gloriosus* as Popular Drama." *Rivista di studi classici* 28:185–209.

Lefèvre, E. 1991. *Plautus barbarus: Sechs Kapitel zur Originalität des Plautus.* Script Oralia 25. Tübingen.

———. 2011. *Plautus'* Bacchides. Script Oralia 138. Reihe A: Altertumswissenschaftliche Reihe, Bd 40. Tübingen.

Leonard, M. 2015. *Tragic Modernities.* Cambridge, MA.

Loman, P. 2006. "Mercenaries, Their Women and Colonisation." *Klio* 87:346–365.

Lowe, J. B. 1985. "Cooks in Plautus." *Classical Antiquity* 4:72–102.

———. 1987. "Tragic Space and Comic Timing in Menander's *Dyskolos.*" *Bulletin of the Institute of Classical Studies* 34:126–138.

———. 2001. "Greek and Roman Elements in *Epidicus'* Intrigue." In Auhagen 2001:57–70.

Luppe, L. 1993. "Nochmals zur 'Imbroi'-Didaskalie." *Zeitschrift für Papyrologie und Epigraphik* 96:9–10.

Luraghi, N. 2006. "Traders, Pirates, Warriors: The Proto-History of Greek Mercenary Soldiers in the Eastern Mediterranean." *Phoenix* 60:21–47.

———. 2012. "Commedia e politica tra Demostene e Cremonide." In *La commedia greca e la storia: Atti del Seminario di studio Urbino, 18-20 maggio 2010,* ed. F. Perusino and M. Colantonio, 353–375. Florence.

Luria, S. 1965. "Menander kein Peripatetiker und kein Feind der Demokratie." In *Menanders* Dyskolos *als Zeugnis seiner Epoche,* Schriften der Sektion für Altertumswissenschaft 50, ed. F. Zucker, 3–31. Berlin.

Lynch, J. P. 1972. *Aristotle's School: A Study of a Greek Educational Institution.* Berkeley.

Ma, J. 2004. "You Can't Go Home Again: Displacement and Identity in Xenophon's *Anabasis.*" In Fox 2004:330–345.

MacCary, W. T. 1972. "Menander's Soldiers: Their Names, Roles, and Masks." *American Journal of Philology* 93:279–298.

MacDowell, D. M. 1990. "The Meaning of ἀλαζών." In *"Owls to Athens": Essays on Classical Subjects Presented to Sir Kenneth Dover,* ed. E. Craik, 287–292. Oxford.

Major, W. E. 1997. "Menander in a Macedonian World." *Greek, Roman, and Byzantine Studies* 38:41–73.

———. 2004. Review of *Reproducing Athens: Menander's Comedy, Democratic Culture, and the Hellenistic City*, by S. Lape. https://bmcr.brynmawr.edu/2004/2004.06.39/.

———. 2006. "Aristophanes and *Alazoneia*: Laughing at the Parabasis of the *Clouds*." *Classical World* 99:131–144.

———. 2013. *The Court of Comedy: Aristophanes, Rhetoric, and Democracy in Fifth-Century Athens*. Columbus.

Mann, C. and P. Scholz, eds. 2011. *"Demokratie" im Hellenismus: Von der Herrschaft des Volkes zur Herrschaft der Honoratioren?* Die hellenistische Polis als Lebensform 2. Berlin.

Manuwald, G. 2004. "Die ungleichen Schwestern in Plautus' *Poenulus*." In Bair 2004:215–233.

———. 2011. *Roman Republican Theater*. Cambridge.

Marasco, G. 1984. *Democare di Leuconoe: Politica e cultura in Atene fra IV e III sec. a.c.* Studi e testi 4. Florence.

Marinovič, L. P. 1992. *Le mercenariat grec au ive siècle avant notre ère et la crise de la polis.* Trans. Jacqueline et Yvon Garlan. Paris. Orig. pub. 1975.

———. 1989. "Les mercenaires de la guerre lamiaque." *Dialogues d'histoire ancienne* 15.2:97–105.

Marshall, C. W. 2006. *The Stagecraft and Performance of Roman Comedy*. Cambridge.

Marshall, H. and C. W. Marshall, eds. 2020. *Greek Drama V: Studies in the Theatre of the Fifth and Fourth Centuries BCE.* London.

Mason, H. J. 2002. "Chaireas in Chariton and New Comedy." *Classical Bulletin* 78:21–27.

Mastromarco, G. 2009. "La Maschera del Miles Gloriosus dai Greci a Plaut." In *Lecturae Plautinae Sarsinates XII:* Miles Gloriosus, ed. R. Raffaelli and A. Tontoni, 17–40. Urbino.

May, R. 2005. "'The Rape of the Locks': Cutting Hair in Menander's *Perikeiromene*." *Spudasmata* 102:275–289.

McKechnie, P. 1989. *Outsiders in the Greek Cities in the Fourth Century B.C.* London.

———. 1994. "Greek Mercenary Troops and Their Equipment." *Historia* 43:297–305.

Meineck, P. 2009. "'These are Men Whose Minds the Dead Have Ravished': Theater of War / The Philoctetes Project." *Arion* 17:173–191.

———. 2012. "Combat Trauma and the Tragic Stage: 'Restoration' by Cultural Catharsis." *Intertexts* 16:7–24.

———. 2016. "Combat Trauma and the Tragic Stage: Ancient Culture and Modern Catharsis?" In *Our Ancient Wars: Rethinking War through the Classics*, ed. V. Caston and S-M. Weineck, 184–208, Ann Arbor.

———. 2018. *Theatrocracy: Greek Drama, Cognition, and the Imperative for Theatre.* London.

Meineck, P. and D. Konstan, eds. 2014. *Combat Trauma and the Ancient Greeks.* New York,

Meineck, P. and P. Woodruff. 2007. *Sophocles: Four Tragedies*; Ajax, Women of Trachis, Electra, Philoctetes. Indianapolis.

Miller, H. F. 1984. "The Practical and Economic Background to the Greek Mercenary Explosion." *Greece & Rome* 31:153–160.

Moloney, E. 2014. "*Philippus in acie tutior quam in theatro fuit* … (Curtius 9.6.25): The Macedonian Kings and Greek Theatre." In Csapo, Rupprecht Goette, Green, and Wilson 2014:231–248.

Moore, T. J. 2004. "Music in a Quiet Play." In Bair 2004:139–161.

———. 2012. *The Meters of Roman Comedy.* Cambridge.

———. 2020. "The State of Roman Theater, c. 200 BCE." In Franko and Dutsch 2020:17–29.

Mueller, M. 2016. *Objects as Actors: Props and the Poetics of Performance in Greek Tragedy.* Chicago.

Nervegna, S. 2013. *Menander in Antiquity: The Contexts of Reception*. Cambridge.

———. 2014. "Performing Classics: The Tragic Canon in the Fourth Century and Beyond." In Csapo, Rupprecht Goette, Green, and Wilson 2014:157–188.

———. 2020. "Plautus and Greek Drama." In Franko and Dutsch 2020:31–45.

Nesselrath, H.-G. 1990. *Die attische Mittlere Komödie: Ihre Stellung in der antiken Literaturkritik und Literaturgeschichte*. Untersuchungen zur antiken Literatur und Geschichte 36. Berlin.

———. 1993. "Parody and Later Greek Comedy." *Harvard Studies in Classical Philology* 95:181–195.

Ober, J. 1989. *Mass and Elite in Democratic Athens: Rhetoric, Ideology, and the Power of the People*. Princeton.

———. 1994. "Power and Oratory in Democratic Athens: Demosthenes 21, *Against Meidias*." In *Persuasion: Greek Rhetoric in Action*, ed. I. Worthington, 85–108. London.

Ober, J. and B. Strauss. 1990. "Drama, Political Rhetoric, and the Discourse of Athenian Democracy." In Winkler and Zeitlin 1990:237–270.

O'Bryhim, S. 2001. "Dance, Old Man, Dance! The Torture of Knemon in Menander's *Dyskolos*." In *Greek and Roman Comedy*, 96–111. Carbondale.

———. 2020. "Stock Characters and Stereotypes." Franko and Dutsch 2020:123–133.

Olson, S. D. 2007. *Broken Laughter*. Oxford.

———. 2015. "On the Fragments of Eupolis' *Taxiarchoi*." In *Studi sulla commedia attica*, Paradeigmata 31, ed. M. Taufer, 201-214. Freiburg.

O'Sullivan, L. 2009. "History from Comic Hypotheses: Stratocles, Lachares, and P.Oxy. 1235." *Greek, Roman, and Byzantine Studies* 49:53–79.

Owens, W. M. 2011. "The Political Topicality of Menander's *Dyskolos*." *American Journal of Philology* 132:349–378.

Palagia, O. 2005. "A New Interpretation of Menander's Image by Kephisodorus II and Timarchos." *Annuario della Scuola Archeologica di Atene* 83:287–296.

Papaioannou, S. 2010. "Postclassical Comedy and the Composition of Roman Comedy." In *New Perspectives on Postclassical Comedy*, ed. A. Petrides and S. Papaioannou, 146–175. Newcastle upon Tyne.

———. 2020. "Plautus and the Topography of His World." In Franko and Dutsch 2020:287–300.

Papastamati-von Moock, C. 2007. "Menander und die Tragikergruppe: Neue Forschung zu den Ehrenmonumenten im Dionysostheater von Athen." *Mitteilungen des Deutschen Archäologischen Instituts, Athenische Abteilung* 122:273–328.

———. 2014. "The Theatre of Dionysus Eleuthereus in Athens: New Data and Observations on Its Lycurgan Phase." In Csapo, Rupprecht Goette, Green, and Wilson 2014:15–76.

Parke, H. W. 1933. *Greek Mercenary Soldiers from Earliest Times to the Battle of Ipsus*. Oxford.

Parker, D. 1992. "WAA—an Intruded Gloss." *Arion*, third series, 2 (2/3):251–256.

Pernerstorfer, M. J. 2009. *Menanders* Kolax: *Ein Beitrag zu Rekonstruktion und Interpretation der Komödie*. Untersuchungen zur antiken Literatur und Geschichte 99. Berlin.

Pertsinidis, S. 2018. *Theophrastus'* Characters: *A New Introduction*. London.

Peterson, A. 2019. *Laughter on the Fringes: The Reception of Old Comedy in the Imperial Greek World*. Oxford.

Petrides, A. K. 2005. "Masks in Dialogue: The First and Second Episeistos Masks in New Comedy." In *Il personaggio e la maschera: Atti del convegno internazionale di studi, Napoli, Santa Maria Capua Vetere, Ercolano, 19–21 giugno 2003*, ed. R. Grisolia and G. M. Rispoli, 161–174. Naples.

———. 2014a. *Menander, New Comedy and the Visual*. Cambridge.

———. 2014b. "Plautus between Greek Comedy and Atellan Farce: Assessments and Reassessments." In Fontaine and Scafuro 2014:424–443.

Petzl, G. 2002. "Neue Inschriften aus Lydien (IV): Kulturbeflissenes Nordostlydien." *Epigraphica Anatolica* 34:93-102.

Philipp, G. B. 1973. "Philippides, ein politischer Komiker in hellenistischer Zeit." *Gymnasium* 80:497–509.

Podlecki, A. T. 1985. "Theophrastus on History and Politics." In *Theophrastus of Eresus: On His Life and Work*, vol. 2, ed. W. W. Fortenbaugh, P. M. Huby, and A. A. Long, 231–249. New Brunswick.

Poe, J. P. 1996. "The Supposed Conventional Meanings of Dramatic Masks: A Re-examination of Pollux 4.133–54." *Philologus* 140:306–328.

Potter, D. 1987. "Telesphoros, Cousin of Demetrios: A Note on the Trial of Menander." *Historia* 36:491–495.

Powers, M. 2014. *Athenian Tragedy in Performance: A Guide to Contemporary Studies and Historical Debates*. Studies in Theatre History and Culture. Iowa City.

———. 2018. *Diversifying Greek Tragedy on the Contemporary US Stage*. Oxford.

Puchner, W. 2017. *Greek Theatre between Antiquity and Independence: A History of Reinvention from the Third Century BC to 1830*. Cambridge.

Raaflaub, K. 2001. "Father of All, Destroyer of All: War in Late Fifth-Century Athenian Discourse and Ideology." In *War and Democracy: A Comparative Study of the Korean War and the Peloponnesian War*, ed. D. McCann and B. Strauss, 307–360. Armonk.

———. 2014. "War and the City: The Brutality of War and Its Impact on the Community." In Meineck and Konstan 2014:15–46.

———. 2016. "Lysistrata and War's Impact on the Home Front." In Caston and Weineck 2016:37–73.

Race, W. 2014. "Phaeacian Therapy in Homer's *Odyssey*." In Meineck and Konstan 2014:47–66.

Raubitschek, A. E. 1962. "*Demokratia*." *Hesperia* 31:238–243.

Rawlings, L. 2011. "Army and Battle during the Conquest of Italy (350–264 BC)." In *A Companion to the Roman Army*, ed. P. Erdkamp, 45–62. Oxford.

Reiss, W. 2012. *Performing Interpersonal Violence: Court, Curse, and Comedy in Fourth-Century BCE Athens*. MythosEikonPoiesis 4. Berlin.

Revermann, M., ed. 2014. *The Cambridge Companion to Greek Comedy*. Cambridge.

Ribbeck, O. 1873. *Scaenicae Romanorum poesis fragmenta.* 2nd ed. Vol. 2. Leipzig.

Richlin, A. 2017. "The Ones Who Paid the Butcher's Bill: Soldiers and War Captives in Roman Comedy." In *Brill's Companion to Loss and Defeat in the Ancient World*, ed. J. M. Clark and B. Turner, 213–239. Leiden.

———. 2018. *Slave Theater in the Roman Republic: Plautus and Popular Comedy.* Cambridge.

Rop, J. 2019. *Greek Military Service in the Ancient Near East, 401–330 BCE.* Cambridge.

Rosen, R. and H. Foley, eds. 2020. *Aristophanes and Politics: New Studies.* Columbia Studies in the Classical Tradition 45. Leiden.

Rosivach, V. J. 1998. *When a Young Man Falls in Love: The Sexual Exploitation of Women in New Comedy.* London.

Roy, J. 2004. "The Ambitions of a Mercenary." In Fox 2004:264–288.

———. 2017. "Mercenaries in Aineias Tacticus." In *Brill's Companion to Aineias Tacticus*, ed. N. Barley and M. Pretzler, 206–213. Leiden.

Ruffell, I. 2011. *Politics and Anti-Realism in Athenian Old Comedy: The Art of the Impossible.* Oxford.

———. 2014. "Character Types." In Revermann 2014:147–167.

Scafoglio, G. 2017. *Ajax, un héros qui vient de loin.* Amsterdam.

Scafuro, A. 1997. *The Forensic Stage: Settling Disputes in Graeco-Roman New Comedy.* Cambridge.

———. 2014a. "Comedy in the Late Fourth and Early Third Centuries BCE." In Fontaine and Scafuro 2014:239–257.

———. 2014b. "Menander." In Fontaine and Scafuro 2014:218–38.

Schaps, D. M. 1979. *The Economic Rights of Women in Ancient Greece.* Edinburgh.

Schröder, S. 1996. "Die Lebensdaten Menanders (Miteinem Anhangüber die Aufführungszeit seines Εαυτὸν τιμωρούμενος)." *Zeitschrift für Papyrologie und Epigraphik* 113:35–48.

Schwartz, E. 1929. "Zu Menanders *Perikeiromene.*" *Hermes* 64:1–15.

Scodel, R. 1993. "The Tragic Sacrifice and Menandrian Cooking." In *Theater and Society in the Classical World*, 161–176. Ann Arbor.

Segal, E. 1968. *Roman Laughter: The Comedy of Plautus*. Cambridge, MA.

Shay, J. 1994. *Achilles in Vietnam: Combat Trauma and the Undoing of Character*. New York.

———. 2002. *Odysseus in America: Combat Trauma and the Trials of Homecoming*. New York.

———. 2014. "Moral Injury." *Psychoanalytic Psychology* 31:182–191.

Shear, T.L., Jr. 1978. *Kallias of Sphettos and the Revolt of Athens in 286 B.C.* Hesperia Supplement 17. Princeton.

Sherman, N. 2014. "'He Gave Me His Hand but Took My Bow': Trust and Trustworthiness in the Philoctetes and Our Wars." In Meineck and Konstan 2014:207–224.

Slagowski, B. 2015. "Menander and War Trauma." Paper presented at Annual Meeting of the Classical Association of the Middle West and South, Boulder, CO. https://camws.org/sites/default/files/meeting2015/Abstracts2015/375.MenanderAndWarTrauma.pdf.

Slater, N. W. 1994. "The Fabrication of Comic Illusion." In *Beyond Aristophanes: Transition and Diversity in Greek Comedy*, ed. G. W. Dobrov, 29–45. Oxford.

———. 2020. "Stratophanes the Ephebe? The Hero's Journeys in Menander's *Sikyonioi*." In Marshall and Marshall 2020:205–214. London.

Smith, S. D. 2019. *Greek Epigram and Byzantine Culture: Gender, Desire, and Denial in the Age of Justinian*. Cambridge.

Sommerstein, A. H., ed. 2014a. *Menander in Contexts*. London.

———. 2014b. "Combat Trauma in Athenian Comedy: The Dog That Didn't Bark." In Meineck and Konstan 2014:225–236.

Starks, J. H. 2013. "*Opera in bello, in otio, in negotio*: Terence and Rome in the 160s BCE." In Augoustakis and Traill 2013:132–155.

Storey, I. 2003. *Eupolis: Poet of Old Comedy*. Oxford.

Bibliography

Tarn, W. W. and G. T. Griffith. 1935. *Hellenistic Civilization*. London.

Taylor, C. 2017. *Poverty, Wealth, and Well-Being: Experiencing* Penia *in Democratic Athens*. Oxford.

Tordoff, R. 2013. "Actors' Properties in Ancient Greek Drama: An Overview." In *Performance in Greek and Roman Theatre*, ed. G. W. M. Harrison and V. Lapis, 89–110. Leiden.

Traill, A. 2008. *Women and the Comic Plot in Menander*. Cambridge.

Tritle, L. 2000. *From Melos to My Lai: War and Survival*. London.

Trundle, M. 1998. "*Epikouroi, Xenoi* and *Misthophoroi* in the Classical Greek World." *War and Society* 16:1–12.

———. 1999. "Identity and Community among Greek Mercenaries in the Classical World: 700–322 BCE." *Ancient History Bulletin* 13:28–38.

———. 2004. *Greek Mercenaries from the Late Archaic Period to Alexander*. London.

———. 2013. "The Business of War: Mercenaries." In *The Oxford Handbook of Warfare in the Classical World*, ed. B. Campbell and A. Tritle, 330–350. Oxford.

Turner, A. J., and G. Torello-Hill, eds. 2015. *Terence between Late Antiquity and the Age of Printing: Illustration, Commentary and Performance*. Leiden.

Ustinova, Y., and E. Cardeña. 2014. "Combat Stress Disorders and Their Treatment in Ancient Greece." *Psychological Trauma: Theory, Research, Practice, and Policy* 6:739–748.

Victor, B. 2012. "*Terentius orator an poeta*: The Endings of *Eunuchus* and *Adelphoe*." *Classical Quarterly* 62:671–691.

Webster, T. B. L. 1970. *Studies in Later Greek Comedy*. 2nd ed. Manchester.

Weiberg, E. L. 2018. "Weapons as Friends and Foes in Sophocles' *Ajax* and Euripides' *Heracles*." In *The Materialities of Greek Tragedy: Objects and Affect in Aeschylus, Sophocles, and Euripides*, ed. M. Telò and M. Mueller, 63–78. London.

Welles, C. B. 1970. *Alexander and the Hellenistic World*. Toronto.

Wellesley, K. 1955. "The Production Date of Plautus' *Captivi.*" *American Journal of Philology* 76:298–305.

Whitehead, D. 1991. "Who Equipped Mercenary Troops in Classical Greece?" *Historia* 40:105–113.

Wiles, D. 1984. "Demetrius of Phalerum's Dilemma." *Greece & Rome* 31:170–179.

———. 1991. *The Masks of Menander: Sign and Meaning in Greek and Roman Performance.* Cambridge.

Wilkins, J. 2000. *The Boastful Chef, The Discourse of Food in Ancient Greek Comedy.* Oxford.

Williams, J. 1997. "Ideology and the Constitution of Demetrius of Phalerum." In Polis *and* Polemos*: Essays on* Polites*, War, and History in Ancient Greece in Honor of Donald Kagan,* ed. C. D. Hamilton and P. Krentz, 327–346. Claremont.

Winkler, J. J. and F. I. Zeitlin, eds. 1990. *Nothing to Do with Dionysus? Athenian Drama in Its Social Context.* Princeton.

Witzke, S.S. 2020. "Gender and Sexuality in Plautus." In Franko and Dutsch 2020:331–346.

Xenophontos, S. 2012. "Comedy in Plutarch's Parallel Lives." *Greek, Roman, and Byzantine Studies* 52:603–631.

Zagagi, N. 1994. *The Comedy of Menander: Convention, Variation and Originality.* London.

Zanetto, G. 2014. "La tragedia in Menandro: dalla paratragedia alla citazione." In *Menandro e l'evoluzione della commedia greca: Atti del Convegno internazionale di studi in memoria di Adelmo Barigazzi nel centenario della nascita (Firenze, 30 settembre-1 ottobre 2013),* ed. A. Casanova, 83–103. Florence.

Zanker, P. 1995. *The Mask of Socrates.* Trans. A. Shapiro. Berkeley.

Index Locorum

General Index

Achilles: moral injury of, 6
actors: serving as soldiers, 1, 160
Aelian, 38
Agamemnon: homecoming of, 14
Agathias, 78–79
Agnoia (*Perikeiromene*). *See* Ignorance
Ajax: cultural narratives of, 71–72;
    as influence on M., 14, 71–72,
    116; laughter of, 4, 71–73; moral
    injury of, 8; sword and shield of,
    74; theatrical tradition of, 71–73.
    See also suicide
alazones. *See* braggarts; cooks; *miles
    gloriosus*
Alexander the Great, 20–21, 30–31
Alexis, 29–30, 57–58; *Karchedonios*,
    143; *Parasitos*, 146
amnesty: granted to M., 32
Anderson, W. S., 136–137, 139, 142,
    143
Anhalt, E. K., 75n35
Antigonus the One-Eyed, 20–21
Antipater, 35
Antiphanes, 58–59
anxiety: about mercenaries, 11, 14,
    19, 47–54, 76, 93, 111, 113, 121,
    137–138, 160
Aquila Theatre, 9
Archedikos, 28–29
Aristophanes, 9–10, 69; *Acharnians*, 55
Aristophanes of Byzantium, 2

Aristotle, 34–35; on Ajax, 71; on
    hubris, 39; on mercenaries, 50n4
Arnott, W. G., 56, 63, 96n27, 127,
    133n7, 143n31, n32, 144, 149
Arrian, 103–105, 108
Athenaeus: as evidence for M., 31,
    60–61
Athens: as cultural center, 20;
    Macedonian control of, 11–13,
    19–21, 32, 41, 47; M. as citizen of,
    3, 5, 20–21; mercenaries in, 51;
    political upheaval in, 3–4. *See also*
    democracy

Baragwanath, E., 52
Barsby, J., 144n35, 145, 151n43, 156,
    158
Bayliss, A. J., 21, 23n11
Berthaume, G., 63
betrothal, 100–101, 113. *See also*
    marriage; weddings
Bias (*Kolax*), 16, 144–147, 150, 154
Biers, W. R., 139n22
Billings, J., 23
biography: of M., 3–4
Blanchard, 77n2
braggart characters: types of, 5–6,
    16, 57–59. *See also* cooks; *miles
    gloriosus*
Brown, P., 136n14, 139
Brown, P. G. McC., 157n50